Access to Justice for Minority Language Communities

TRANSLATION, INTERPRETING AND SOCIAL JUSTICE IN A GLOBALISED WORLD

Series Editors: **Philipp Angermeyer**, *York University, Canada* and **Katrijn Maryns**, *Ghent University, Belgium*

Translation, Interpreting and Social Justice in a Globalised World is an international series that welcomes authored monographs and edited collections that address translation and interpreting in settings of diversity, globalisation, migration and asylum. Books in the series will discuss how translation and interpreting practices (or their absence) may advance or hinder social justice. A key aim of the series is to encourage dialogue between scholars and professionals working in translation and interpreting studies and those working in other linguistic disciplines, such as sociolinguistics and linguistic anthropology. Books in the series will cover both translation and interpreting services provided by state and corporate entities, as well as informal, community-based translation and interpreting. We welcome proposals covering any combinations of languages (including Sign languages) and from a wide variety of geographical contexts. A guiding aim of the series is to empower those who may be disadvantaged by their lack of access to majority or official languages, and as such proposals which bridge the gap between theoretical and practical domains are particularly encouraged.

Topics which may be addressed by books in the series include (but are not limited to):

- Medical settings (including care settings and provision of public health information)
- Legal settings (law enforcement, court, prison, counselling)
- Educational settings (including community-based education)
- Asylum and migration procedures
- Access to democracy and citizenship
- Interactions with business and private-sector institutions
- The media and minority-language broadcasting and publishing
- Ethical and political considerations in translation
- Cultural translation
- Translation and language rights
- Translation and intercultural relations and conflict

Intended readership: academic and professional.

All books in this series are externally peer-reviewed.

Full details of all the books in this series and of all our other publications can be found on http://www.multilingual-matters.com, or by writing to Multilingual Matters, BLOCK, The Fairfax, Pithay Court, Bristol, BS1 3BN, UK.

TRANSLATION, INTERPRETING AND SOCIAL JUSTICE IN A GLOBALISED WORLD: 5

Access to Justice for Minority Language Communities

Experiences of Irish Speakers and Irish Sign Language Users

Gearóidín McEvoy

MULTILINGUAL MATTERS
Bristol • Jackson

DOI https://doi.org/10.21832/MCEVOY9094
Library of Congress Cataloging in Publication Data
A catalog record for this book is available from the Library of Congress.

Library of Congress Control Number: 2026011414

British Library Cataloguing in Publication Data
A catalogue entry for this book is available from the British Library

ISBN-13: 978-1-80041-909-4 (hbk)

Multilingual Matters
UK: BLOCK, The Fairfax, Pithay Court, Bristol, BS1 3BN, UK.
USA: Ingram, Jackson, TN, USA.
Authorised Representative: Easy Access System Europe - Mustamäe tee 50, 10621 Tallinn, Estonia, gpsr.requests@easproject.com

Website: https://www.multilingual-matters.com
Bluesky: @multi-ling-mat.bsky.social
X: Multi_Ling_Mat
Facebook: https://www.facebook.com/multilingualmatters
Blog: https://www.channelviewpublications.wordpress.com

The policy of Multilingual Matters/Channel View Publications is to use papers that are natural, renewable and recyclable products, made from wood grown in sustainable forests. The FSC and/or PEFC logos will appear on those books where full certification has been granted to the printer concerned.

Typeset by SAN Publishing Services.

This book is dedicated to the memory of Dr Vicky Conway, a friend, a mentor, a feminist, an academic, a warrior.

For Lasse, Laika and Séamus.

Contents

Acknowledgements ix

Glossary of Terms xi

1 Introduction 1
1.1 Introduction 1
1.2 Understanding a Minority 3
1.3 The Right to a Fair Trial 6
1.4 Ireland, the Criminal Justice System and Language 7
1.5 Access to Justice 7
1.6 Research Questions 8
1.7 Research Parameters 10
1.8 Methodology 11
1.9 Chapter Summary 14

2 Identity Construction and the Criminal Justice System 16
2.1 Introduction 16
2.2 Identity: The Internal and the External 17
2.3 Cop Culture and the External Identity 21
2.4 Judicial Bias 23
2.5 Chapter Summary 25

3 Deaf and Irish Speaker Identity Construction 27
3.1 Introduction 27
3.2 Minority Language-User Identity 27
3.3 Deaf Identity 28
3.4 Irish Speaker Identity 36
3.5 Tropes in the Data 41
3.6 Chapter Summary 42

4 Access to Justice 44
4.1 Introduction 44
4.2 Aspects of Access to Justice 45
4.3 Chapter Summary 53

5 The Right to an Interpreter and Procedural Access 55
5.1 Introduction 55
5.2 Entitlement to an Interpreter 56
5.3 Interpreter Standards 64

5.4 Interpreters in the Data 71
5.5 Chapter Summary 81

6 Minimum Standards of the Right to a Fair Trial and Procedural Access 84
6.1 Introduction 84
6.2 Justifying the Selection of Minimum Standards 85
6.3 Trial Without Undue Delay 85
6.4 Communication with Counsel 92
6.5 Presence at Trial 96
6.6 Chapter Summary 100

7 Substantive Access and Legislation, Training and Inclusion 102
7.1 Introduction 102
7.2 Legislation 103
7.3 Training 109
7.4 Chapter Summary 121

8 Symbolic Access and the External Identity: The Slíbhín and the Créatúr 124
8.1 Introduction 124
8.2 Defining the 'Créatúr' Trope 125
8.3 Defining the 'Slíbhín' Trope 129
8.4 Chapter Summary 141

9 Symbolic Access and Recognising Internal Identity 142
9.1 Introduction 142
9.2 Culturally Deaf 143
9.3 The True Gael 146
9.4 Interacting with the CJS – Pass or Punish 150
9.5 Known-About-ness and Symbolic Access 154
9.6 Chapter Summary 157

10 Concluding Remarks 159
10.1 Introduction 159
10.2 How do Minority Language Users Experience the Right to a Fair Trial? 159
10.3 How do Minority Language Users Experience the CJS? 161
10.4 How do Minority Language Users Experience Access to Justice? 162
10.5 Recommendations 163
10.6 Summary 164

References 166

Index 178

Acknowledgements

This work began its life as my PhD thesis and as such, it has been part of my life for almost 10 years. In a way, it is odd to be closing this chapter, and in another way, it feels right. This work is the embodiment of the notion that it takes a village. My village over the past nine years has been small but mighty. I have a multitude of people to thank and to be grateful for. I will do my best to express how profoundly grateful I am, but as my work shows time and again, sometimes language is limited in what it can do.

Firstly, I would not be the researcher, the feminist or the woman I am today were it not for the constant support, encouragement and guidance from my two PhD supervisors, Dr Tanya Ní Mhuirthile and Dr Vicky Conway. During my tenure as their supervisee, both went above and beyond for me, supported me through the toughest times, through a lonely and isolating pandemic, through self-doubt and imposter syndrome. I could not have done this work without them. To Dr Tanya Ní Mhuirthile, who believed in the greater meaning of this work before I could even see it myself, who introduced me to Goffman, hermeneutic phenomenology, Judith Butler, Zotero, and so many other aspects of my academic life that are now foundational. Go raibh mile, mile maith agat! Your support since we met has been phenomenal and it is always a joy to get to work side by side. This work would not be what it is without you.

My other PhD supervisor, Dr Vicky Conway is no longer with us to thank. Vicky, I hope you knew how much you impacted my life, how much you supported me, how much you meant to me, and still mean to me. I regularly guide myself by asking 'What would Vicky do right now?' I know you were proud of this work at its earlier stages, and I can only hope that you would have been proud what it is now. I miss you. Thank you, wherever you are.

Thanks must also go to Dr Vinita Joseph. Without your guidance and support, I might never have gathered the courage to put this work out there for consideration and certainly would not have written this book. Thank you for your wise words, your clear delivery, your introspection and your assistance.

I must thank Professor Karen McAuliffe. You have been an excellent mentor, friend and colleague for years. Thank you for believing in me, for teaching me to value myself, my work, my time, my personal boundaries and my expertise, and for helping me with the practicalities of writing a book proposal.

Thank you to my editor, Rosie, for being so patient with me as I galivanted off for a whole year to have a baby after we agreed to do this! Your kindness, support and interest in this work have been incredible.

Thank you to my friends and family, to my parents Colm and Dolores, who have supported me from the very beginning, who always believed in me. To my mother for her lifelong encouragement in learning, to my father, who has never failed to find my work interesting. To my wonderful husband Lasse, who has been here since before this was even the seed of an idea, who has supported me in every possible way throughout this work, and all my work since I have known you. Thank you for believing in me far more than I believe in myself. You are my loudest cheerleader, my biggest supporter, my best friend. Tack tack. To my wonderful son Séamus who has never failed to make me smile at the end of a hard day, who brings so much joy to my life. Go raibh míle maith agat, mo thaisce. Grá mo chroí thú. To my dog Laika, who was there for almost 14 years until she suddenly wasn't – she is responsible for a major part of my sanity during the pandemic, during this writing process and throughout my entire adulthood. It is in the closing stages of writing this manuscript that I must regretfully relegate her to the past tense. I will forever be thankful for having had her in my life as my unofficial emotional support husky.

I wish to thank the interpreters who made my research possible. I am indebted to your work, skill and professionalism. Finally, and most importantly, I am indebted to the participants to this research. To Dr Mary Phelan, Dr Seán Ó Conaill, Dr John Bosco Conama and Prof Lorraine Leeson. Go raibh míle maith agaibh as bhúr n-am agus bhúr n-eolas. Thank you for your time and expertise. Your contributions made my work better and deepened my understandings. I am grateful to the lawyers and other experts who participated. I appreciate you all for sharing your time, expertise and knowledge with me and for showing the compassion you have for the people and groups you serve.

And lastly, to the participants who experienced the criminal justice system firsthand. I cannot express to you all how much your participation meant to me, and how truly thankful I am. Put simply, this work would not have been possible without you. You gave me your time, your trust and your stories. I am eternally grateful for this. I hope that I have done justice to you, your stories, and your community. This work is as much yours as it is mine. Thank you.

Agus ar deireadh, de bharr na rannpháirtithe ar a raibh táithí leis an gcóras dlí coiriúil. Ní féidir liom mo bhuíoch a chur síos in fhocail go ceart, i ndáiríre. Go shimplí, ní tharlófaí an obair seo gan bhur rannpháirtíocht. Thug sibh bhur am dom, chuir sibh bhur muinín ionam agus d'inis sibh bhur scéalta dom. Agus beidh mé buíochasach go deo asaibh. Tá súil agam gur thug mé cothrom na Féinne daoibh, do bhur scéalta agus don phobal. Is libhse an obair seo. Go raibh míle maith agaibh.

Glossary of Terms

Irish Politics

Coimisinéir Teanga The language commissioner for the Irish language in Ireland. The office was established under the Official Languages Act, 2003 and the role of the commissioner is to monitor compliance under the Official Languages Act.

Dáil The lower house of Parliament in Ireland.

Seanad The upper house of Parliament in Ireland.

TD Teachta Dála A member of the Irish Parliament.

Irish Courts

Circuit Court Intermediate court of local and limited jurisdiction

District Court Lowest court, responsible for hearing minor claims and minor criminal offenses.

High Court Serious crimes and claims court for first instance cases

Supreme Court Highest judicial authority in Ireland and the court of final appeal

solicitor A professional lawyer who is the first point of contact for a client, and deals with out-of-court legal matters, but may also work in court advocacy.

Irish Police

An Garda Síochána The Irish police service. Literally translates to English as 'guardians of the peace'. Often abbreviated to Gardaí, the Guards or an individual police officer of any rank may be referred to as a 'guard' or 'Garda'

Member in charge The ranking officer who is in charge of a particular Garda Station. They are responsible, among other things, for the safety and rights of people detained at the Garda Station

Garda/guard An individual police officer of any rank.

Gardaí/The Guards A group of police officers of any rank, or a shortened name for the police service, An Garda Síochána

International law

in absentia To be absent, particularly in the context of a trial. An accused person may be tried *in absentia* when they are not present for the trial.

inter alia In addition to

violation When a right, law, or entitlement is denied or rejected.

monitoring body An organisation tasked with ensuring laws or treaties are followed by states who are members of those laws or treaties.

jurisprudence The philosophy of law

Precedent A decision that serves as an authority for courts when deciding subsequent identical or similar cases

UN Human Rights Committee The body of independent experts that monitors implementation of the International Covenant on Civil and Political Rights by its States parties.

ICCPR International Covenant on Civil and Political Rights

UN General Comment Interpretations of provisions or human rights in a treaty by the treaty body. For example, the HRC publishes general comments about the ICCPR.

Council of Europe Europe-wide organisation for the protection of human rights with 47 member states

ECHR European Convention on Human Rights. The main human rights document of the Council of Europe

European Court of Human Rights The international court that hears claims related to violations of the European Convention on Human Rights

International Criminal Court International tribunal based in The Hague which tries war crimes, crimes against humanity, genocide and other most serious international crimes

1 Introduction

1.1 Introduction

On the 15th December 1882, a man named Maolra Seoighe from county Galway (Ó Cuirreáin, 2017) Ireland, was hanged in punishment for a crime he did not commit. Maolra was tried, convicted and sentenced to death for the murder of five people in Mám Trasna (Kelleher, 2018). He did not speak English (Kelleher, 2018). He spoke only Irish and yet was represented by a barrister who did not speak Irish. He was tried by an English-speaking court (Bairéad, 2018). There was no interpreter present to bridge the momentous gap in understanding for the accused (Kelleher, 2018). Maolra Seoighe was in fact innocent and had been convicted on the basis of perjured information (Bairéad, 2018). And yet he sat, isolated and powerless in a court, unable to comprehend and to defend himself, only for the supreme power of the justice system to punish him with the ultimate price. In 2018, over 130 years after his unjust trial, wrongful conviction and wrongful execution, the President of Ireland issued a pardon to Maolra Seoighe (Kelleher, 2018). This is a story of colonial rule, of outdated justice systems and power imbalances. But it is also a story of today. Linguistic discrimination and language as a barrier to accessing justice are still realities in courts and criminal justice systems.

In 2016, a deaf man and Irish Sign Language (ISL) user in Donegal, Ireland, was arrested and detained by An Garda Síochána (the police service in Ireland) and brought to court on charges of harassment (Harkin, 2016). John McGrotty, like Maolra Seoighe, did not speak English (Cradden, 2016). Like Maolra Seoighe, John McGrotty was subjected to an English-speaking criminal justice system. And like Maolra Seoighe, John McGrotty was not provided with an interpreter (Cradden, 2016). Only when activists in the deaf community intervened was an ISL interpreter provided (Cradden, 2016). While the penalty in Mr McGrotty's case was not as severe as that in Maolra Seoighe's case, the lack of access bears a striking resemblance. A man engaging with the criminal justice system as an accused person, was denied the opportunity to comprehend or participate. Both men epitomise a lack of awareness of, or a willingness to overlook, the risks associated when a language barrier is allowed to remain in the criminal justice system (CJS). Both men, I would argue, experienced injustice and a denial of their human rights.

Language is a core aspect of human life. It is through language that people find community and kinship. As stated in the Canadian Supreme Court in *Re Manitoba Language Rights*:

> The importance of language rights is grounded in the essential role that language plays in human existence, development and dignity. It is through language that we are able to form concepts; to structure and order the world around us. Language bridges the gap between isolation and community, allowing humans to delineate the rights and duties they hold in respect of one another, and thus to live in society. (*Re Manitoba Language Rights*, 1985)

Language allows us to understand the world around us and to connect with others. In terms of the law, it is through language that laws are formed, cases are heard and matters are adjudicated. Not only a medium through which law operates, the two vignettes above show that language can be a contested issue in law, and pose a barrier to fairness and justice.

In analysing their experiences, both Maolra Seoighe and John McGrotty represent minority language users, the focus of this book. In particular, they are an Irish speaker and an ISL user, respectively. English is the dominant majority language in Ireland. It was the dominant language of power and authority in Ireland during Maolra Seoighe's time. These stories demonstrate how minority language usage can cause tension when it interacts with the organs of the state, and in particular, the CJS.

Irish is a Celtic language native to Ireland. While once the vernacular language of Ireland, after colonisation by Britain, wherein laws were put in place which prevented the use of Irish (Phelan, 2019), Irish saw a steady decline in usage over the years, through deliberate efforts to circumvent the use of the language by the colonial powers, and through corresponding lack of opportunity associated with the use of Irish (Crowley, 2005). An Irish language revival movement at the end of the 19th century coincided with increased efforts for Irish independence (C.C. O'Reilly, 2014). This culminated the establishment of the Republic of Ireland in 1937, where Irish was given the primary constitutional status as the first official language of Ireland (Article 8, Constitution of Ireland, 1937). Learning Irish is a mandatory part of the Irish primary and secondary education systems, with certain exceptions.[1] This has not resulted in widespread resurgence of the language or a growth in fluency, but rather a general familiarity with the language (Romaine, 2006). In the most recent statistics, about 1.5% of the population in the Republic of Ireland are reported to speak Irish daily (*Irish Language and the Gaeltacht Census of Population 2016 – Profile 10 Education, Skills and the Irish Language – Central Statistics Office*, 2021).

Irish is currently listed as 'definitely endangered' by the United Nations Educational, Scientific and Cultural Organization (UNESCO) (*Irish*, 2024).

Irish Sign Language is the indigenous language of deaf people in Ireland (Rose & Conama, 2018). At the outset, the reader should note that ISL, like other signed languages, is its own distinct language (Leeson & Saeed, 2012). It is not a signed form or English or Irish (Minogue, 2021). The language is used by approximately 5000 deaf people and an estimated 40,000 others (*Irish Sign Language*, 2021). Not all deaf people have ISL as a language, and it should be noted that for generations in Ireland, signed language usage was discouraged or banned in institutions which educated and housed deaf people, based on the belief that signing was detrimental to the ability to acquire spoken language (Rose & Conama, 2018). This policy, known as 'oralism' prioritised spoken language acquisition in deaf people (Rose & Conama, 2018) and discounted signed languages as actual languages (Gertz & Boudreault, 2016). This policy is similar in effect to the prohibitions on Irish-usage under colonial rule. As a result of this policy of oralism, many deaf people experienced language deprivation (Glickman & Hall, 2018a), were unable to acquire spoken language, and were denied any opportunity to learn a signed language. ISL was recognised in legislation in Ireland in 2017. There is no mandated learning of ISL in schools like that for Irish.

Both Irish and ISL are minority languages, indigenous to Ireland, where English is the majority language. In this book, I call both ISL and Irish regional or minority languages. Briefly, it is important to discuss the development of the concept of a minority and to understand how minorities are constructed and understood.

1.2 Understanding a Minority

A minority necessarily exists as a contrast to a majority. The concept of a minority within a state, as we know it, coincides with the development of the nation-state. The idea of nation-states and nationhood began with the French Revolution. It was during this time that the concept of 'nation=state=people' came into being (Hobsbawm, 1992). Part of that equation included a recognition of homogeneity among the people who formed part of the state. The notion of one nation, one people and one language took hold, as May notes:

> ...the model of the linguistically homogeneous nation-state...is actually only a relatively recent historical phenomenon, arising from the French Revolution of 1789 and the subsequent development of European nationalism. Previous forms of political organization had not required this degree of linguistic uniformity. For example, empires were quite happy for the most part to leave unmolested the plethora of cultures and languages subsumed within them – as long as taxes were paid, all was well. Nonetheless, in the subsequent politics of European nationalism – which,

> of course, was also to spread throughout the world – the idea of a single, common, 'national' language...quickly became the leitmotif of modern social and political organization. (May, 2012: 261)

Hobsbawm also notes that in addition to its connection to geography and territory, nationhood was also inherently connected to language: 'In a sense acquiring French was one of the conditions of full French citizenship (and therefore nationality) as acquiring English became from American citizenship' (Hobsbawm, 1992: 18). This can be extrapolated to mean that as a people, the citizens of France were French-speaking. 'French was essential to the concept of France' (Hobsbawm, 1992: 60). The French Revolution, 'through its democratic aspects, had a negative effect on regional minority cultures' (Alcock, 2000: 23). Since then, the 'use of minority languages [in France] has...been perceived as anti-revolutionary, anti-republican and consequently, also anti-democratic' (Trenz, 2007: 162). This negative effect manifested itself through attempts to 'mould society into one culture', a mode of governance that became globally popular (Alcock, 2000: 23).

Minority groups pose an opposition to the concept of a nation-state. They exist as a counter to some or all aspects of nationalism and are thus treated as '*problems* for the nation-state' (Eriksen, 2010: 314). The nation-state promotes ideals of sovereignty, unity and oneness. The other is anything beyond that. As Hylland Eriksen states, the 'nation-state represents itself through nationalist ideology; that is, an ideology proclaiming the essential cultural unity of all its citizens' (Eriksen, 2010). In spite of this ideology, the idea that any nation is entirely homogenous in terms of race, religion, culture or language is wholly unsubstantiated in reality, 'since most states contain minorities who do not define themselves as members of the group represented through state nationalism' (Eriksen, 2010: 314). These groups may be indigenous, present in the territory long before the development of the state itself, descendants of colonial settlers, migrants to the state, etc. Therefore, there will necessarily be an objection to the *status quo* of a nation-state from the minority group who cannot fully identify with what is required of homogenous nationalism of their state. 'Several rivalling nationalisms may exist within one nation-state; usually one of them is dominant and may refer to the others as "ethnic", "secessionist", "regionalist", or even "tribal"...' (Eriksen, 2010: 314). The concept of nation-state then is rooted in a specific identity (the majority, homogenous, national identity) whereby a minority represents an othered, exceptional identity. By its make-up and definition:

> ...the 'democratic' unity of a modern nation-state is nearly always parasitic on those whom it excludes from its unity – be they outsiders or insiders – or those who are compelled to join against their will. (Eriksen, 2010: 314)

The minority groups who do not fit the mould are outsiders and the other. They are the ones who do not, cannot or will not conform to the unity of the nation and are therefore at risk of persecution or isolation as punishment. Coulmas as a result, describes 'the nation-state as it has evolved since the French Revolution [as] the natural enemy of minorities' (Coulmas, 1998). In discussing minority issues, it is important to address terminology. Defining a minority is somewhat of a contested term in the space (Packer, 1993). At present, the UN Special Rapporteur on Minority Issues defines a minority as follows:

> An ethnic, religious or linguistic minority is any group of persons which constitutes less than half of the population in the entire territory of a State whose members share common characteristics of culture, religion or language, or a combination of any of these. A person can freely belong to an ethnic, religious or linguistic minority without any requirement of citizenship, residence, official recognition or any other status. (*About Minorities and Human Rights*, 2024)

It is reiterated that the main criteria for defining a minority under the Special Rapporteur's mandate is a numerical one, whereby the population constituting a minority must be less than that of the majority (*About Minorities and Human Rights*, 2024). Caportoti provided a well-known definition of minorities in 1977. This definition is described as the 'best approximation of a generally applicable authoritative definition of minority' (Jackson-Preece, 2014: 5). Caportoti's definition differs from the above in the requirement that minorities do not hold a position of dominance in their state:

> ...a group numerically inferior to the rest of the population of a state, in a non-dominant position, whose members – being nationals of the state – possess ethnic, religious or linguistic characteristics differing from the rest of the population and show, if only implicitly, a sense of solidarity directed towards preserving their culture, traditions, religion or language. (Capotorti, 1977: 96)

Caportoti links minority status to both population and power, therefore. Packer offers a far shorter definition, in explaining the concept of a minority as:

> ...a group of people who freely associate for an establish purpose where their shared desire differs from that expressed by the majority rule. (Packer, 1993: 45)

Packer positions minorities as defined by the majority, and their otherness to that majority. There is truth and accuracy in all of these definitions. In this research, I would err closer to that of Caportoti's definition, believing that a minority is not only defined by its numerically inferior status, but also by its lack of political power. However, in acknowledging that minority status is an identity, perception is also at the centre of understanding what constitutes a member of a minority group. Alfredsson notes in discussing minorities, where he states that there are 'two poles: an individual decides that he/she is a member of a minority and a group accepts an individual as its member' (Alfredsson, 1991: 10). A minority must therefore involve an element of self and group determination, whereby an identity is assumed, and that identity is accepted by others with that same identity as being legitimate.

1.3 The Right to a Fair Trial

To continue the discussion of Maolra Seoighe and John McGrotty, there were two major issues which emerge from the facts of both cases. Both men were minority language users and both stories centre around the CJS and issues of the right to a fair trial. Briefly, it is important to layout these issues in the context of this research.

The right to a fair trial is of basic importance and constitutes a fundamental right in many human rights documents. It is featured in the European Convention on Human Rights (ECHR) from the Council of Europe and the International Covenant on Civil and Political Rights (ICCPR) from the UN (Articles 6 at 14 respectively), which are the focus of this book. It is part of the African Charter on Human and People's Rights under Article 7, the American Convention on Human Rights under Article 8, and the Charter of Fundamental Rights of the European Union under Article 47.

Under both the ICCPR and the ECHR, minimum standards under the right to a fair trial are laid down. These minimum standards exist as safeguards for fairness because of the risks posed when a person stands accused of a crime (Council of Europe, Guide on Article 6 of the European Convention on Human Rights: Right to a Fair Trial (Criminal Limb), 2019). Primarily, an accused person faces the potential to be deprived of their liberty, but there is also the risk of fines, damage to their reputation and the risk that a criminal conviction for certain crimes might impact their lives for years to come.[2] The right to a fair trial seeks to safeguard against all of these risks and ensure that a certain level of fairness is achieved in proceedings. The right to a fair trial encompasses a wide range of protections including the right to be free from undue delay, the right to communicate with counsel, the right to be present at trial and the right to an interpreter.

The minimum standards under the right to a fair trial in the ICCPR and the ECHR make specific protections for those who do not speak the language of the court. They ensure that an interpreter will be provided, free of charge, and that the accused is informed of the charges against them in a language they understand. These rights show a recognition in the ICCPR and the ECHR that language can pose a barrier to accessing fairness of trial, and that in ensuring fairness of trial, allowances for language need to be made. In this book, I explore how the right to a fair trial is experienced for minority language users when they use their language, and whether their experiences are sufficiently protected by the minimum standards currently in place.

1.4 Ireland, the Criminal Justice System and Language

To very briefly preface the reader, Ireland is a common law republic. Ireland has a foundational constitution, called *Bunreacht nah Éireann* or *The Constitution of Ireland*, written in 1937. This constitution is then supported by laws in the form of legislation or often by judicial precedent, or decisions made by judges which become part of the law. Criminal law in Ireland is governed by the police service in Ireland, An Garda Síochána and people charged with crimes may go forward to any number of courts of first instance, depending on the severity of the crime. Suspects of crime are entitled to legal assistance if they cannot afford one, and, in theory, an interpreter if they do not speak the language of the court.

In Ireland, English is the dominant spoken language. Irish is the native language to Ireland, which is a Gaelic language. It is not similar to English in terms of structure, grammar or syntax. Irish is taught as a mandatory subject, with exceptions, to all school children in Ireland from primary to secondary schools. That being said, it is a minority language with most people having limited interactions with the language on a meaningful, regular basis.

Irish Sign Language (ISL) is the native signed language of Ireland. It is used by many members of the Irish Deaf Community, but not all deaf people sign. ISL is not taught as part of any national curriculum in Ireland. ISL is permitted to be used with interpreters in courts in both criminal and non-criminal proceedings under the Irish Sign Language Act, 2017.

1.5 Access to Justice

Access to an interpreter was at issue for both Maolra Seoighe and John McGrotty. I would argue that on analysis of their cases, neither man could be said to have accessed justice. Access to justice is understood in this research as encompassing a holistic view of how a person experiences fairness within a justice system. It means that the barriers which exist in the justice system itself are removed. It also means that barriers which exist in society outside of the justice system, which nevertheless impact on a person's ability to arrive before the justice system, are removed.

For John McGrotty and Maolra Seoighe, we must look to the socio-economic and historic realities which surrounded their cases, and how these realities impacted their access to justice. Maolra Seoighe's trial took place under colonial rule, where Irish usage was oppressed and devalued for generations, by way of outlawing the use of Irish in courts, and banning Catholics (who were most likely to be Irish speakers) from working in the legal system (Phelan, 2019). John McGrotty's case came after generations of state-sanctioned language deprivation in the deaf community (Rose & Conama, 2018) before any legal recognition of ISL. In analysing their experiences, we must investigate what it means to have access to justice.

As it is understood in this research, access to justice is threefold (Bahdi, 2007). It includes being able to participate in the justice systems which are already in place (Flynn, 2015). Neither John McGrotty nor Maolra Seoighe could participate as accused persons in the systems in place because they were denied interpreters. But access to justice must also include laws and systems that were created with marginalised people in mind (Flynn, 2015). Neither Maolra Seoighe nor John McGrotty experienced a CJS that was built for them or for their needs as minority language users. Neither man had their language recognised in law, and so their needs went unknown to the CJS. Finally, access to justice must also include a wider, societal acceptance of a marginalised identity (Flynn, 2015). Where marginalise people are accepted and valued in society, then their needs are more likely to be understood and implemented into the systems built into society. Neither Maolra Seoighe nor John McGrotty lived in a society where their identities as minority language users were valued or included. When considering access to justice, we need to look beyond the four walls of the courtroom or the police station and examine how they exist as minority language users in society. This research will examine the wider application of access to justice for minority language users and investigate how their language and their identities impact that access to justice.

1.6 Research Questions

This research looks at how minority language users access their right to a fair trial under the United Nations and Council of Europe systems of human rights. It is clear from the discussion thus far that minority language usage can cause a tension in the CJS, as a disruption to the norm and a demonstration of othered behaviour by an accused. Where that tension manifests, there is a risk to the fairness of the trial for an accused minority language user. This research is interested in investigating that tension.

The research is sociolegal in nature, conducting a case study by way of empirical research on individuals from two specific language groups: Irish speakers in Ireland and Irish Sign Language users in Ireland. Academic experts, members of the police service, lawyers who have worked with minority language users and minority language users who have experienced the criminal justice system firsthand as suspects were interviewed for this research. In doing so, I aim to tackle the following research questions:

(1) How do minority language users experience the right to a fair trial when using their language?

(2) How do minority language users experience the CJS when using their language?
(3) How do minority language users experience access to justice?

These questions will provide insight into how individual minority language users themselves engage with the justice system. They will provide a unique insight into the lived experiences of minority language users who have navigated the CJS using their language. In order to answer these questions, I conducted two case studies, one on Irish speakers in Ireland and one on deaf, ISL-users in Ireland. As minority groups in Ireland who use languages which are not the dominant language of the state, both groups fall within the understanding of minority language users in this research.

The right to a fair trial, as it exists under Article 14 of ICCPR and Article 6 of the ECHR, is the focus of this book. Underpinning these rights is the principle of access to justice. I understand access to justice as it is articulated by Flynn (2015), Bahdi (2007) and Beqiraj *et al.* (2017). In this literature, access to justice is understood as having three major components: procedural access; substantive access and; symbolic access. Procedural access refers to a traditional view of access to justice and relates to 'the process by which claims are adjudicated, generally in legal or administrative systems' (Flynn, 2015: 15). Substantive access 'requires the development of laws and policies which promote substantive equality and stresses that this cannot usually be achieved without the involvement of the disadvantaged group' (Flynn, 2015: 14). Symbolic access, which is sometimes known as promotional access (Bahdi, 2007; Flynn, 2015) ensures that 'individuals from marginalised communities are fully included and empowered to participate as equal citizens' (Flynn, 2015). Seen this way, symbolic access ensures that marginalised people are empowered in society itself. The three aspects of access to justice underpin the right to a fair trial – without all of the aspects catered for, there is a lack of access to justice. If rights are provided for the benefit of all people, including the minority language users as it relates particularly to the right to a fair trial, then this furthers procedural access. If those laws are not created with minority language user input, with their specific needs and desired outcomes in mind, then substantive access is not achieved.[3] Additionally, if these laws exist but are gate-kept or impacted by wider societal barriers (such as stereotyping, biases, culture, etc) then there is a lack of symbolic access. Therefore, the prevalence of stereotypes about identities, particularly minority identities, and the impact these stereotypes have on the individual's journey through the criminal justice system. Without access to justice, the right to a fair trial remains theoretical and illusory.

It ought to be noted that while this research began initially as an exploration of human rights norms, and in particular, the right to an interpreter for accused minority language users, on collection and analysis of the data, it became clear that such a focus would be too narrow an approach to understand the lived experiences of those interviewed, and the a sociological understanding of their experiences would be necessary. As such, this research is sociolegal, with an emphasis on the holistic way in which minority language users experience the CJS and being accused persons, under the lens of access to justice, which in itself is a holistic view of fairness and human rights.

The research in this book is unique in that it combines literature on identity and the self with literature on policing, the judiciary and with literature on access to justice in order to explore the experiences of minority language users as they navigate the CJS using their language. The multi-disciplinary approach will provide a richer understanding of how linguistic identity can inform how an individual is perceived in the CJS, how that perception will manifest in terms of the fairness of trial, and how their overall experience is underpinned by access to justice.

1.7 Research Parameters

At the outset, the parameters of the research should be borne in mind by the reader. Primarily, the research herein is not a representative study and cannot speak to the experiences of all Irish speakers, deaf people or all minority language users who encounter the CJS. The research presents only the experiences of those who have been interviewed.

Additionally, the research focuses only on the right to a fair trial, rather than on rights relating to arrest and detention. While rights regarding arrest and detention could apply to many instances which are described in this work, the right to a fair trial encompasses these instances also, and so it has been the only human right analysed.

In terms of the literature informing the research, the work in this book is contextualised through literature on identity, with a notable focus on the work of Erving Goffman. Undoubtedly, it would have been possible to contextualise the work through engagement with other fields, such as linguistics, psychology or criminology. The focus here, however, is limited to a discussion on identity. As a result of the focus on identity, this research does not seek to define what it means to be a minority, or who is or is not a member of a specific minority. It is not the aim of this book to define what it means to be an Irish-speaker or a deaf person.

It is important to highlight the limitations to this work. Firstly, this study is not representative of the experiences of all or most Irish speakers, deaf people, or minority language users in engaging with the criminal justice system. It can only attest to the experiences of those individuals interviewed (Adams, 2015). If the study had been representative, it would have been unlikely to have taken the current form. Surveys would have been a more useful method to ascertain representativeness, but this would have come at the detriment of the lived experiences, which were revealed in interviews (Nardi, 2018).

As will be discussed below, I spoke Irish during interviews with Irish speakers and was able to then directly communicate with those participants without an intermediary, and in their language of choice. This was not possible for ISL users who participated in the research, as I did not have sufficient ISL and as such, interpreters facilitated the interviews. Although all interpreters were trained and qualified and chosen by participants, direct communication in ISL would have been preferable to ensure nothing was lost in translation.

The lived experiences in this research are also limited to an Irish context. Initially, this research set out to have a more international scope, with research planned for the USA and Finland in addition to Irish speakers and deaf people in Ireland. I had planned to conduct the same research on the Blackfoot people in Montana, USA and Swedish-speaking Finns in Finland. However, due to difficulties in creating networks with these minority language communities in the USA and Finland, as well as financial and time constraints, the international element to this work was abandoned. It would have been of benefit to see whether the same tropes uncovered in this work also extended to Finland and the USA, or whether there are different discourses that impact minority language users in these countries.

In terms of the methods used, open questioning was not always a useful method. In particular, it was necessary to be more direct in questioning some deaf participants, as described above. Deaf people are direct, and directness is a feature of deaf culture. Open questioning did not always lend itself to this culture, and there were instances where deaf interviewees were confused by the open question techniques. I had to adjust my interview techniques to engage in more 'deaf friendly' questions at times. I had not encountered any research detailing the use of open questioning with deaf people, facilitated by an interpreter as a research method and, in fact, this may be a topic that requires further research in the future.

1.8 Methodology

For the methodology, I have looked at this research through the lens of hermeneutic phenomenology (Heidegger *et al.*, 2008) as I believed it would be the best way to engage with the research questions. In doing so, it should be noted that my own experiences as a researcher are relevant to how the research has been conducted and analysed. The reader should expect to encounter my identity throughout the work, in line with the chosen methodology.

In terms of the methods used for this work, I conducted 23 semi-structured interviews with 'criminal justice subjects' who were Irish speakers or deaf people, lawyers and experts (see Table 1.1 for a detailed breakdown of the participants). Criminal justice subjects refer to people who have had experiences being accused, suspected or convicted of crimes and who have otherwise engaged with the criminal justice system either through An Garda Síochána or the courts or both. Table 1.1 shows the breakdown of the interviewee profiles.

These interviews were conducted between 2017 and 2018. For Irish speakers and deaf people, participants were recruited through social media advertisements about the interviews, posted in Irish and in ISL and via snowballing (Parker *et al.*, 2020). The posts sought participation from adults who had interacted with the criminal justice system in Ireland as accused or suspected persons, and who had attempted to use their language while doing so. For lawyers, specific targeted contact was made with Irish lawyers practicing who either specialised in working with Irish speakers, or who were known to have had experience representing deaf clients. For experts, targeted invitations were put out to individuals with

Table 1.1 Breakdown of research participants

Participant Type	Irish Speaker Group	Deaf Group
Criminal Justice Subjects	Gael1	Deaf1
	Gael2	Deaf2
	Gael3	Deaf3
	Gael4	Deaf4
	Gael5	Deaf5
	Gael6	
	Gael7	
	Gael8	
Lawyers	Dlíodóir1	Lawyer1
	Dlíodóir2	Lawyer2
Experts	Dr Seán Ó Conaill (SÓC)	Prof. Lorraine Leeson
	Dr Mary Phelan (MP)	Dr John Bosco Conama (JBC)
	AGS1	AGS2

expertise in the field. Two members of An Garda Síochána were interviewed after one member reached out with interest in the project and recommended contact with a second member. Interviews were recorded using a Dictaphone for spoken language interviews and video recorded for ISL interviews, with the exception of one interviewee who chose not to be recorded. Fieldnotes were taken in all interviews. Consent forms and plain language statements were presented to all participants in Irish or English prior to their participation in interviews.

As stated above, I am an Irish speaker and so interviews with Irish speakers were conducted in Irish. I am hearing and at the time of this research, my ISL was poor and basic, at best. As such, interviews with ISL users were conducted using trained and qualified ISL interpreters of the participant's choice. No interpreter used for this work accepted payment for their work. The first interpreter used enquired about whether or not the project had specific funding for interpretation. When I told them it did not, they said that they knew the importance of such research and as such, would be waiving their fee. In fact, this same interpreter went on to inform their colleagues that I was not to be charged for this work. I am immensely grateful to the interpreters for their generosity, their belief in this work and their professionalism.

In terms of my positionality in this work, I consider myself both an insider and an outsider. I am an insider in the Irish-speaking community. Irish is not my first language, and I am what might be considered a 'newspeaker'. Nevertheless, I am involved in the community and speak the language daily at work and at home. I view myself as a Gael and an Irish speaker and, for the most part, I have felt that this identity is accepted by others within my community as legitimate. That being said, I did not grow up in an Irish speaking environment, I am not a native speaker and I cannot implicitly know the lived experiences of those who are native speakers, who grow up in Irish speaking communities and who have Irish as their first language. Therefore, when I speak, I do not speak for the entirety of the community, or even an entirety of newspeakers, but rather I am guided by the lived experiences of individual participants in this work and beyond.

In terms of the Deaf community, at the time of this work, and even now, many years later, I consider myself an outsider. I am not deaf or hard of hearing, I do not have any familial or historical links to the deaf community. In fact, it was through this work itself that I came to know the deaf community. Certainly, I see similarities between the plight of Irish speakers and that of deaf people seeking to sue one's language in engaging with the State – hence the project itself. But ultimately, I do not claim membership to the deaf community, despite how kind and welcoming the community has been to me during this work and ever since. My aspiration is to act as an ally to the deaf community and to use what privilege I have as a hearing, white, English-speaking academic to platform deaf issues.

For this research, semi-structured interviews were conducted with 23 individuals. I interviewed Irish speakers and deaf people who had been suspected, accused or convicted of crimes in the past (referred to here as 'criminal justice subjects'), lawyers who had worked with Irish speaking or deaf clients, members of An Garda Síochána and academic experts on the issue of engagement with the CJS as a minority language user.

All recorded interviews were transcribed by me in order to assure confidentiality for participants. Irish language interviews were transcribed into Irish and ISL interviews were transcribed into English to aid with analysis. Certain parts of transcripts were redacted, and these redactions may be seen throughout the work. For criminal justice subjects, lawyers and members of An Garda Síochána, codenames were given and personal or identifying information was redacted but it was made known to participants that if a person with in-depth knowledge of their situation was to read this work, even in its redacted format, they may be able to surmise the identity of a participant.

The redacted transcripts were input into NVivo, a data analysis software for qualitative data, wherein they were analysed. Data analysis involved identifying 'codes' or themes within each transcript. I read through the transcripts and then did a closer reading of each in order to highlight relevant codes. As above, hermeneutic phenomenology was the guiding principle for this analysis, as it allows for the reader to find meaning in the normal lives of individual people (Dibley *et al.*, 2020; Laverty, 2003).

In placing these parameters around the work, I have been able to more closely consider the research questions and provide more robust and well-rounded research.

1.9 Chapter Summary

Language binds us to each other and to culture. It is through language that people can connect to a culture. According to Ríos, 'the blueprint for a culture is embedded in language' (Gillon *et al.*, 2018). In respect of Maolra Seoighe and John McGrotty, both men were bound to their communities and to themselves through their languages. But both men experienced injustice because of their language and culture, and because of the CJS's failure to account for that language and culture. In this research, I aim to investigate experiences like those of Maolra Seoighe and John McGrotty and to shine a light on their experiences as they engage with the CJS.

Moving forward from this point, I begin to engage with the research questions as posed above. Central to this research is the belief that languages are important cultural and identity markers, and their use in criminal law settings is significant. In using their language, minority language users are not just communicating with the CJS, but they are also communicating their identity and themself to the CJS. It is significant then how they are treated on the foot of that communication. This book aims to explore this phenomenon, beginning with a discussion on identity, before moving on to a discussion of the law and finally, an analysis of the data collected. Access to justice, as it is understood herein will constitute the main lens through which these phenomena are understood.

These three aspects of access to justice are connected. If one aspect is lacking, then access to justice cannot be said to have been guaranteed, based on Bahdi and Flynn's descriptions of access to justice. If a minority language user has a right to use their language with police (procedural access), but no training has been provided to police to facilitate their ability to respond (substantive access), or the negative stereotypes which police may harbour about such minority language users (symbolic access) interfere, then there is a lack of access to justice. When viewing the right to a fair trial only in terms of purely procedural access, we fail to see the actual lived experiences and real-world access to justice. This research aims to provide a holistic view of the lived experiences of the right to a fair trial, in terms of access to justice for minority language users.

Notes

(1) Notably for this research, Irish is not taught in Deaf schools to Deaf children.
(2) Convictions for certain crimes may bar a person from working in certain fields, and the impact of a criminal past can have a great impact on an individual's life, from job prospects to social and family life.
(3) See, for example, the disparity in drafting between Article 27 of the ICCPR where minorities were generally depicted as an 'othered' problem for 'other states', versus the inclusive input from disabled people in the creation on the CRPD. See Thornberry, *International Law and the Rights of Minorities* (Clarendon Press, 1991) at 155 and *supra* note 71 at 14.

2 Identity Construction and the Criminal Justice System

2.1 Introduction

Minority language users and their experiences are at the core of this research. It is through the lens of minority language users' experiences that the right to a fair trial and the criminal justice system (CJS) will be considered. As such, this chapter interrogates what it means to be a minority language user. In doing so, I explore literature on identity and the self to understand how identity is constructed, how it exists and is communicated, allowing for a richer understanding of the experiences of specific minority language users.

This chapter and the next look at the identity of minority language users. In this chapter, I address the literature on identity. Goffman's work on the self and stigma is addressed in detail to provide a foundational understanding of what identity means and how it is constructed in society. Second, I engage with literature on policing to gain an understanding of how police view the world and, in turn, how they come to view minority language users. Third, I mirror this approach in respect of judges and explore literature on judicial bias in an effort to understand how judges might view minority language users as accused persons. While there are other actors in the CJS, the focus in this research is on police and judges, as the two main professions which arose as issues in interviews.

At the outset, it is acknowledged that Goffman's work is old at this point, and particularly as it relates to this work, contains outdated language to refer to and deal with marginalised groups, including deaf people (Goffman, 1986: 20). That being said, Goffman's work is still notable and central in sociological study. His work has been the basis for other work which is referred to in this chapter (Butler, 2004; Katz, 1981; Millen & Walker, 2001; Newton, 1979). Goffman's work still holds great relevance and is the source of much of the sociological research contained herein. As such, I will be using Goffman and his theories on stigma, identity, known-about-ness and passing going forward.

The purpose of this chapter is to provide an understanding of the nature of identity construction and how othered identity is perceived in the CJS. It acts as a foundation for the following chapter, where the identity of both deaf people and Irish speakers is addressed.

2.2 Identity: The Internal and the External

While many of us will profess to know our own identity, I am sure that many will also struggle to define identity itself. Constructing a catch-all concept for identity is fraught with difficulty. Identity is both individual and collective. Riley explains that on:

> ...the one hand, we use 'identity' to talk about what makes individuals just that, individual. What makes 'me' *me,* as opposed to all other individuals, the agent of my actions, the continuing locus of my thoughts and memories, separately embodied in a numerically and physically distinct organism...On the other hand, we use 'identity' to talk about what makes this individual like other individuals in terms of shared characteristics, memberships...[etc.]. (Riley, 2007: 87, 88)

A person can understand their own identity, but that must also include an understanding of a group to which that person belongs, and what makes that group and that person different from others. Community and belonging are important elements of identity. As philosopher and psychologist William James noted in 1890, personal identity is the 'consciousness of personal sameness' (James, 1995: 331). This implies that identity requires a link to others who also subscribe to the same characteristics, establishing it as a group-based concept. Hogg refers to a social group as:

> ...more than two people who share the same social identity. They identify and evaluate themselves in the same way and have the same definition of who they are, what attributes they have, and how they relate to and differ from people who are not in their group... (Hogg, 2006: 111)

In this way, identity is about sameness. It is formulated through commonality and connection. But it is also fundamentally formulated through difference:

> Identity is always and everywhere formed in the dialogue with others, symbolic or real, who are different, whose difference from you and yours from them is made manifest in the claim for identity. In other words, the only fixity in the process of identification is the necessary connection, the relationship, with the other who is different. (Blot, 2003: 8)

As people, we can only know what we are by comparison to what we are not. We find commonality with peers only through difference from others. Goffman refers to those in the majority or those who do not depart from society's expectations as 'the normals' and those beyond that are in possession of an otherness or a stigma (Goffman, 1986). A stigma, an essential concept in this space, is a deviation from the anticipated norm. Goffman says that there are three different types of stigma: first, 'abominations of the body' which are 'physical deformities'; second, 'blemishes of individual character' which denote weakness of will or 'unnatural passions' such as addiction or criminality (Goffman, 1986); third, there is 'tribal stigma' which constitutes inherited otherness, such as race, religion and nationality (Goffman, 1986). A minority group has a particular stigma or set of stigmas which sets them apart as different to the normal or the majority. They are identifiable through this otherness. However, what is understood by this otherness and differentiating factor or factors is subjective.

What this means is that a person's identity is both personal and public. There is an internal and an external element to identity. Famously, Goffman notes in *The Presentation of the Self in Everyday Life* that the individual 'intentionally or unintentionally *expresses* himself, and the others will in turn have to be *impressed* in some way by him' (1969: 14). What individuals understand by their presentation of their self or their otherness, what meaning they seek to express to the world by their performance is not always aligned with what the world understands, or is impressed by, from that same performance. This is an important feature of this research. What an individual or minority group might see as a source of pride, identity and unity, the majority may see otherwise, potentially as destructive, deviant or undesirable.

This disconnect between what one internally perceives as their self and what is externally perceived is linked to what Goffman calls the 'known-about-ness' of a stigma (Goffman, 1986). 'Known-about-ness' is what society perceives of an othered person or group, based on the expression of their otherness, but also the previous knowledge that the observers had about the otherness. 'Known-about-ness' may be 'derived perhaps from gossip or a previous contact with the person when the stigma was visible' (Katz 1981: 3). As such, 'known-about-ness' can be informed by stereotypes in society, or visible tropes about particular groups. If the major understanding of a group comes from an oversimplified, possibly derogatory trope dominant in society, this will inform the known-aboutness of that group. Cusack *et al.* (2003) notes that:

> ...stigma is this gap between the virtual and the actual...one of the important features of Goffman's work is its emphasis on the way in which others make demands on us on the basis of our public image. (2003: 299)

This gap, which forms the basis for stigma, is the disconnect described above. An oversimplification or a generalisation of a particular group can mean that a person's language, religion, ethnicity, sexuality or race, etc.

is misunderstood and subsequently a source of discrimination. Minority groups can then experience treatment which is informed by their known-about-ness, rather than by their true selves (and true needs) (Goffman, 1986). In the context of criminal justice, it can lead to a situation whereby a marginalised, minority group is seen as deviant and troublesome at face value, and they are treated as such. This matter will be discussed below in respect of police and judges and their views on stigma and othered persons, but it is also the core of the empirical work which will be introduced in this book. It will show the disconnect between how minority language users see themselves and how they are treated by the CJS.

2.2.1 Passing and pride

It is important to address how people with a stigma respond to that disconnect between the internal and external identity and manage that stigma in society. Those with a stigma may seek to hide their otherness to safely exist in society, free from the negative consequences of a visible otherness. 'Passing' is one such a phenomenon where stigma is concealed and managed, and people 'pass' as non-stigmatised people. Goffman describes passing as 'the management of undisclosed discrediting information about self' (Goffman, 1986). It is connected to the self as a performance and involves downplaying or 'undercommunicating' (Goffman, 1969) a stigma before a particular audience. It can be seen in the context of sexuality where queer people might seek to undercommunicate stereotypical queer characteristics and 'pass' as heterosexual to live safely in a hostile environment. Leary refers to passing as a 'cultural performance whereby one member of a defined social group masquerades as another' (Leary, 1999: 85). It may be a conscious or subconscious performance or masquerade, with self-preservation at its core. Leary describes the situations where passing might occur:

> Passing occurs when there is perceived danger in disclosure. At its most extreme, it is a form of camouflage to sequester the self from expected trauma. It represents a form of self-protection that nevertheless usually disables, and sometimes destroys, the self it means to safeguard. (Leary, 1999: 85)

Passing then can constitute behaviour that acknowledges the stigma associated with a particular identity and seeks to hide that identity to avoid the stigma. While passing may be about self-preservation in the moment, the effect of passing may ultimately cause damage to the self. Millen and Walker explain the phenomenon of passing as follows:

> ...people adopt coping strategies generically called 'passing', that are a cluster of social interactions employed to protect themselves and their senses of self from detection by normal others and avoid the full weight of stigma. (Millen & Walker, 2001: 92)

Passing is about navigation through the world, and about protecting oneself from the treatment associated with one's identity. There are spaces where overt communication of identity and stigma is welcome and safe, and there are those spaces where it is safer to pass. In her sociological study on drag queens or female impersonators, Newton encountered this navigation among 'stage impersonators' or performing drag queens who all admitted to passing, and avoiding other stage impersonators in their off-stage life (Newton, 1979). In their off-stage life, the performing drag queens tended to 'look like bland, colorless men' (Newton, 1979) in contrast to their on-stage lives. The drag bar was a safe space to overtly communicate this aspect of their identity, whereas in the largely heterosexual, heteronormative society outside of this space, it was safer to pass.

Passing can be seen in minority language communities as well. Users of other languages may seek to disguise their accents when using the majority language so as to pass as a member of that linguistic community and conceal their otherness. A common feature within the deaf community is a phenomenon known as the 'deaf nod'. Vernon *et al.* explain it as such:

> the deaf person will behave as a hearing person does when talking to a non-English-speaking person in a foreign country. Rather than appear stupid and continually ask the speaker to repeat or explain, the deaf person tends to smile, nod his/her head, and, in general, acquiesce. (Vernon *et al.*, 1996: 350)

The deaf nod is behaviour to facilitate passing in a hearing-dominant world. In the context of the CJS, if police or judges are unfamiliar with the deaf nod, it can give rise to grave situations where deaf people acquiesce to confessions, convictions or the waiving of certain rights without fully understanding the process (Miller & Vernon, 2002). For Irish speakers, passing can be a daily occurrence and even a necessity, where they speak English in public and when engaging with society,[1] rather than overtly displaying their identity as Irish speakers.

Since Goffman first wrote about stigma, there have been multiple, high-profile movements from minority groups rejecting the expectation of shame and stigma, and responding to expectations of stigma by embracing the othered identity. Civil rights movements among Black people in the USA, the Stonewall riots, disability rights movements, etc. have all contributed to minority groups taking ownership and pride in their alleged stigma. Erikson writes about a 'revitalisation movement' among indigenous Sámi communities in Norway 'reminiscent of the "Black is beautiful" movement in the US' (Eriksen, 2010). Some Sami people, traditionally shamed and stigmatised for their ethnicity, have taken to embracing their ethnic identity. So there have been movements to encourage pride in deaf identity (Eriksen, 2010), disabled identity (Martin, 2012), and minority language identity. Pride movements encourage acceptance of the alleged stigma. As with passing, embracing and communicating one's identity with pride is a method of stigma management, where the expectation of shame is rejected and the othered identity is celebrated. That is not to say, however, that overt communication of pride in an identity is constant. Depending on the arena, communication of certain aspects of identity will be more or less appropriate, as with Newton's example above (Newton, 1979). In the context of this research, while an individual might be a proud member of their linguistic and cultural community, they may also favour passing as a member of the majority linguistic community before police or judges, lest they be met with the stigma (known-about-ness) associated with that identity. There are a range of responses to stigma available to individuals which may be applied contextually to manage that stigma and navigate daily life. The following sections address stereotypes and the external construction of minority identity, which flow from the police and the judiciary.

2.3 Cop Culture and the External Identity

It has been established that identity is made up of two parts: the internal, true self, and the external, perceived self (Goffman, 1986). In the context of the CJS then, it is important to explore how operatives of the CJS might be likely to perceive othered persons and their external identity, and whether this occurs at an occupational, rather than individual level. I look at police and the intersection of police culture with minorities and identity.

Reiner's research on 'Cop Culture' provides a comprehensive breakdown of police behaviour. When we can understand how police operate, we can better understand how and why they perceive an individual or group in a certain way. Therefore, we can understand how a person's identity is likely to be treated by police and within the CJS itself. Reiner argues that the police have their own occupational culture or set of beliefs and values, which influences how they utilise their powers. There are common characteristics to be found in 'cop culture' (Reiner, 2010), which informs the use of police discretion. While discretion is a necessary aspect of policing to allow for specific situations and individual circumstances, it also leaves space for the potentially negative aspects of policing. Research has upheld the existence of this cop culture among police forces globally (Loftus, 2010). Reiner describes seven characteristics of police culture, which shape police perspectives and actions.

The first characteristic combines mission, action, cynicism and pessimism. The job of policing is viewed by police as more than just a job, but as a way of life, where they represent the thin blue line between order and chaos. Police have a thirst for action, which can be a fun game of wit and skill, where they represent the 'good guys'. Police also tend to develop bitterness, viewing 'social trends in apocalyptic terms, with the police as a beleaguered minority about to be overrun by the forces of barbarism' (Reiner, 2010: 120). Second, Reiner talks about suspicion as a characteristic of cop culture. Inherent to policing is constant and unrelenting suspicion. Being constantly on the lookout for crime, however, leads to stereotyping. This stereotyping then leads to self-fulfilling prophecies, whereby groups suspected of criminality are over-policed, which leads to a 'vicious cycle of deviance amplification' (Reiner, 2010: 121). Isolation from those outside the police and solidarity among police represent a third characteristic of cop culture, where there is a tendency to close ranks against scrutiny. This isolation and solidarity against the outside gives rise to categorisation of people with whom the police interact. They include 'good class villains' (Reiner, 2010: 123) or professional criminals who are worth police time; 'police property' (Reiner, 2010: 123, 124) who are marginalised groups in society who pose a problem to the public; there is also rubbish (people who are seen by police as messy and unworthy of police time); challengers (people who have access to police society beyond what is publicly visible, such as doctors, lawyers, social workers, researchers); disarmers (people who are hard to deal with because they are socially vulnerable); do-gooders (people who are critical of the police) and politicians (Reiner, 2010). A fourth characteristic, which Reiner talks about, is pragmatism (Reiner, 2010). Police have a down-to-earth, anti-theoretical attitude in carrying out their duties. There is a preference for less paperwork, less convoluted course of action. Police will opt for the most straightforward option. Additionally, there is an aversion to innovation, experimentation or research because of this pragmatism. Other characteristics of police culture which Reiner (2010) describes are police conservatism, machismo and racial prejudice.

Beyond Reiner's research, there is other work which informs us how police perceive the world around them and react in certain situations. In his work on police discretion, Brown refers to the idea that police will negatively react to others or othered behaviour. Brown refers to the process of identifying deviance as an 'attitude test' conducted by police:

> One of the most frequently used, though rarely acknowledged, criteria that a patrolman uses in making decisions is what has been euphemistically called the 'attitude test.' A rough but accurate definition of the attitude test is that the person confronted by police authority must exhibit acceptance of that authority and deference to the officer and his admonishments. It is rooted in two requirements of police work: the necessity of maintaining control on the street and the necessity of assessing an individual's willingness to mend his ways. These two requirements are not mutually exclusive and they are often combined; but circumstances may enhance the emphasis on one rather than the other. (Brown, 1988: 196)

Where an individual fails the attitude test then, by failing to display appropriate deference to police authority, police can react negatively, and this is an example of how the culture (specifically the characteristics of conservatism and stereotyping) can influence the use of powers. Similarly, in 2010, Christy Lopez coined the term 'contempt of cop' (Lopez, 2010) to describe negative reaction from police to attitudes they perceive as deviant or malicious. 'Contempt of cop' refers to the phenomenon whereby 'in response to disrespect or non-cooperation, officers too often respond with verbal abuse, use of force and/or arrest' (Walker & Archbold, 2020: 86). Excessive force, rather than de-escalation, has been shown to be a reaction to 'contempt of cop' (Lopez, 2010).

To relate this research to language usage then, there are many reports under the ECRML showing that users of minority languages often fear that their linguistic identity will be interpreted as troublesome behaviour.[2] It can be that 'linguistic paranoia' causes individuals to perceive use of another language in their presence is inherently suspicious and done so purely to secretly conspire 'against' the non-speaker (Haviland, 2003). In her research, Chan also showed that non-English-speaking groups were perceived as deviant by police in New South Wales in Australia (Chan, 2009). The research shows that police are culturally predisposed to view others and othered language usage as deviant, troublesome or difficult behaviour. The characteristics of cynicism, suspicion, solidarity and isolation merge to permit this stereotype, stigma and otherness to emerge. This literature informs us on how police can view minority language users' identities externally, and that these are not opinions derived from individual officer's world views but formed through a collectively shared culture. The literature shows how police externally perceive identity and their responses to that perception of identity. Based on that literature, it is possible to understand how minority language users might be perceived when encountering the police in the CJS. Remembering that identity is formed of both internal and external views, then in encounters with the police, cop culture can therefore shape how minority language users experience the CJS.

2.4 Judicial Bias

In continuing the discussion on external perceptions of identity, I now address literature on how judges might perceive others and othered person. Judicial benches tend to be made up from homogenous groups, who in turn, hold homogenous perspectives (Hunter, 2015). As Cahillane shows, the Irish judiciary consists of a demographic that is largely upper-class, white and male (Cahillane, 2016). As such, it is understandable that the perspectives in Irish jurisprudence demonstrated by Enright reflect those of upper-class, white men (Enright *et al.*, 2017). The right to a fair trial will be discussed in greater detail later on. But for now, it is enough to note that the right to a fair trial includes, *inter alia*, the right to a trial before an impartial judge (Article 14.1 of the ICCPR and Article 6.1 of the ECHR). Judges are human, and inherently susceptible to human conditions. While work has not been conducted to reflect on judicial culture in as coherent a way as with the police, we can consider how factors such as bias can be a feature of judicial decision making.

In discussing judicial impartiality, Nugent has stated that:

> Judges are expected to be rigorous in excluding personal bias when making decisions; hence, there are few judges who would readily admit that they have biases which interfere with their impartiality. Indeed, judges are typically appalled if their impartiality is called into question. After all, most judges believe themselves to be consistently objective, impartial and fair. Judges generally believe that they have taken great strides to be equitable and that they have granted full latitude to each side in a controversy, allowing both sides the opportunity to fully present their case...But it is exactly through this blind faith in their impartiality that judges may gain a false sense of confidence in their decisions. They may fail to take into account the unavoidable influences we all experience as human beings and disregard the limits of human nature and the difficulty of bringing to the conscious level subjective motivations, beliefs and predilections. (Nugent, 1994: 5)

Nugent points to a danger in a presumption that judges can always put aside their biases for the sake of objectivity. A blind faith that judges will always behave objectively is not necessarily based in reality. Enright refers to a similar perception that some judges believe 'that law and its associated techniques of reasoning are largely autonomous from questions of identity' (Enright *et al.*, 2017). Judges may perceive themselves to be without bias, uninfluenced by their identities or by society, but this is not necessarily the case. Enright shows that in particular, a Catholic ethos has informed and shaped judicial reasoning in Ireland and Northern Ireland, resulting in 'a variety of serious consequences for women' (Enright *et al.*, 2017). She shows how judicial decisions are informed by the dominant societal identity and judicial identities, and how those identities, imposed on law, can have negative consequences for marginalised people (Enright *et al.*, 2017). In addition to the harmful impact these identities and perspectives have on marginalised people, they also go unnoticed because of the pervasive belief of objectivity among the judiciary (Enright *et al.*, 2017).[3]

Studies show that globally, marginalised people experience the CJS more harshly than the majority population. In the US, African Americans and Hispanic/Latinx people represent a disproportionate amount of the prison population (*Criminal Justice Fact Sheet | NAACP*, 2021). Indigenous people in Canada (Canada, 2020), Australia (*Over-Representation*, 2018), Ireland (Holland, 2017) and New Zealand also make up a disproportionate amount of the prison populations (O'Brien, 2018). While there are multifaceted reasons for such overrepresentations in CJSs, research shows that bias exists in among judiciaries and impacts on how othered people experience the CJS (Bergova, 2016).

Specific to language usage, Piller argues that linguistic discrimination or bias is inevitable among judges. Once a person speaks (or indeed, does not speak) in court, the justice system will be able to 'form a view of the speaker's socioeconomic status, their level of education, their ethnicity, their gender, their age and their country of origin' (Piller, 2016: 4). To connect to the research above, language immediately allows an observer – in this case, a judge – to form an opinion about the language user, which can certainly be based on the known-about-ness of that language or its users (Goffman, 1986). And a judge is not just an observer, but an officially empowered person with a great deal of powers over that person.

Just as was argued with the police and the external aspect of identity, judges have been shown to have a biased attitude about othered people, including minority language users (Piller, 2016). From this, we can extrapolate that it could be possible to show a disconnect between the internal identity held by a minority language user and the external identity understood or likely to be understood by a judge.

2.5 Chapter Summary

This chapter has looked at external identity and its forms in various contexts. Identity is a complicated notion. It is both a personal and a public performance. It is about how the player perceives their own performance, but also about how that performance is received by an audience (Goffman, 1969). This has been referred to as the internal and the external aspects of identity. Goffman states that what is perceived of the self is not necessarily what is perceived by society (1969). Communication of identity is constantly in flux. Depending on the audience, an individual may seek to conceal or communicate their identity (Eriksen, 2010). Passing is a form of stigma management where the stigmatised identity is undercommunicated or concealed, and it generally represents a form of self-preservation. Pride in the stigmatised self is a counter form of stigma management, whereby the othered identity is embraced and overcommunicated, denouncing the expectation of shame. Both are responses to stigma, where an individual seeks to manage and control how they are perceived (Leary, 1999). The stigmatised self can be a source of pride and a source of shame, depending on the audience and the circumstances.

Literature detailing the actions and culture of actors in the CJS can help us understand the possible external aspects of identity. Police culture or cop culture literature provides us with a detailed understanding of the traits which govern policing and police behaviour. In navigating the CJS, people who interact with the police must also navigate the cop culture and the externally imposed perceptions about their identity which flow from it. Similarly, literature on instances of judicial bias can indicate how we can expect judges to perceive othered and minority persons who appear before them. Evidence shows us that both police and judges can show suspicion and distrust of minorities and the other. This suspicion and distrust can then manifest as unfair treatment or bias, which then impacts how marginalised people will experience the CJS. If we can understand how minority language users might be perceived externally by police or judges, then we can understand how they might subsequently transition through the CJS.

In the following chapter, I extend this discussion on identity and explore the identity, grounded in research, which is held by the two groups which are at the centre of this research: deaf people and Irish speakers.

Notes

(1) While it is possible that there are some monoglot Irish speakers or speakers who do not have English, the vast majority of Irish speakers also speak English to the native level and engage with English regularly.

(2) Committee of Experts report, Finland 2001 at para 76, Committee of Experts report, Hungary 2001 at paras 16 and 46, Committee of Experts report, Norway 2001 at para 68, Committee of Experts report, Germany 2002 at para 442, Committee of Experts report, Norway 2003 at para 105, Committee of Experts report Sweden 2003 at para 102, Committee of Experts report, United Kingdom 2004 at para 135, Committee of Experts report Sweden 2011 at para 240, Committee of Experts report, Austria 2012 at para 207, Committee of Experts report, Romania 2012 at para 435 Committee of Experts report, Spain 2012 at para 536, Committee of Experts report, Bosnia and Herzegovina 2013 at para 125, Committee of Experts report, Slovenia 2014 at para 202, Committee of Experts report, Ukraine 2014 at para 131, Committee of Experts report, Croatia 2015 at para 96, Committee of Experts report, Czech Republic 2015 at paras 44, 68 and 111, Committee of Experts report, Bosnia and Herzegovina 2016 at para 159, Committee of Experts report, Ukraine 2017 at para 28, Committee of Experts report, Austria 2018 at para 31, Committee of Experts report, Croatia 2020 at para 48.

(3) See also GRECO 'Corruption prevention in respect of members of parliament, judges and prosecutor' Greco Eval IV Rep (2014) 3E at para 3. This is notwithstanding the recent scandal from Judge Séamus Wolfe, who attended a golfing gala in Clifden while ongoing COVID-19 restrictions on movements were in place, which arguably affected public confidence in this sect of the judiciary. See Keena '"Golfgate" has damaged public's view of Supreme Court, say legal academics' *The Irish Times* (08 October 2020).

3 Deaf and Irish Speaker Identity Construction

3.1 Introduction

Following on from the previous chapter, I now continue the discussion on identity. This chapter explores the identity of minority language users, and in particular, the two case studies at the core of this research. This chapter discusses the construction of identity of these specific groups. Moving beyond how minority language users can be perceived in the CJS as presented in the previous chapter, this chapter explores both how Irish speakers and deaf people are viewed externally in society and how they view themselves internally.

3.2 Minority Language-User Identity

In keeping with the belief that defining a group involves exclusion, as discussed in Chapter 2, no clear-cut definition of Irish-speaking or deaf communities will be provided.[1] Doing so would inevitably exclude, but it would also position me as an authority on defining these communities, which I am not. Both of the groups studied herein are minority language communities, as noted in Chapter 1. Their identity is constructed in some way in terms of their language and culture. Kramsch explains the connection between language, culture and identity as follows:

> ...language is a system of signs that is seen as having itself a cultural value. Speakers identify themselves and others through the use of language; they view their language as a symbol of their social identity. (Kramsch, 2011: 3)

This is true for both Irish speakers and deaf people. Their language forms an inherent part of that identity. In his book on colonialism and language, Ngũgĩ states that language is something that can be 'central to a peoples' definition of themselves' (Ngugi wa Thiong'o, 2005). It can 'symbolize group identity and become emblems of that identity, especially when there is contact with other groups whose ways of being are different' (Hansen & Liu, 1997: 569, citing Heller). It may also overlap, however, as an additional identifying factor for groups who are based in ethnicity, race, religion, or particularly, nationality (Caldas & Caron-Caldas, 1999; Fishman, 1985). Therefore, it needs to be maintained that although it can sometimes be the sameness over which a group connects, it may also be a bi-product or inherent part of another identifying factor.

No one person has a singular identity. People are multifaceted beings, and their identity is an intersection of characteristics and traits to formulate an individual or a group. Irish speaking is not specific to ethnically Irish people, nor is being a deaf person in Ireland who uses ISL. Crenshaw famously coined the term 'intersectionality' to describe the unique perspectives of Black women, who shared in and compounded the struggles of being both a woman in a patriarchy and a Black person in a racist society. Neither the singular identifiers of Black experience or women experiences encapsulated the lived realities of a Black woman (Crenshaw, 1993). Race, religion, disability, sexuality, language, political beliefs, etc., intersect to create layers to an individual's identity. Criminality is an identity marker too, and is at the core of this research. Goffman's three types of stigma were mentioned in Chapter 2: 'abominations of the body', 'blemishes of individual character' and 'tribal stigma' (Goffman, 1986). Criminal behaviour would fall into the category of 'blemishes of individual character' (Goffman, 1986). A person who commits or is thought to have committed a crime can be ostracised from the community which they are part of. Goffman writes that:

> In general, the tendency for a stigma to spread from the stigmatized individual to his close connexions provides a reason why such relations tend either to be avoided or to be terminated, where existing. (Goffman, 1986: 43)

Their identity becomes spoilt by criminality, least they contaminate those who also share that identity. This is particularly relevant when it comes to smaller minority groups and identities. As the focus of this research is on minority language users who have interacted with the criminal justice system, it is important to bear in mind the complexity and intersectionality of identities at play. I now turn to exploring the concepts of deaf identity and deaf culture.

3.3 Deaf Identity

As with the parameters of any identity, understanding what is meant by a 'deaf identity' or 'deaf culture' is a complex effort. At the outset, it is important to note that for generations, discourse around deaf people, sign language and deaf culture has been articulated largely by hearing people, without input or consideration from deaf people. As Ladd explains, it is 'important for the lay reader to understand that virtually all discourses about deaf people have been conceived, controlled and written by people who were not themselves Deaf' (Ladd, 2003). I am hearing. I am not seeking to define or set parameters on who is or is not D/deaf (Note that the d/Deaf distinction is discussed below). Rather, this section will look at some of the literature that discusses deaf identity and culture. This section seeks no more than to position in the mind of the reader that establishing a deaf identity is complex. In 1978, Baker and Padden provided a helpful understanding of a deaf identity, which can be applied to minority communities generally:

> The most basic factor determining who is a member of the deaf community seems to be what is called 'attitudinal deafness'. This occurs when a person identifies him/herself as a member of the deaf community, and other members accept that person as part of the community. (Baker & Padden, 1978: 41–42)

A person belongs in a community when they themselves feel part of that community and they are recognised by the community itself, similar to the point of view held by Alfredsson, as detailed in Chapter 1 (Alfredsson, 1991). The deaf community in Ireland includes a multitude of people from all backgrounds and walks of life. It includes, but is not limited to; ISL users; those who do not sign; people with hearing aids or cochlear implants; those who are profoundly deaf; those with partial hearing; those who are hard of hearing (HoH); those who were born deaf; those who became deaf later in life; those who are Deaf; those who are deaf; those who come from a family of deaf people; those who come from a family of hearing people; children of deaf adults (CODAs); parents of deaf children; and interpreters.

Further, it is important to note that this research looks at the deaf community from the perspective of a cultural group and users of ISL as a linguistic minority group. The emphasis is not on any medical aspect of deafness, nor is it on deafness as a disability *per se*. In the data collected, at no point did I solicit information about participants' level of hearing or their medical status. Rather, participants responded to a call for the participation of deaf people, and as such, self-identified as deaf. In respect of disability, Skelton and Valentine state that 'there is an important discourse within deaf culture that being deaf is not to be disabled, but rather to be part of a linguistic minority' (Skelton & Valentine, 2003: 453). Ladd also alludes to this, noting that disability discourse inherently medicalises deaf people and positions being deaf as an impairment rather than as a culture (2003). It is also notable that no participant in this research identified as being disabled.

Leigh *et al.* explained the concept of being culturally deaf as follows:

> ...becoming culturally Deaf means using signed languages, being upfront as a Deaf person, being comfortable with other Deaf people, and wanting to interact with them. (Leigh *et al.*, 2018: 8)

Thus, being culturally deaf means embracing one's community and identity as a deaf person. Much of the literature positions the culturally deaf identity as the antithesis of a purely medicalised notion of deafness.

However, there are those in the deaf community who do identify as disabled, or who view the hearing world around us as disabling to deaf people. This work in no way attempts to negate or invalidate that identity. Additionally, in the mainstream, deafness is widely acknowledged as a disability – the external known-about-ness of deaf people is that being deaf is a disability. It may be that many hearing readers of this book will have viewed being deaf as disabled without much thought to what that means. Therefore, it is necessary to understand what is meant by 'disabled'. Often, there is a paternalistic association with disability. This association stems from what is known as the 'medical model' within disability studies. Degener explained how the medical operates in practice:

> [The medical model] regards disability as an impairment that needs to be treated, cured, fixed or at least rehabilitated. Disability is seen as a deviation from the normal health status. Exclusion of disabled persons from society is regarded as an individual problem and the reasons for exclusion are seen in the impairment. For example: Because a person is deaf and blind, it is assumed that she or he cannot participate in political or cultural life. Disability according to the medical model remains the exclusive realm of helping and medical disciplines: doctors, nurses, special education teachers, rehabilitation experts, etc. (Degener, 2017a: 32–33)

This perception sees disabled people as lacking capacity outright and medicalises disability. For deaf people, this would entail perceiving deafness purely as a medical problem (a lack of hearing) to be fixed, via hearing aids or cochlear implants (Erard, 2017; Ladd, 2003). Disability literature has moved on from this medical model, most notably towards a 'social model' developed in the 1970s in Britain (Lawson & Priestley, 2017), which views disability as a social construct (Oliver, 2017). This view was explained by Charlton in attempting to define 'disability' through the social model lens 'Disability is socially constructed. For example, if a particular culture treats a person as having a disability, the person has one' (Charlton, 2004: 8). This view sees the world around a disabled person as the disabling factor: a person in a wheelchair is disabled by a lack of ramps; a deaf person is disabled when there is no access to deaf education or sign language instruction.

Degener herself has contributed to an update in disability discourse. With the development of the UN Convention on the Rights of Persons with Disabilities (CRPD), a 'human rights model' emerged. 'The human rights approach affirms that all people with disabilities are holders of rights and have the right to participate in all areas of society on an equal basis with others' (McNamara, 2018: 73). Degener states that the human rights model improves on the social model of disability, in that it acknowledges the intersectionality of identity in a way that the social model has not done (Degener,

2017a). Disabled people can hold multiple identities (racial, religious, gender, sexuality, etc.) which all intersect with the disabled identity and how their identities are experienced. The CRPD acknowledges these variations in how people experience disability in that there are specific rights for disabled children (Article 7 of the CRPD), disabled women (Article 6 of the CRPD), deaf people (Article 30.4 of the CRPD), etc. The human rights model is the foundation on which the CRPD is built.

It must be noted though, that in spite of the development of a discourse on models of disability, the archaic medical model still persists in attitudes to disability among contracting states (Degener, 2017a). The attitude that disability is an inability to effectively participate in society is still largely prevalent. The frequency of content which portrays 'fixing' or 'curing' deafness is evidence of this prevalence (Erard, 2017).

deaf culture is a specific culture within the deaf community. As for many minority cultures, in explaining what deaf culture is *not*, we can understand what it *is* (Eriksen, 2010). Glickman and Hall explain being culturally deaf as being distinct from those who are deaf and consider their deafness as a loss of hearing:

> ...culturally Deaf people, most of whom became deaf early in life, are a relatively small subset of a larger group of people who have hearing loss but experienced it postlingually (i.e., largely as older adults) – thus, the distinction between deaf and Deaf is important to this work. We can talk about culturally Deaf people more positively not by saying they have 'hearing loss' but that they have a visual orientation to life, a form of 'Deaf gain'...The larger group of people with post-lingual hearing loss, however, do generally experience this as a loss of hearing and a disability. (Glickman & Hall, 2018a: 2)

From this, we can see that being culturally deaf is distinct from being deaf, in that deaf culture is embraced and celebrated, whereas it is experienced as a loss by those who become deaf later in life[2] (Ladd, 2003). Not all people who are deaf are culturally deaf. Similarly, those who are culturally deaf are a diverse community of varied backgrounds, hearing levels and sign language competency and are not merely the 'homogenous opposite of hearing', as explained by Leach Scully (Leach Scully, 2012: 114).

Leach Scully also distinguishes the culturally deaf community from disability communities:

> Deaf culture is not just about a peculiarity of language form; it refers to a rich background of distinctive social practices, a shared past and a network of social organizations ranging from schools for the deaf and D/deaf social clubs, to today's virtual D/deaf groups operating online and through video blogs. While similar institutions exist for other kinds of impairment, for example schools for the blind, claims to a distinct community or culture have never been made for these impairments in the way they have for Deaf people. (Leach Scully, 2012: 111)

Here, we can see that there is a collectiveness in deaf culture that is not limited to a lack of hearing. Being culturally deaf is a culture and identity in itself, distinct from disability communities, based around community, social groups and practices and history which exists beyond merely being the opposite of hearing.

To this point, the reader may have noted the varied usage of a capitalised 'D' versus lowercase 'd' in spelling 'deaf'. In fact, there is a longstanding discourse within Deaf Studies on the matter. Some authors will use a lowercase 'd' and some will use an uppercase 'D'. In explaining the general difference, Napier states that:

> 'Deaf' people are those who identify themselves as members of the Deaf community and regard themselves as culturally Deaf, whereas 'deaf' people are those who do not sign and regard themselves as having a hearing impairment. (Napier, 2002: 141)

Skelton and Valentine note that the use of Deaf versus deaf is commonly used to indicate the 'two dominant discourses at play in definitions and identities of deafness', those being a social (indicated by the use of a capital 'D') and a medical model (indicated by the use of a lowercase 'd'), respectively (2003: 454, 455). Ladd says that:

> The lowercase 'deaf' refers to those for whom deafness is primarily and audiological experience. It is mainly used to describe those who lost some or all of their hearing or late in life and who do not usually wish to have contact with signing Deaf communities, preferring to try and retain their membership of the majority society in which they were socialised. 'Deaf' refers to those born Deaf or deafened in early (sometimes late) childhood, for whom the sign language, communities and their cultures of the Deaf collective represents their primary experience and allegiance, many of whom perceive their experience as essentially akin to other language minorities. (2003: xvii)

It is also common to see the variation 'D/deaf' in literature when referring to people who identify as Deaf and people who identify as deaf. Skelton and Valentine prefer this variation, explaining that the 'boundary between Deaf and deaf identities, meaning and construction can be fluid. At different times people may identify as Deaf or as deaf' (2003: 455). For the purposes of this research, however, I follow the understanding of Deaf and deaf laid down by Padden. She says:

> ...the capitalized 'Deaf' is used when referring to cultural aspects, as in the culture of Deaf people. The lower case 'deaf', on the other hand, refers to non-cultural aspects such as the audiological condition of deafness. (Padden, 2002: 44)

Being Deaf is inherently connected to an identity in one's Deafhood (Ladd, 2003: xvii). Ladd explains how the hearing world has understood 'being deaf' as something negative and a burden that one ought not wish on another:

> 'How dare you wish more Deaf children into the world?', they cry. To which the response is 'If by "deaf" you mean people who were born

> hearing but whose daily reality is now one of forever being condemned to live on the margins of existence, where, to adapt an old advertisement, "*the edge of a conversation is the loneliest place in the world*"; who have to cling to the coat-tails of the hearing world and numbly accept being reduced to imbecilic status in the eyes of the media, by cartoonists and comedians', yes indeed, who would wish that isolated and unhappy existence on anyone? (2003: 37, Emphasis in original text)

Ladd is showing that externally, the known-aboutness of being deaf is viewed in terms of disability and stigma, and undesirable otherness (Goffman, 1986). This view of deaf people would indicate at least a problem of integration into society (Woehrling, 2005), whereby society is built for hearing people, and deaf people are on the outside, exceptional to that society. However, Ladd demonstrates the difference between deaf as understood externally by hearing society and what being Deaf means internally to a vibrant and thriving deaf community:

> But if, like us, you mean 'Deaf' as a national and international community of people with their own beautiful languages, their own organisations, history, arts and humour, their own lifelong friends whom otherwise we would not have met, then perhaps you will understand our pride in what we have created, our desire to pass this on to future generations of Deaf children. And if you can comprehend this pride, then you will understand the longstanding Deaf belief that if societies learn these languages and become able to participate on what we have created, barriers can come own, and all may benefit from the unique skills of Deaf existence. (2003: 37)

However, the reader might also note that in recent years, the discourse around Deaf vs deaf has evolved and many scholars are moving away from this distinction (Kusters *et al.*, 2017). In discussing the use of 'Deaf', Kusters, De Meulder and O'Brien state that it was 'initiated in the early years of Deaf Studies, within a certain political and academic landscape that has changed and evolved considerably since then' (Kusters *et al.*, 2017: 21). They note that capitalisation is a norm that is typical in English, but that this is not so in all languages, and that it is also 'paternalistic, obscuring and imposing' and that it is improper to use this Deaf label to describe people who do not necessarily use it themselves.

In fact, Woodward (1975), who originated the deaf/Deaf distinction, noted in follow-up work that his original intention id being misapplied:

> a rigid taxonomy of deaf/Deaf is dangerous, colonizing, ethnocentric, and reinforces tautological and spiral debates with no positive constructions to the understanding of what it means to be deaf/Deaf. It starts with the misunderstanding of the origins of deaf/Deaf and why this distinction was originally made. (Woodward & Horejes, 2016: 286)

Woodward and Horejes (2016) state that it is no longer useful to make this distinction. In the space, there are still those who will use Deaf and those who will use deaf. In fact, until recently, I positioned my writing firmly within the Deaf camp, wishing to identify my work with a cultural identity of being Deaf, as opposed to a medical assessment. However, upon greater reflection and with the development of the discourse in the field, I have begun to question this usage, wondering whether it is exclusionary or isolating. There are many people who may consider themselves deaf, rather than Deaf, and still be impacted by the subjects I write about. It is not for me to draw distinctions or boundaries around the deaf community, and as such, for this work, I am using a lowercase deaf generally, unless citing or referring to specific instances or proper nouns. I take the same stance as Kusters, De Meulder and O'Brien (2017), whereby they

> define 'deaf' as a term describing all kinds of deaf persons, including those who are hard of hearing. Yet, we want to emphasize that we acknowledge that there are benefits and values connected to capitalizing 'Deaf'. (2017: 22)

I use deaf to refer people who are born deaf, who became deaf later in life or in adulthood, those who are hard of hearing, those who sign and those who do not sign, cochlear implantees and hearing aid wearers, and all those who see themselves as being deaf.

When viewed outside the lens of a majority hearing perspective, deaf identity can be a source of unity, togetherness and pride, as well as a linguistic identity, connected to sign languages.

In discussing deaf identity from this linguistic perspective, it is necessary to discuss some aspects of deaf history. In an Irish context, Rose and Conama noted that ISL has a longstanding history as a language in Ireland, predating the introduction of deaf schools (Rose & Conama, 2018). The history of the Irish deaf community is complex and painful. It is necessary at this juncture to highlight the prevalence of oralism and its effect on the deaf community and a collective deaf identity, as alluded to in Chapter 1. Rose and Conama explain how the policy of oralism in Irish schools impacted – and still impacts to this day – the education provided to deaf children:

> Oralism refers to a system of teaching, where Deaf people are encouraged to communicate via the use of speech and lip-reading, rather than sign language. The philosophy was imported to Ireland from continental Europe and was manifested in a range of measures within Irish schools from the methods of instruction in classrooms to the counselling of parents of Deaf children. A common practice of oralism was a blanket ban on children, who were deemed to have oral language potential, from using sign language in any context, and a deep

> intolerance for such children caught using ISL in school settings. The rationale behind the ban was an erroneous belief that using sign languages would hinder a child's ability to learn listening and speech skills. However, no such research to date has supported this rationale. (Rose & Conama, 2018: 390)

This shows how ISL was demonised in Ireland for many deaf people. Under this policy of oralism, being deaf was positioned as inferior to speech and spoken language. ISL usage was clandestine (see the description of children being 'caught' signing) and to be discouraged (Rose & Conama, 2018). Rose and Conama show that even though an oralist method is no longer the educational policy for instructing deaf children, it still remains an attitude present in Ireland (2018). There is still a prevailing perception that spoken language – and in particular, English – is superior to ISL, and consequently, that ISL is an inferior 'crutch' or language tool, rather than a complete language in itself. This perception can be described as 'audism'. Humphries explains audism as a:

> ...bias and prejudice of hearing people against deaf people. It is the bias and prejudice of some deaf people against other deaf people...It appears... in the form of people who continually judge deaf people's intelligence and success on the basis of their ability in the language of the hearing culture. It appears when the assumption is made that the deaf person's happiness depends on acquiring fluency in the language of the hearing culture. It appears when deaf people actively participate in the oppression of other deaf people by demanding them the same set of standards, behaviour and values that they demand of hearing people. It appears in the class structure of the deaf culture when those at the top are those whose language is that of the hearing culture or closest to it. It appears when deaf people in positions of power keep that power by oppressing other deaf people. (Humphries *et al.*, 2012: 394, 395)

Audism, therefore, informs a known-about-ness of deaf people. But rather than just impacting the external, hearing view of deaf people, audism can also be internalised by deaf people. Gertz calls this 'dysconscious audism', which is the:

> ...acceptance of dominant hearing norms, privileges and cultural values by Deaf individuals, and the subsequent perception of hearing society as being more appropriate than Deaf society. Individuals who manifest dysconscious audist behaviour and beliefs have an awareness of the of the oppression facing themselves and other Deaf individuals, yet the still don't fully reject all forms of that oppression, nor do they develop their own Deaf consciousness and identity to its maximum potential. By internalizing dysconscious audism, Deaf people disempower themselves, and contribute to a continued perception that being Deaf and promoting the values and norms of Deaf Culture is an obstacle to success. They may believe the only way to succeed is to become 'like hearing'. (Gertz & Boudreault, 2016: 64–65)

This concept of dysconscious audism can feed into the idea that being deaf is indeed the stigma that Goffman depicts, and in order to thrive in society, one may need to pass as hearing (Goffman, 1986).

This research is inclusive of its understanding of deaf people, deaf culture, deafness and disability. A deaf person can be both Deaf and deaf, abled and disabled. They can belong in both hearing and deaf worlds or feel that they do not belong in either. The Deaf/deaf experience is as varied as individual Deaf/deaf people themselves. This research interrogates how deaf people are perceived in the CJS and how the conflict between their internal and external identity impacts on their experiences in the CJS.

3.4 Irish Speaker Identity

As with the discussion above, this research stops short of providing a catch-all definition of who is or in not an Irish speaker, and what identity as an Irish speaker means. Nevertheless, there is literature which seeks to define and categorise Irish speaker identity, and this is discussed here, in order to understand the discourses about the language and its users. Irish speakers are often broken into two general groups for distinction; new speakers and native or old speakers (S. Brennan & O'Rourke, 2019). According to Brennan and O'Rourke:

> ...the term 'new speaker' has come to be used as a lens for studying individuals who did not learn a (minority) language through family transmission in the home or through exposure to its use within their local community, but instead acquired it through the education system or as adult learners, often in the context of language revitalisation projects. (2019: 132)

Walsh *et al.* expand on new speakers to include in their understanding of new speakers:

> ...speakers who have active competence in Irish because it was spoken to them at home, or because both English and Irish were spoken to them, but Irish was not the language of the community in their vicinity i.e. people raised with Irish outside the Gaeltacht... (Walsh *et al.*, 2015: 5)

These definitions show a broad application from people who did not have Irish in the home and learned it through education or other avenues, to those who had Irish in the home but not the community. They show the varied experiences of Irish speakers and the varied understanding of terms associated with language competency.

The inverse of new speakers then is native or old speakers. Following Walsh *et al.* (2015), these people largely come from Gaeltacht (primary Irish-speaking region) areas, growing up in Irish-speaking communities and environments where Irish is the vernacular. They might be described as *cainteoirí dúchais* (native speakers) or may also refer to themselves as people who have Irish as a *máthairtheanga* (mother tongue) or *príomh teanga* (first language). However, the divide between new speakers and old speakers is not necessarily clear cut. While terms such as 'native language', 'first language' and 'mother tongue' may all be considered to synonymously mean the language one acquires from infancy onwards, in fact they can be deeply complex (C.C. O'Reilly, 2014). Walsh *et al.* state that:

> It is often impossible to easily create a distinction between new speakers and native speakers of Irish and we do not mean to imply that there is always a clear division between them. (Walsh *et al.*, 2015: 5)

New speakers and native speakers may well be useful identifiers in some contexts, but they are not definitive categories within Irish speaker identity. Irish speakers (both new speakers and native speakers) are sometimes referred to as 'Gaeilgeoirí'. The term is often used in the English lexicon or media when referring to Irish speakers, but it will not be used here. According to O'Rourke, the 'gaelgeoir' can often be used in a derogatory sense to 'describe learners of Irish and/or Irish language enthusiasts' (O'Rourke, 2011), rather than as a catch-all term for people who speak Irish. Therefore, for the purposes of this research, the broader term 'Irish speaker' or 'Gael' will be employed. These terms will refer to people who speak Irish and include: people who grew up speaking Irish in the home; people who learned Irish as a child outside the home; people who learned Irish outside the home later in life; people from the Gaeltacht; people from outside the Gaeltacht. To apply Padden and Baker's definition of 'attitudinal deafness' above, membership of the Irish-speaking community could be defined by 'attitudinal gael-ness' in that it occurs:

> ...when a person identifies him/herself as a member of the [Irish-speaking] community, and other members accept that person as part of the community. (Baker & Padden, 1978: 4)

A Gael or an Irish speaker as they are understood in this research, is a person who identifies as such, and who is accepted by the Irish-speaking community as a member.

In terms of the history, Irish and Irish-speaking has traditionally been linked to the national identity in Ireland. O'Reilly explains how independence movements from 1880–1920 adopted Irish into the struggle, driven mainly by the Gaelic League (C.C. O'Reilly, 2014). It was 'during this period that an association between the Irish language and Irish cultural and political nationalism crystallized' (C.C. O'Reilly, 2014: 79). Brennan and O'Rourke say that the promotion of Irish, particularly in Gaeltacht areas has its origins:

> ...in the Romantic nationalism that contributed to the movement for Irish independence: at end of the nineteenth and beginning of the twentieth century, cultural and then political nationalists in Ireland had constructed these peripheral areas in which Irish was still spoken as both a symbol

> and a repository of the unbroken linguistic heritage and the traditional culture that set the Irish nation apart. (O'Rourke, 2017: 128)

Gaeltacht regions would exist to preserve the Irish language and a traditional way of life. However, with this purpose comes an association that Irish exists only in this specific space (Gaeltacht area) and this specific time (the Ireland of old). The connotation gives rise to perceptions that 'Irish is a dead language' (Conradh na Gaeilge, 2017), whereby it is argued that Irish no longer has significance, use or function in society. The external perception of Irish then, can be that it is a relic of old, rather than a functional language through which people conduct their lives.

The known-aboutness of Irish also includes negative stereotypes about the language and its speakers (Goffman, 1986). Irish usage can be connected to violent republicanism,[3] most notably through the paramilitary organisation the Irish Republican Army (IRA), who popularised the slogan 'Tiocfaidh Ár Lá' (Translation: Our Day Will Come) and the use of Irish in Long Kesh prison by IRA prisoners (Mac Giolla Chríost, 2012). But there is also a multitude of more mundane, less political criticism about Irish, such as investment in the language being wasteful or that the language lacks functionality.

Irish usage and Irish speakers have been connected to perceptions of troublemaking, which has its origins in colonialism, as O'Higgins explains:

> Since the Tudors, the English government had pursued a generally hostile (though inconsistently executed) policy towards the Irish language. The overall effect – and purpose – of the seventeenth-century plantations had been to supplant troublemakers with orderly English speaking loyalists. By the mid eighteenth century in Britain, Anglo-Irish writers argued that the English language was essential for unifying the 'nation' of Britain, comprising Scottish, Welsh, and Irish subjects, as well as the vast range of English dialect speakers. (O'Higgins, 2007: 431)

This perception of Irish as deviant and bad continued throughout the colonisation of Ireland such that at independence (Madaraka Festival, 2019), there was a concerted effort to reverse this perception and take ownership of the language once more through the revival movement. As shown below, a multitude of Irish organisations (many of which were founded around the time of Irish independence) have Irish language names. This reflected a desire to forge a distinct Irish identity in the post-colonial landscape (Grin *et al.*, 2003). Irish was encouraged in private (Foras na Gaeilge, 2020) and public life. Nevertheless, negative stereotypes about Irish persist (Boland, 2016). Discussions about the cost of language services (De Barra, 2017), the necessity (Delaney, 2019; Irish Examiner, 2020; Walshe, 2003) of Irish and allegations of elitism (Fitzpatrick, 2014; Holden, 2007), commonly feature on local and national media (Cooper, 2019; Gilligan, 2019; Rousseau, 2019). It must be noted that generally the public has positive attitudes towards Irish (Walsh *et al.*, 2015), but there is a distinct dislike and distrust of Irish speakers and Irish in relatively mainstream sectors of society.

In terms of modern visibility of Irish, Brennan and O'Rourke refer to the phenomenon of the *cúpla focal* (a few words) where Irish is most visible. It sees Irish being used:

> ...at the beginning of a speech and then often peppered throughout the following (otherwise English-only) oration, the *cúpla focal* has been characterised as a way of 'flavouring one's speech'. (S. Brennan & O'Rourke, 2019: 129)

Seen in this way, Irish can be positioned in society as a language without function beyond ceremonial purposes. Post-colonialism plays an important role in the development of the *cúpla focal* in society. In an attempt to forge a distinct Irish identity, separate from British identity, emphasis was placed on the furtherance of Irish at the foundation of the Republic of Ireland. Under Article 8 of the Constitution of Ireland, Irish is the 'national' and 'first official language' of the state (Article 8.1). English is then 'recognised as a second official language' under the constitution (Article 8.2). Attempts to put Irish forefront of communicating Irishness is common since the foundation of the state. But these attempts are often underpinned by the tokenism of the *cúpla focal*. It can be seen in the naming practices of state organisations and businesses in Ireland. It is common to see organisations (state bodies, semi-state bodies or former state bodies in particular) with Irish names, who largely do not conduct their affairs in Irish, or have historically not engaged with the public in Irish in spite of legislative requirements to do so and in spite of the constitutional position of supremacy held by Irish. An Garda Síochána is one example of this, where the name of the service is Irish (meaning 'guardians of the peace') but the working language of the service is English. In particular, An Garda Síochána have repeatedly failed to comply with obligations to use Irish under the *Official Languages Act, 2003* (Ó Caollaí, 2021).

Examples of organisations with Irish names who largely do not conduct business in Irish include Fáilte Ireland (Translation: Welcome Ireland), the Irish tourism body; Bord Gáis Energy (Gas Board Energy), a supplier of gas and electricity; Bord Iascaigh Mhara (Sea Fish Board), the Irish marine fisheries organisation; An Post (The Post), the Irish post office; Bord na Móna (Peat Board), the body overseeing Irish peatlands; Bord Bia (Food Board), the body promoting Irish food; Aer Lingus (Air Fleet), the Irish national airline; Bus Éireann (Bus Ireland), the national bus transportation company and; Raidió Teilifís Éireann (Radio Television Ireland), the Irish national broadcasting company. The use of Irish language names in politics is also extremely common, where those naming practices do not reflect Irish language usage: The major Irish political parties are Fianna Fáil (Soldiers of Fortune), Fine Gael (Family of the Irish) and Sinn Féin (Ourselves); The Irish Prime Minister is called the Taoiseach (Chief); the deputy Prime Minister is the Tánaiste (Second/Number two); the Irish Parliament is called Dáil Éireann (Assembly of Ireland); the Irish senate is called the Seanad Éireann (Senate of Ireland) and; the legislature is called the Oireachtas (Gathering). It should be noted that for the most part, these bodies and organisations operate in English and have varying degrees of dedication to actually using Irish. These uses of Irish point to a performativeness and tokenism (S. Brennan & O'Rourke, 2019), where Irish could be said to demonstrate Irishness, but not to actually indicate the use of Irish as a working language. These examples are a common interaction that the majority English-speaking population has with the language. As such, the perception and known-aboutness of Irish is easily connected to this performativeness and tokenism (S. Brennan & O'Rourke, 2019).

This tokenism is underpinned by statements from the judiciary in respect of Irish speakers who attempt to use their language with the state. In *Ó Beoláin v Fahy,* Haridman J acknowledged that there is a difficulty associated with the use of Irish in the legal system. He argued that it would take a certain type of strong personality to cope with the pressures of that difficulty. He states that:

> If such a person seeks a statute in Irish from the official Government outlet he or she is more than likely to be told it is not available. There is no Irish version of the forms required to institute a simple claim in Irish in the District Court, nor of the forms to enable a person, for example, to summon a witness or commence an appeal. The practical experience of the cases cited in this judgment indicates that, very frequently, only litigation or the threat of litigation will produce these documents. *This state of affairs is a constant, officially tolerated, discouragement or actual preclusion from the conduct of legal business in the national language.* (*Ó Beoláin v Fahy,* 2001: 155)

Here, Hardiman J points out that there is a practice of tolerating a negative attitude about Irish and alludes that it is difficult to conduct proceedings in Irish because of this negative attitude. In spite of the dominant position in the constitution, the use of Irish is actively discouraged. This furthers the notion that Irish – and its constitutional preference – is tokenistic among Irish society at large (S. Brennan & O'Rourke, 2019).

Similarly, Ní Raifeartaigh J summarised the complexity of the external Irish speaker identity in Ireland in *Ó Cadhla v. Minister for Justice:*

> Ireland today has a peculiar and complex relationship with the Irish language...[among non-Irish speakers] there are substantial numbers of people within the population who, while favourably disposed towards the language in a general sort of a way, have little fluency and no commitment to speaking it in their daily lives. There are also many people who are either indifferent to whether or not the language survives or, in some instances, (whether due to its compulsory educational status or, more

likely, for other more complex reasons) are actually hostile to the language. The Irish-speaking minority in society sometimes faces surprising intolerance towards its rights from quarters usually more respectful of minority rights. (*Ó Cadhla v. Minister for Justice*, 2019: 4)

Justice Ní Raifeartaigh highlights here that there exists an element of hostility from some in society towards Irish speakers. That the mere act of speaking Irish can be met with intolerance and bigotry. Irish speaking is often treated as extraordinary and faces intolerance, irrespective of its position as a traditional language in Ireland. Again, as with deaf people, this attitude would point to a problem of integration, where Irish is not accepted in society (Woehrling, 2005).

In this research, Irish speakers or Gaels refer to those people who define themselves as such and who are understood by the Irish-speaking community to be part of that community. It is immaterial whether they are old or new speakers, or what specific label they apply to themselves. The internal identity is one of an Irish speaker or Gael. The external perception of Irish users is as twee or suspicious, or somewhere between these extremes. This concept of tokenism is something which I wish to explore in my research. I will interrogate whether the perception of the *cúpla focal* impacts on a person a person who seeks to conduct their affairs through Irish. If the external expectation of a *cúpla focal* does not match with the internal identity as an Irish speaker using their language, then conflict potentially arises.

3.5 Tropes in the Data

Conflict between the expected external identity and the internal, true identity arose repeatedly in the data. In categorising the instances of this conflict, I have created two tropes which help to describe the experiences of deaf people and Irish speakers in the CJS. These tropes are the 'créatúr' and the 'slíbhín'. The créatúr is a pitiful, poor wretch who is paternailised when they interact with the CJS. The créatúr is treated as incapable of self-advocacy and autonomy. By contrast, the slíbhín is a sneaky, untrustworthy person who uses whatever tools they have at their disposal to attempt to evade justice and cause problems for the CJS. These tropes are caricatures of the true internal identities held by Irish speakers and deaf people.

How these tropes played out in the data collected will be the focus of Chapters 8 and 9. For now, it is sufficient to know that the créatúr and the slíbhín arose in interviews with criminal justice subjects, lawyers and experts. The slíbhín trope featured mostly in reference to Irish speakers, but it was also present for some deaf people, whereas the créatúr trope only applied to deaf people. However, there are historical references in the literature which show Irish speakers being treated as créatúir[4] in the past where under colonial rule from Britain, speaking Irish was seen as the practice of the peasant classes (Phelan, 2019). In this research, the slíbhín trope in respect of Irish speakers has been further categorised into three subtropes, representing the various aspects of identity at play. These three subtropes are the 'Good Gael' the 'Bad Gael' and the 'True Gael'. The Good and the Bad Gaels represent an external identity visited upon Irish speakers. The Good Gael is the person who uses Irish only in the context of the *cúpla focail*. They use Irish in private and in public only as a greeting or formality. They do not force their language on others or require state operatives to engage with them in Irish. By contrast, the Bad Gael is obstreperous and uses Irish as a means to frustrate proceedings and cause annoyance. They insist on using Irish and drain resources, despite being fully competent in English. Both the Good and the Bad Gaels are external identities projected onto Irish speakers that do not necessarily reflect the true, internal identity. The True Gael is the internal identity held by Irish speakers in this research. For the True Gael, Irish is directly connected to their sense of self, and their use of their language is not a conscious choice, but their most natural form of expression.

3.6 Chapter Summary

The groups considered for this research represent minority language using groups. They are the users of the othered languages and they are othered people. They are generally without any major political power and dominated by a larger language group. There may be pressure from the national, homogenous group to assimilate into that culture and the minority culture is deemed as a troublesome upstart that needs to be managed, rather than developed and promoted. The minority only becomes relevant when discussing the majority – it is only when one defines what a state ought to be, who the people are and what language they speak that we define and recognise those who fall beyond it. Both Irish speakers and the deaf community have a long and complicated history with the Irish state, from the tokenistic use of Irish to the complete oppression of ISL. Both languages have their own distinctive communities and cultures and both groups have their own struggles to have their voices heard, as will be illustrated throughout this research. Both language communities have faced problems of integration, whereby they are not welcome parts of Irish society. Internal identity in both groups is complex and varied and informed by the historic, social and economic realities of the group. Externally, both groups face misunderstandings about their identity and that misunderstanding is demonstrated in this research through the use of tropes of the créatúr and the slíbhín.

The following chapters will discuss access to justice, the right to a fair trial and the right to an interpreter in depth. These sections will focus on the parameters of the legal provisions and case law. These chapters will be necessary to understand the current scope of rights as it relates to minority language users. Bringing this understanding of identity to bear on understanding the scope of human rights will allow an original and rich analysis. While the right to a fair trial does not explicitly refer to identity, the conflict between the internal and the external aspect of identity are central. Law, and one's journey through a legal system does not exist in a vacuum. The realities of the individual and how they are perceived by the police or by judges will inevitably impact their experiences. So too, will past experiences have a bearing on the individual. In reading the law, we must simultaneously read in the lived realities of minority language user identity and how these people are likely to experience the CJS. Only then can we understand a holistic picture of the lived experiences of minority language users in the CJS.

Notes

(1) As an outsider to the Deaf community, it is not for me to decide who is or is not part of a specific minority community. Although an insider in the Irish-speaking community, I will not place a boundary around my community, as such a boundary risks excluding those who legitimately feel they belong.

(2) Typically, a condition known as presbycusis, for example, which involves the slow loss of hearing in both ears.

(3) This association is perhaps stronger in Northern Ireland than in the Republic of Ireland.

(4) The plural of créatúr is créatúir.

4 Access to Justice

4.1 Introduction

This chapter explores the concept of 'access to justice'. Access to justice is a central aspect of the right to a fair trial. The Human Rights Committee (HRC) has stated that the right to a fair trial:

> ...encompasses the right of access to the courts in cases of determination of criminal charges and rights and obligations in a suit at law. Access to administration of justice must effectively be guaranteed in all such cases to ensure that no individual is deprived, in procedural terms, of his/her right to claim justice...A situation in which an individual's attempts to access the competent courts or tribunals are systematically frustrated *de jure* or *de facto* runs counter to the guarantee of article 14, paragraph 1, first sentence. (Human Rights Committee, General Comment 32, Article 14, Right to Equality before Courts and Tribunals and to a Fair Trial, 2007: 3)

Seen in this way, access is built into the right to a fair trial. The first sentence of Article 14.1 of the ICCPR reads that '[a]ll persons shall be equal before the courts and tribunals' and the HRC has interpreted this to ensure access. While the HRC has focused on procedural issues, I will demonstrate how this approach is too narrow to ensure actual access to justice.

Access to justice is experienced differently by different people. As the previous two chapters showed, identity plays a role in how people are perceived and treated in the CJS. The circumstances which guarantee access to justice for the abled, white, cisgender male who speaks the language of the court do not guarantee access to justice for everyone. The experiences of othered persons in attempting to access justice need to be considered if we are to analyse effective access to justice. As such, I will rely on literature around women's rights and disability human rights, both of which have engaged extensively with the concept of access to justice and what it means to provide access to marginalised people.

Going forward from this point, access to justice underpins the discussion on the right to a fair trial to follow, and the data analysis. I rely on Bahdi (2007), Flynn and Lawson (2013) and Flynn (2015) for their detailed assessments of access to justice as having three distinctive aspects: substantive access, procedural access and symbolic access (Bahdi, 2007).

I address these three elements of access to justice by exploring what is meant by each and how they relate to the right to a fair trial. Finally, I address how each aspect relates to the research at hand.

4.2 Aspects of Access to Justice

Access to justice is frequently referred to in discussions on the right to a fair trial (Flynn, 2015). It generally refers to an accused's ability to go to court and access justice in a physical sense. In this research, access to justice is understood on a deeper level. Ortoleva actually states that the principle is not just relevant for the right to a fair trial, but that it 'is intrinsic to all human rights treaties' (Ortoleva, 2011). Francioni notes that it appears in a multitude of human rights treaties and documents (although the term 'access to justice' is not generally used) and formulates part of customary international law (Francioni, 2007). The EU Agency for Fundamental Rights explains the intrinsic link between all human rights generally and access to justice:

> [t]he possibility of enforcing a right is central to making fundamental rights a reality. Access to justice is not just a right in itself but also an enabling and empowering right in so far as it allows individuals to enforce their rights and obtain redress. In this sense, it transforms fundamental rights from theory into practice. (Access to Justice in Europe, 2011: 3)

Thus, access to justice is more than just a stand-alone right: it is an underlying principle that ensures the realisability of rights. Defining what is understood by 'access to justice' can be a complicated task (Farrow, 2014). And in fact, according to Francioni, it can mean a number of different things to a number of different people (2007). He notes that quite commonly, it is used in reference to the right to seek a remedy before the court or the right to have legal representation, but this is a limited view of access to justice (Francioni, 2007). This application of access to justice references individual minimum standards, and does not encompass the accessibility of the justice system itself. It is necessary to take a broader view to understand access to justice as a principle which transforms rights from theory into practice (Access to Justice in Europe, 2011). As Lord *et al.* noted, access to justice must be understood in the following way:

> 'Access to justice' is a broad concept, encompassing people's effective access to the systems, procedures, information, and locations used in the administration of justice. Persons who feel wronged or mistreated in some way usually turn to their country's justice system. In addition, persons may be called upon to participate in the justice system, for example, as witnesses or as jurors in a trial. (Lord *et al.*, 2012: 284)

Access to justice is more than just the right of an accused; it is an encompassing concept. Literature on disability rights can be instructive here as noted above. This is largely because the first (and to date the only) acknowledgement of a right of access to justice – separate to it being a part of other rights, such as the right to a fair trial – appears in the CRPD. Therein, Article 13 reads that:

(1) States Parties shall ensure effective access to justice for persons with disabilities on an equal basis with others, including through the provision of procedural and age-appropriate accommodations, in order to facilitate their effective role as direct and indirect participants, including as witnesses, in all legal proceedings, including at investigative and other preliminary stages.
(2) In order to help to ensure effective access to justice for persons with disabilities, States Parties shall promote appropriate training for those working in the field of administration of justice, including police and prison staff.

Access to justice literature is often intrinsically intertwined with disability rights literature. This is the case with Beqiraj *et al.*, who have explained access to justice in light of three components:

> [Article 13] reflects the general UN expanded notion of access to justice, which entails 'much more than improving an individual's access to courts... It must be defined in terms of ensuring that legal and judicial outcomes are just and equitable'. Accordingly, it has been pointed out that the concept of access to justice encompasses not only *procedural* access (ie, effectively engaging in and using the established legal system), but also *substantive* access (ie, equitable and beneficial judicial outcomes) and *promotional* access (ie, promotion of citizens' belonging and empowerment)… (Beqiraj *et al.*, 2017: 14)

In fact, Beqiraj *et al.* are basing their understanding of access to justice on the work done by Bahdi on women's rights in the Middle East. Bahdi says that access to justice boils down to three components: substantive access, procedural access and symbolic access (2007). Flynn has built on Bahdi's work (Flynn, 2015), and so too have Bates *et al.* who described access to justice in the following terms:

> …procedural access to justice (defined as an ability to invoke and participate in justice processes); substantive access to justice (defined as an ability to attain fair outcomes); and symbolic access to justice (defined as being accorded respect and recognition by the system as a whole)… (Bates *et al.*, 2016: 9–10)

These three components work together to provide a holistic approach to access to justice, which extends beyond the parameters of the court room or the police station interview room. I now explore these three aspects of access to justice in turn.

4.2.1 Procedural access

Procedural access, according to Flynn, is closer to a more traditional concept of access to justice as it is 'the process by which claims are adjudicated, generally in legal or administrative systems' (Flynn, 2015: 15). Larson defines procedural access as focusing:

> on both the processes that are available to help people enforce their rights and privileges under the law and the effectiveness of those processes. When one explores procedural access to justice, for example, one might examine access to the physical locations of justice administration (such as courthouses and police stations), individuals' ability to understand and participate in proceedings (such as court hearings, police interviews, and conversations with one's attorney), and due process of law. (Larson, 2015: 1)

This mirrors what Flynn states in that procedural access is the traditional understanding of access to justice: it focuses on the minimum standards of the right to a fair trial as they exist, the physical accessibility of locations in the CJS. If access to justice is a triangle (see Figure 4.1), procedural access represents the top-most layer, with a narrow application, proximate to the CJS as it currently exists.

Flynn explains that procedural access has an application beyond the parameters of the CJS:

> procedural access to justice requires the removal of barriers to bringing justice claims and the introduction of supports to enable people to

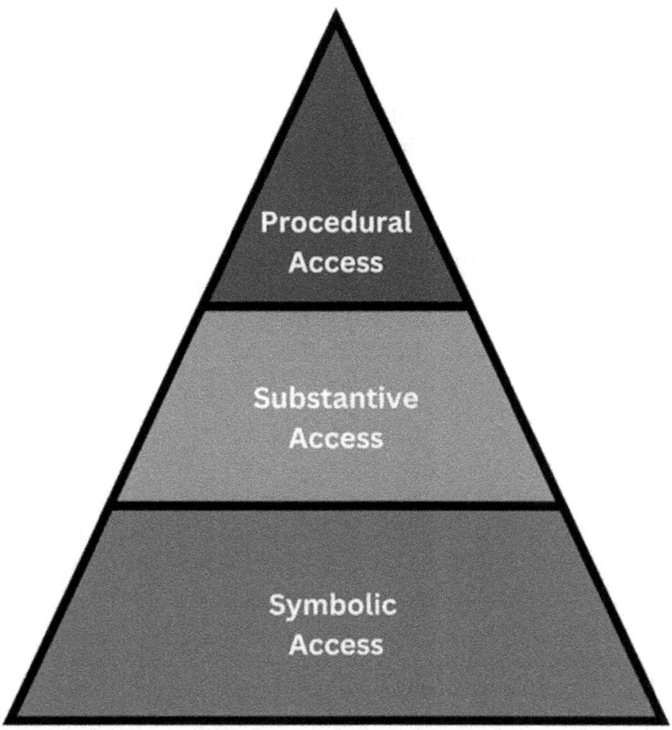

Figure 4.1 Access to justice triangle

> participate effectively in proceedings designed to administer justice...the dismantling of these disabling barriers 'will demand that attention be given to structures which are outside the classic justice system (such as schools, residential establishments, social services and the political sphere) which provide the context in which complaints or claims might first be voiced'... (Flynn, 2015: 15)

Therefore, in pursuing procedural access, people must be familiar with their rights and entitlements as they currently exist. In ensuring this, people must be able to learn about these rights and entitlements in schools, or raise such claims with social services, etc. to begin the process of accessing justice.

Bahdi states that procedural access needs to address the 'opportunities and barriers to getting one's claim into court (or other dispute resolution forum)' (2007: 28). Even before an individual gets to court, there may be an array of barriers which prevent them from accessing justice, which need to be addressed. Procedural access in this way is intertwined with substantive access (Genn, 2010) which is addressed below. Removing the barriers to access must tackle those other barriers which prevent marginalised people from partaking in the CJS as a whole, such as the associated costs, access to information, access to counsel, etc. (Bahdi, 2007).

Procedural access ensures that the wider societal context is taken into account when considering access to justice. Barriers within the system must be removed to ensure access for marginalised people. Therefore barriers beyond the system must also be removed. Flynn notes how this must necessarily include improvements in respect of representation and removal of barriers that prevent marginalised people from partaking in the CJS, beyond just as parties to a trial. She states that in the context of disability:

> ...procedural access to justice would require attention to be given to removing the barriers which prevent people with disabilities from participating in the justice system in a wide variety of roles, for example, as lawyers, witnesses, judges, jurors and observers. (Flynn, 2015: 16)

Flynn is showing the importance of visibility in ensuring access to justice: if an individual can see themselves as part of the system, as welcome in the system, then their being in the system (as a defendant or accused, for example) is less obscure. Procedural access must ensure participation beyond just participation as an accused. The barriers that exist to this wide participation need to be removed to ensure the 'effective' engagement with an established legal system that Beqiraj *et al.* call for (Beqiraj *et al.*, 2017: 14).

Lack of appropriate legal terminology in their language, for example, poses a major barrier to engaging with a legal system for minority language users (Pirotta, 2017: 19). Similarly, a lack of appropriate training and regulation around the use of interpreters can act as a barrier for minority language users when engaging with the criminal justice systems. But in addition, minority language users can experience a lack of access to appropriate education (Nogueira López, 2012: 250), language deprivation (Glickman & Hall, 2018b) and poor representation in the CJS (An Garda Síochána, 2019), all of which will pose a problem for procedural access. Laws and policies which directly or indirectly prohibit minority language users from becoming police (An Garda Síochána, 2019), or serving on juries (C. Gallagher, 2020) need to be tackled in the interests of procedural access, so as to create a CJS environment that is accessible to marginalised people.

Procedural access, as described by Flynn and Bahdi, is concerned with the functioning of the CJS and the provision of minimum standards of the right to a fair trial as they currently exist. Procedural access is an important aspect of access to justice but cannot be the sole focus. If the legal system concerns itself only with the immediate and physical barriers to accessing justice, then it misses those instances where access to justice has been barred much earlier.

4.2.2 Substantive access

Secondly, there is substantive access, which centres on the ability to achieve a fair outcome. Bahdi states that substantive access concerns 'assessment of the rights claims that are available to those who seek a remedy' (Bahdi, 2007: 3). Bahdi explains that substantive access needs an innate understanding of context (2007: 28). She states that substantive access approaches must recognise:

> that patterns of disadvantage and oppression exist in society and requires that law makers and government officials take this into account in their actions. It examines the impact of law to make sure that it promotes full participation in society by everyone, regardless of personal characteristics or group membership. Substantive equality requires that rights be interpreted, and that policies and programs – through which rights are implemented – be designed in ways that take [marginalised people's] socially constructed disadvantage into account. In short, laws and policies must secure equal benefits for [marginalised people]. (2007: 27)

Bahdi is highlighting that for laws and policies to effectively impact the lives of marginalised people, they must take into account their realities and lived experiences. Building on this, Flynn notes how it is essential to include affected persons in the decision-making process and in the CJS generally. This is broader than procedural access in that it includes marginalised people in the decision-making processes who then create the systems found in procedural access. Flynn states that including marginalised people in this way resonates deeply with the 'Nothing About Us Without Us' movement in disability activism (2015: 16). She notes how such an approach resulted in the creation of the CRPD, which has been commended for its inclusivity during the drafting process (2015: 16). The benefit of this inclusion through substantive access is articulated by Lawson and Flynn, again in the disability context:

> Without the active participation of people with disabilities, attempts to design laws and policies which will achieve disability equality and inclusion at domestic level are unlikely to succeed. There is a high risk that particular dimensions of the disadvantage and exclusion experienced by disabled people would go unnoticed or unaddressed...Substantive access to justice for disabled people can be achieved only by facilitating their entry into, and full participation in, the legal professions, the legislature and other public offices; and by involving disabled people's organizations in the design and delivery of laws, policies and services. (Flynn & Lawson, 2013: 15)

Beyond the inclusion of marginalised people in rules which ensure procedural access, as noted above, substantive access ensures that they are included in the processes which design the system itself. Measures ensuring access to justice for marginalised people are likely to be ineffective when they are not drawn up with the participation of marginalised people. By ensuring substantive justice, the effectiveness of provisions for minorities is ensured. The specific needs of marginalised people can only be properly taken into account during law-making (Manhart, 2019), when the marginalised people are listened to (Flynn, 2015: 14). As an example of a failure of substantive access, Bahdi refers to laws which provide for no-fault divorce for women in Egypt (Bahdi, 2007: 26). In spite of the apparent improvement in the law on the surface, there was a failure to consider the socioeconomic and cultural realities that existed for women availing of divorce in Egypt (Bahdi, 2007: 26). Laws created to improve the lives of marginalised people must actually provide these people with the power to enforce these laws (Manhart, 2019: 16). As such, in interpreting substantive access to justice, we must ask who has been involved in the decision-making process and if the lived experiences of impacted persons are being included in the decisions being made? If a provision or law was created for the benefit of a marginalised group, does it do so in reality? And has that marginalised group actually been consulted in bringing about these laws? And as Lawson and Flynn note, such involvement leads to better participation by those marginalised people in the legal system itself, not just as accused persons, but as lawyers, judges, jurors, clerks, etc. To continue the triangle analogy from above, substantive access represents the second level of the triangle: it is wider and more far-reaching than procedural access (see Figure 4.1) in that it alters the systems already in place and seeks to ensure marginalised people are included and involved and that their needs are heard and met.

Where the marginalised groups have been consulted in the policies which guide them through the CJS, the outcomes ought to have their experiences in mind. Thus, the laws and policies created should reflect their needs substantively. Their experiences in the CJS will be coloured by whether or not their experiences have been catered for. It will be discussed later on in Chapter 5, but when considering the implementation of the right to an interpreter, there are no requirements that an interpreter be trained or qualified. There are no defined parameters for who is or is not entitled to an interpreter. This is a lack of substantive access, but it has an effect on procedural access: an accused is not automatically entitled to an interpreter where their language differs from that of the court (Human Rights Committee, General Comment 32, Article 14, Right to Equality before Courts and Tribunals and to a Fair Trial, 2007). As will be shown, this can have a grave impact on the progression of the trial and can impact on the actual accessibility of the CJS for a minority language user. A right to an interpreter, without guaranteeing the right to quality interpretation renders the right ineffective. And yet this reality has largely not been discussed by the HRC or the ECtHR (*Baytar v Turkey*, 2014; *Michael and Brian Hill v. Spain*, 1997). Neither institution has connected the right to an interpreter to the need for that interpretation to be effective. The failure to include this proviso in the provisions of the right to an interpreter shows that the specific pitfalls of poor interpretation, and thereby the needs of minority language users were not considered.[1]

Substantive access must entail 'equitable and beneficial judicial outcomes' (Beqiraj *et al.*, 2017: 14). Yet equitable and beneficial outcomes alone do not indicate substantive access. Where a system must bend to accommodate a marginalised person in order to ensure equitable and beneficial outcomes, then there is no substantive access. Substantive access measures ensure that the specific needs of marginalised groups have been considered in the creation of the systems, laws and policy, so that the system does not need to bend to accommodate them. While it is possible to obtain just outcomes in the absence of substantive access, doing so is through coincidence or exception, rather than being a built-in part of the system.

4.2.3 Symbolic access

Finally, we move on to symbolic access. Beqiraj *et al.* refer to this as 'promotional access', where they describe it as promoting citizens' belonging and empowerment outcomes' (Beqiraj *et al.*, 2017: 14). Flynn and Bahdi both refer to this aspect as 'symbolic' access (Bahdi, 2007: 3; Flynn, 2015: 16). Bahdi says that this aspect steps outside the realm of the justice system and asks how society itself promotes citizens' belonging and empowerment (2007: 3). Flynn defines symbolic access as entailing a:

> ...society in which, due in part at least to its laws and justice system, individuals from marginalised communities are fully included and empowered to participate as equal citizens... (2015: 16)

Flynn is showing how access to justice stems beyond the justice system itself. Where marginalised people are valued members of society, this lays the groundwork for them to be valued members of a CJS. It refers to a broad, societal understanding of access to justice, whereby individuals and groups are empowered, valued and active members of society (Flynn & Lawson, 2013: 16). Empowerment has been defined by Purkey in the context of refugees:

> ...as the process through which protracted refugee populations become able to use the law and legal mechanisms and services to protect and advance their rights and to acquire greater control over their lives, as well as the actual achievement of that increased control. (Purkey, 2014: 260)

This definition can be extrapolated for the research here: minority language using groups can be said to be empowered when they are able to use the law to protect themselves and their communities, to achieve their rights and to have control over their lives and their communities. This empowerment extends beyond merely the CJS, and in fact, it ought to be present in order to manifest itself in the form of access. When there is symbolic access, a group is included and accepted in society. They are confident and capable of asserting their rights and freedoms. Again, using the triangle (see Figure 4.1), symbolic access is the bottom foundational layer. It has a much broader application, going beyond the CJS entirely, applying to society at large. It is also the foundation, as true access to justice within the system is unlikely to occur without it.

Symbolic access is symbiotic in the sense that it needs to feature co-operation from the majority outside the group and the minority group itself. It is insufficient if the minority group alone tries to assert itself in a society which is unwelcoming towards it. Known-aboutness, therefore, plays a role in the pursuit of symbolic access (Goffman, 1986). If a group is predominantly seen in a negative light in society, or there is a persistent negative stereotype which attaches to that group, then it will impact their attempts to become empowered, valued members of that society. Manhart refers to the growth in xenophobic rhetoric regarding refugees and asylum seekers arriving in Greece and how it impacts symbolic access:

> Anti-migration rhetoric, populism, and xenophobia have created a political climate in Europe (and beyond) that rarely will grant symbolic access to justice to asylum seekers. (Manhart, 2019: 14)

The growth of anti-migrant rhetoric in society and in the political sphere inhibits symbolic access. Migrants cannot be truly valued and empowered when there is a dominant (or growing) known-aboutness that demonises their existence.

Symbolic access flows into the other two aspects of access to justice. Where individuals are empowered and valued, they can be involved in the assertion of their needs and in the creation of laws and policies which affect them (substantive access) (Bahdi, 2007). Where they are empowered and valued, they can assert their rights in the criminal justice system, removing the barriers to accessing justice (procedural access) (Flynn & Lawson, 2013). Symbolic access is symbiotic in this way, and so those administering justice (either politicians creating law, or Gardaí, judges, etc. administering law) perceive these people as empowered and valuable. Therefore, those administering justice do not block procedural access in that they can perceive the barriers within the CJS as they exist for marginalised people and remove them. Nor do they block substantive access in that they will welcome and seek the participation of interested parties.

Flynn states that symbolic access aims to harness the power of law to encourage social change (2015: 17). It can be difficult to measure whether symbolic access is inspired by substantive access, or vice versa (Bahdi, 2007). Writing in the context of disabled people, Basser-Marks and Jones note that law does not always translate to social change:

> Lawyers have a tendency to believe that law will provide solutions to complex social and political problems. While there is clearly a place for well thought-out laws, and having appropriate law is, in fact, very important to disadvantaged or vulnerable members of the society, law is at best only part of any strategy required to provide rights for people with disabilities. (Basser Marks & Jones, 1997: 3)

There are complexities in finding cause-and-effect relationships between social change and marginalised people participating in the justice system (Bahdi, 2007). Nevertheless, an empowered people who are respected and valued in a society are more likely to be considered and have their concerns heard by law and policymakers, or even to be law and policymakers themselves. Where a group has the opportunities and tools to assert themselves and be heard through symbolic access, then they are in a better position to pursue substantive access for themselves, which will then lead to procedural access.

In recognising the need for symbolic justice, minority language users should be empowered to use and assert their language and identity. Biases and stigma surrounding their identity in wider society must be tackled to ensure symbolic access. For symbolic access to be achieved for minority language users, they must be given control over their own language, its instruction and given access to education in that language (Nogueira López, 2012). When minority language users are empowered in their language and identity, they can better engage with the criminal justice system in an empowered way, using their language and displaying their identity.

4.3 Chapter Summary

Access to justice is a commonly used phrase in legal discourse. But it is a scarcely defined phrase. It seems that it is the concept that everyone knows, but which no one attempts to explain. The sociologist Pierre Bourdieu comes to mind here when he said that it 'goes without saying because it comes without saying' (Bourdieu, 2010: 167). Generally, when access to justice is talked about, the focus is on a limited understanding of procedural access, the narrowest part of access to justice overall. Access to justice is referred to in terms of the physical aspects of entering a court room or the administrative aspects of court or police stations (LawUCC, 2020). Little attention has been paid to the individual person's wider experiences with the CJS, the justice system generally, or society overall (LawUCC, 2020).

Access to justice is a core component of the right to a fair trial, and of human rights generally. When we consider access to justice, we must look beyond merely assessing whether or not an individual went to court and availed of a remedy. There are a wide ranging, societal aspects which must be considered if true access to justice is to be ensured for marginalised groups. By combining this perspective on access to justice, with the concept of identity as outlined in Chapters 2 and 3, a deeper assessment of the effectiveness of human rights in this space can be achieved. Those rights will be the subject of the next part of this thesis, where human rights law will be discussed in the context of identity and access to justice.

Note

(1) In searching through the travaux préparatoires for both the ICCPR and the ECHR, I was unable to locate specific references to qualified interpreters or the needs of other language users in respect of Article 14 of the ICCPR or Article 6 of the ECHR.

5 The Right to an Interpreter and Procedural Access

5.1 Introduction

This chapter and the next focus on language rights as they appear under the right to a fair trial in international human rights law. The focus is specifically on the ECHR and the ICCPR. When considering the right to a fair trial and language or minority language users, the right to interpretation comes to mind immediately. It constitutes one of the minimum standards guaranteed under the right to a fair trial. Interpretation is a central right in accessing a fair trial where language is at issue. This can underpin all other aspects of the right to a fair trial. An interpreter can act as the divide between justice and injustice for an accused who does not have the language of the court. The interpreter may be the bridge from inaccessibility to accessibility. In fact, the other minimum standards are often only achievable for the minority language user when an interpreter has been provided: an accused cannot enjoy the right to counsel where they cannot communicate with counsel, they cannot be said to have availed of adequate time and facilities when there is no interpreter, etc. (Article 14.3(b) of the ICCPR and Article 6.3(c) of the ECHR). As such, I discuss the right to an interpreter first here, before moving on in the next chapter to the other aspects of the right to a fair trial which are impacted by language, which include the right to trial without undue delay, the right to communicate with counsel and the right to be present at trial.

At the core of this chapter is procedural access to justice. As discussed in the previous chapter, procedural access references the structures within the CJS as they currently exist, including the minimum standards of the right to a fair trial. As such, procedural access covers the right to an interpreter. Procedural access ensures that the accused has the opportunity to effectively engage in the proceedings against them (Beqiraj *et al.*, 2017). It calls for the removal of barriers which block engagement for the accused (Flynn, 2015). Where language forms such a barrier, and it is not removed, there is a failure to ensure procedural access and access to justice overall. The provision of an interpreter who is skilled and competent can be the key to ensuring a minority language using accused has procedural access to justice. Note that there are two timelines (Figures 5.1 and 5.2) in Sections 5.3.1 and 5.3.2 which detail the jurisprudence of the HRC and the ECtHR, respectively, on the right to an interpreter.

5.2 Entitlement to an Interpreter

The right to an interpreter recognises that language may present an obstacle to the fairness of trial. This offers a solution to this problem in the form of interpretation. In providing for an interpreter, the language barrier is lifted for the accused. Under Articles 14.3(f) and 6.3(e) of the ICCPR and the ECHR respectfully, the right entitles an accused to 'the free assistance of an interpreter if he cannot understand or speak the language used in court'. I address the scope of the right under the HRC and the ECtHR below.

5.2.1 UN Human Rights Committee

The HRC is the UN monitoring body which, among other functions, hears individual complaints alleging violations of rights under the ICCPR from Contracting Parties. The HRC also issues General Comments elaborating on the scope of rights under the ICCPR. The HRC has discussed on the scope of the right to an interpreter most notably in its General Comments. The HRC has stated that the right to interpretation:

> ...is of basic importance in cases in which ignorance of the language used by a court or difficulty in understanding may constitute a major obstacle to the right of defence. (Human Rights Committee, General Comment 13, Article 14, Right to Equality before Courts and Tribunals and to a Fair Trial, 1994: 13)

Under this standard, an accused person is entitled to an interpreter when they are 'ignorant' of the language of the court, or when they have 'major' trouble understanding the language of the court. This standard is vague. 'Ignorant' is not defined in the commentary. It could be that ignorance is assessed as having no command whatsoever of the language, or it could mean that the accused is competent in some instances but has difficulty understanding the language of the court. Similarly, what constitutes a 'major obstacle' is unclear.

In its individual complaint capacity, the HRC also engaged with the scope of Article 14.3(f). It held in its decision in *Guesdon v France:*

> ...[T]he requirement of a fair hearing [does not] mandate States parties to make available to a citizen whose mother tongue differs from the official court language, the services of an interpreter, if this citizen is capable

> of expressing himself adequately in the official language. Only if the accused or the defence witnesses have difficulties in understanding, or in expressing themselves in the court language, must the services of an interpreter be made available. (1990: 67)

The HRC states that there is no immediate right for the accused to have an interpreter when their mother tongue differs from that of the court's language. Where the accused does not speak the language of the court 'adequately' and where they have difficulty in understanding, then an interpreter must be provided. In addition, what the HRC means by having 'difficulty in understanding' is unclear in this case, particularly given that the HRC went on to say that in not providing an interpreter to Mr Guesdon:

> ...the French courts complied with their obligations under article 14, paragraph 1, in conjunction with paragraphs 3(e)and (f). The author has not shown that he, or the witnesses called on his behalf, were unable to address the tribunal in simple but adequate French. In this context, the Committee notes that the notion of a fair...does not imply that the accused be afforded the possibility to express himself in the language which he normally speaks or speaks with a maximum of ease. (*Guesdon v. France,* 1990: 67)

The Committee's logic here seems to be conflicting. Mr Guesdon's 'simple but adequate' command of French was deemed a sufficient standard to stand trial in the absence of an interpreter. Article 14.3 denotes the minimum guarantees that must be afforded. In writing about the *Guesdon* case, Cardi noted that:

> ...the right to an interpreter does not aim to afford tolerance, protection or promotion for any language or any linguistic identity. Its rationale lies somewhere else: in securing trial fairness. (Cardi, 2007: 4)

While this may be true, it does not guarantee that the HRC actually secured fairness, in spite of their efforts. Again, if we are to hold access to justice and procedural access as central to fairness of trial, then we must ensure the accused is given the opportunity to effectively participate. In the literature, Del Valle states that surely when an accused faces criminal charges, (Del Valle, 2003) one would want to give testimony with the most clarity and accuracy of intent (the language one speaks with 'maximum ease'), rather than relying on the 'simple but adequate' speech that satisfied the Committee in *Guesdon.*

The HRC again referred to the right to an interpreter in *Shukuru Juma v. Australia* (*Shukuru Juma v. Australia,* 2003). The author in this case was a Tanzanian man who spoke Swahili as his first language. English, the language used at trial, was his fourth language, and he claimed that he was 'unable to understand what was taking place during the court hearings and unable to understand the complexities of the legal process' and that in his lack of understanding, he merely agreed with the questions put to him. Nevertheless, it was alleged that the applicant could express himself in 'reasonable' English. The HRC then found that there is no right to an interpreter under Article 14.3(f) where the accused is 'capable of expressing himself adequately in the official language of the court'. Again, these standards of language competency are vague and potentially allow for an accused to be deprived of an interpreter where they need one.

In *Hill and Hill v. Spain,* where interpretation was at issue, a member of the HRC criticised the Committee's decision for failing to elaborate on alleged violation of rights associated with language. He stated that just because

> ...the Committee found a violation of the authors' right to a fair trial under article 14 regarding certain aspects...[it did] not release the Committee from its duty to examine whether other alleged violations of the rights enshrined in article 14. (*Michael and Brian Hill v. Spain*, 1997)

In its General Comment 32, the HRC did update its stance on the scope of the right to an interpreter where it is stated that under Article 14.3(f):

> ...accused persons whose mother tongue differs from the official court language are, in principle, not entitled to the free assistance of an interpreter if they know the official language sufficiently to defend themselves effectively... (Human Rights Committee, General Comment 32, Article 14, Right to Equality before Courts and Tribunals and to a Fair Trial, 2007)

This development followed *Guesdon* in determining that no immediate entitlement to an interpreter existed where the accused's mother tongue differs from the court language.[1] The standard for being denied an interpreter under the ICCPR is set at a command of the language, sufficient enough to allow the accused to form an effective defence, pursuant to General Comment 32. This development is a more accused centric approach and is more reflective of procedural access. The standard is concerned with the accused's ability to form an effective defence not merely a categorisation of whether language poses a 'major obstacle'. The approach can be understood in terms of Flynn's description of procedural access in that it ensures that the accused can participate 'effectively in proceedings designed to administer justice' in respect of a linguistic barrier (2015: 15). Under this development, where the accused could not effectively form a defence because of language, they would be entitled to an interpreter. The HRC has since reiterated this stance in *Zeynalov v. Estonia*. In *Zeynalov v. Estonia*, the accused was highly proficient in the language of court. In fact, the request for an interpreter largely related to a lawyer assisting Mr Zeynalov, who did not speak Estonian. There was no dispute about Mr Zeynalov's abilities in Estonian (*Zeynalov v. Estonia*, 2015). In denying his request for an interpreter, no violation of the right was found by the HRC and the HRC followed the understanding set in General Comment

32, whereby an accused is entitled to an interpreter if they do not understand the language of the court sufficiently enough to defend themselves. It would be interesting to see how the HRC would rule in a case where the author's capabilities in the language were not so obvious. If the HRC is to follow its own jurisprudence, then procedural access should prevail.

While the HRC has had a history of vagueness when considering the right to an interpreter, General Comment 32 shows that there is possibly a shift towards procedural access. They have moved forward from requiring that language pose a 'major obstacle' to considering whether the accused can use the language sufficiently to defend themselves.

5.2.2 The European Court of Human Rights

The ECHR is the primary document of the Council of Europe (CoE), setting out the fundamental rights and freedoms afforded to individuals under its jurisdiction. The ECtHR hears, *inter alia,* individual complains regarding alleged violations of rights under the ECHR. Like the HRC, the ECtHR has also discussed the scope of the right to an interpreter.

In the case of *Hermi v. Italy,* the provision of an interpreter for Mr Hermi was addressed. The Court held that:

> ...interpretation assistance provided should be such as to enable the defendant to have knowledge of the case against him and to defend himself, notably by being able to put before the court his version of the events. (*Hermi v. Italy*, 2006: 70)

The standard here is to have knowledge of the case and to be able to put forward one's version of events. This view followed the jurisprudence seen in *Kamasinski v. Austria* (*Kamasinski v Austria*, 1989), *Lagerblom v. Sweden* (*Lagerblom v. Sweden*, 2003), and was followed again in 2014 in *Baytar v. Turkey* (*Baytar v Turkey*, 2014). In connecting the right to an interpreter with having knowledge of the case against oneself, the Court has set the standard on the basis of the accused's needs. Nevertheless, in *Hermi v Italy*, the Court went on to qualify this by saying:

> The Court has held that, in the context of the application of paragraph 3 (e), the issue of the defendant's linguistic knowledge is vital and that it must also examine the nature of the offence with which the defendant is charged and any communications addressed to him by the domestic authorities, in order to assess whether they are sufficiently complex to require a detailed knowledge of the language used in court... (2006: 71)

Based on this jurisprudence, access to an interpreter is only mandated where the case is 'sufficiently complex' to warrant that access. In *Sąman v. Turkey* (2011), the Court followed this requirement for 'sufficient complexity'. In essence, the ECtHR found that the complexity of the case is directly related to the necessity of an interpreter. This raises certain questions. Court cases are complicated affairs, making use of specific language and conducted in a more formal register, according to the literature (Piatt, 1993). There is research to show that legal proceedings can be difficult to follow, even when conducted in the accused's mother tongue (Hartley, 2000). It could easily be argued that all cases are complex for an accused, particularly if they have a limited command of the language used in court (Piatt, 1993).

The ECtHR has updated its jurisprudence on the right to an interpreter. In 2018, the ECtHR held that having a basic understanding of the language of court is not sufficient to forego the use of an interpreter. The case, *Vizgirda v. Slovenia* revolved around a Lithuanian man residing in Slovenia, convicted of bank robbery (*Vizgirda v. Slovenia*, 2018). The applicant, Mr Vizgirda, was provided with an interpreter who spoke Russian. However, Mr Vizgirda attested to having a weak command of Russian. His native language was Lithuanian, and he complained that the State had made an assumption that he spoke Russian. It is interesting to note that the State alleged that as the applicant had been born in Lithuania in 1980, then part of the Soviet Union where Russian was the official language until Lithuanian independence in 1990, he must have learned Russian at school, thereby insinuating that the applicant *ought to have* knowledge of Russian. This outlook acted as a barrier for Mr Vizgirda against his engagement in the process against him, and as such impacted procedural access. He did not speak Russian sufficiently enough to benefit from a Russian interpreter, and therefore the language barrier was not removed. In coming to its conclusion, the ECtHR held that:

> ...[the duty to provide an interpreter] is not confined to situations where the foreign defendant makes an explicit request for interpreting. In view of the prominent place held in a democratic society by the right to a fair trial...it arises whenever there are reasons to suspect that the defendant is not proficient enough in the language of the proceedings, for example if he or she is neither a national nor a resident of the country in which the proceedings are being conducted. (p. 81)

The Court concluded that it was not the duty of the accused to explicitly request an interpreter. The burden is placed on the State itself to ensure that fairness will still be protected in the absence of an interpreter. This development of jurisprudence puts the accused's proficiency in language at the heart of the right to an interpreter:

> [The Court] would add in this connection that the fact that the defendant has a basic command of the language of the proceedings or, as may be the case, a third language into which interpretation is readily available, should not by itself bar that individual from benefiting from interpretation into a language he or she understands sufficiently well to fully exercise his or her right to defence.

Here, the Court established the standard as being able to 'fully' exercise the right to defence. This line of reasoning is consistent with procedural access, putting the accused's ability to effectively participate in the proceedings at the forefront. The Court elaborated on the command of language necessary to forego an interpreter in a way that has not been done before. In addition, in coming to its conclusion, the ECtHR positively cited the EU Directive 2010/64/EU on the right to interpretation and translation in criminal proceedings, a law which has been passed in most European Union states.[2] The Directive provides for the provision of appropriate systems to ascertain the linguistic needs of accused persons (Article 2.4), systems of appeal against a decision that no interpreter is needed (Article 2.5), and assurance of quality of interpretation (Article 2.8). The Directive provides more detail to the provision of interpretation than is at present available under the CoE system of human rights. It is suggested in the literature that the ECtHR's positive citation of the Directive could possibly point to a European consensus on the Directive (Dzehtsiarou, 2015). A 'European consensus' denotes a norm or right which has become so widespread within Council of Europe states that it can be understood as a right which can be guaranteed by the ECHR, even when it may not have been guaranteed in the past. This is because the ECHR is considered a 'living document' which can be interpreted in light of modern ideals (Dzehtsiarou, 2015), Interpreting the EU Directive as a European consensus would mean that a more detailed understanding of interpreter provision becomes part of the right to an interpreter under the ECHR, particularly given that of the 47 Council of Europe Member States, 26 members are also EU Member States.[3]

The ECtHR has shown development overtime in the jurisprudence in respect of the right to an interpreter. This development from the ECtHR is a promising shift towards a more accused centric approach, where procedural access is at the core.

5.2.3 Understanding 'understanding'

In continuing the discussion on the right to an interpreter under the minimum standards of the right to a fair trial, it is important to briefly discuss the parameters of the right, and what the literature can tell us. If the right to an interpreter is afforded to a person who does not *understand* the language of court, then we need to interrogate what it means to understand a language. Not understanding is the bar for having an interpreter. We need to understand who falls short of this bar, and what it means to be left behind.

We know from literature that there are various layers to language acquisition which vary from person to person (Ellis, 2015). One person's cognitive ability to acquire language may be greatly different to another (Piller, 2016). A number of factors can also affect a person's competency in a language, such as language deprivation (Glickman & Hall, 2018a), educational background, age (Piller, 2016) and disability (Schneider &

Crombie, 2003). Piatt references the high linguistic capacity needed when partaking in a trial when he states that 'because of the sophisticated language level used in [c]ourts, it is necessary to have a minimum of fourteen years of education to understand what goes on in a criminal trial...' (Piatt, 1993: 84) The language used at trial is complex and difficult. It must also be noted that fluency is not a static state of being (Piller, 2016). One is not simply 'fluent' and therefore competent in any arena in that language (Piller, 2016). Fishman has referred to this phenomenon as 'domains' of language (Fishman, 1977). A domain of language refers to the context in which it is used. Humans are competent in certain domains of language. Typical domains are 'family', 'school', 'place of recreation' and 'church' (Berk-Seligson, 1998). Berk-Seligson states that multilingual people will have a better command of their second language in the domain in which they learned that language. She goes on to provide a helpful example of domain in action:

> ...if you learned to play marbles in Spanish, but learned the rules of soccer in English, you probably will have difficulty describing marble game rules in English and similarly, you will have difficulty in describing the soccer game rules in Spanish. (1998: 17)

Language learning and language competency are situational. It is unlikely for a person to be competent in every domain of language. This is particularly true in the legal context, as McCaffrey states.

> The problem of vocabulary becomes even more complex in legal interpreting if highly technical language is involved, such as medical, scientific or other specialized language. (McCaffrey, 1999: 354)

Legal settings can include an overlap of complexities, where one could conceivably require a familiarity with a legal domain and another specialised domain. As such, when the right to an interpreter is qualified by a language the accused 'understands', we must interrogate what the courts have understood by understanding. There have been positive shifts in the jurisprudence of both the HRC and the ECtHR in respect of access to an interpreter as shown. Both have shifted in recent judgments towards a more accused centric approach (*Vizgirda v. Slovenia*, 2018; *Zeynalov v. Estonia*, 2015), with procedural access at the core. But if the jurisprudence of the HRC and the ECtHR is to truly integrate access to justice, then consideration must be given to domain and individual competency. The text of the right guarantees an interpreter where the accused cannot understand or speak 'the language of the court'. The research above shows that the language used in court is a specific and complex domain. Therefore, if the focus is to be on the needs of the accused, then entitlement to an interpreter must consider domains and the accused's individual abilities. If the right to an interpreter is to be effective and ensure procedural access, then it needs to take account of both the ability and the domain of the accused.

It is worth taking time to discuss the issues of necessity and interpretation. From both the ICCPR and the ECHR, interpreters are granted to accused persons on being able to speak the language of court. Allowance of an interpreter is based on linguistic need. As this section shows, language acquisition is complex and language comprehension in a legal setting can be even more complex (Piatt, 1993). In terms of the groups studied herein, it should be understood that for the most part, Irish speakers also speak English with native capabilities (Kelly-Holmes, 2013). In terms of *needing* an interpreter under the parameters of the right to an interpreter for an accused person, there is often no right to an interpreter for an Irish speaker. However, that does not mean there is no entitlement elsewhere to such an allowance.

In Ireland, there is a right to use Irish in interactions with the State under both the Constitution and the *Official Languages Act, 2003*. That right can be executed using an interpreter. In the CJS, where there is no Irish-speaking CJS operative, an interpreter can work to satisfy the right to use Irish for an accused (*Ó Cadhla v. Minister for Justice*, 2019). The domestic law right is not contingent on necessity, or on capability in English, as it might be understood under the ICCPR and the ECHR.

It is worth interrogating, however, what the point of such a requirement is, when Irish speakers can almost exclusively speak English with great competency (Kelly-Holmes, 2013). Surely it is a waste of time and resources to provide an Irish-speaking interpreter when all parties to an interaction share another language? (Ó Deá, 2016) To address this issue, I return to literature on identity. Certainly, the Gael can speak English. But there is a question of identity to consider. In obliging a person to speak another language in order to engage with the CJS, particularly when their identity is so connected to their language, they are being forced to pass (Goffman, 1986). They are being forced to undercommunicate or hide who they truly are in order to avail of fairness (Eriksen, 2010). When we recall what Leary says about passing, the accused must engage in destroying the self they aim to protect at the behest of a powerful CJS (Leary, 1999). It should also be recalled that an accused person does not instigate engagement with the state, *per se*.[4] It is the State which requires an accused to participate in the CJS process. The accused is then required, not only to participate in a process which may result in the denial of their liberty by way of penalty, but also that they must alter their self and pass in order to do so.

Similarly, the right to an ISL interpreter in legal proceedings is guaranteed under the *Irish Sign Language Act, 2017*. However, the right is qualified by necessity. Section 4 reads:

(1) A person may use Irish Sign Language in, or in any pleading in, any court.
(2) Every court has, in any proceedings before it, the duty to do all that is reasonable to ensure that any person competent in Irish Sign Language

and who cannot hear or understand English or Irish appearing in or giving evidence before it may be heard in that language, if that is his or her choice, and that in being so heard the person will not be placed at any disadvantage.

(3) For the purposes of ensuring that no person is placed at a disadvantage as aforesaid, the court may cause such facilities to be made available, as it considers appropriate, for the simultaneous or consecutive interpretation of proceedings into Irish Sign Language.

Section 4.2 notes that an ISL interpreter is permitted where a person cannot hear or understand English or Irish. However, there are many deaf people who will hear to some degree, and who will understand English or Irish. But rather, their preference may be for the use of ISL. While Section 4.2 states what the person seeking the interpreter 'will not be placed at a disadvantage' the determination of what it means to need an interpreter, or what is considered a disadvantage, may well be left up to the courts to decide. If a person communicates using spoken language but prefers an ISL interpreter in court, it may be considered that this is not guaranteed under the *ISL Act*.

It is beneficial then to interrogate what is understood by a 'need' or a 'necessity' to use a particular language, and for the state to provide for the use of that particular language. That necessity can be placed on linguistic ability, or on necessity of protecting the self and identity. In this thesis, I advocate for the latter based on an understanding of the importance of identity and the damage that can be caused by passing.

5.3 Interpreter Standards

In continuing this discussion on the effectiveness of access to an interpreter, I now outline what is meant by the right to an interpreter, and what it entails, with reference to literature on the matter. There is little within Articles 6.3(e) or 14.3(f), or the jurisprudence from the ECtHR or the HRC about who may act as an interpreter, levels of skill or ethical considerations. I address the entitlement to an interpreter at the International Criminal Court (ICC) in Chapter 8. For now, it is sufficient to know that in comparison to the requirements under the right to an interpreter as contained in the ECHR and the ICCPR, interpreters under the provisions of the ICC are required to be 'competent'. In order to work in the language sector of the ICC, it is required that interpreters have university degrees (Koomen, 2014). Consideration is given to the quality of interpretation in providing the right to an interpreter at the ICC. This focus on quality is absent from the ICCPR and the ECHR and their jurisprudences on the matter.

Central to this section is the impact that an interpreter can have on procedural access and how this impact, for the most part, goes unappreciated. Even more significant is the impact that unskilled or faulty interpretation can have on procedural access to justice and how it can have the potential to result in a grave miscarriage of justice. The Association of Translators and Interpreters Ireland (ATII)[5] have noted that a court interpreter:

> ...has to be able to deal with complex legal language, ambiguous questions, slang and references to the media. Poor interpreting can obviously affect a court's perception of a defendant. (Submission from the Irish Translators' and Interpreters' Association to the Working Group on the Jurisdiction of the Courts, 2002: 2)

The ATII here are acknowledging the particularly damaging impact poor interpretation can have on a defendant when they give their own testimony in court. While giving testimony in court is not something a defendant is obligated to do in a criminal case, it can also have an impact on proceedings during the investigation phase. If the interpreter used during police interview with the accused is unskilled, the statement given can risk being inaccurate, misleading or falsely incriminatory. In literature, Shepard notes that 'an inaccurate translation can end a person's liberty or defeat an otherwise meritorious claim' (Shepard, 2007). He goes on to cite examples in which an inaccurate interpretation gave rise adverse outcomes:

> ...[an] interpretation error resulted in a Cuban man's temporary loss of liberty. The Cuban defendant was convicted on drug charges for uttering the words, '¡Hombre, ni tengo diez kilos!' The defendant used these words in response to a request for a loan, and the words can be properly translated as 'man, I don't even have ten cents.' The interpreter, however, mistakenly translated the words as 'man, I don't even have ten kilos.' Fortunately for this defendant, this translation error was caught and the conviction overturned, but these errors often go unnoticed and unpreserved. (Shepard, 2007: 647–648)

There are two important points to take from this example: first, it demonstrates the impact that poor interpretation or misinterpretation can have on the progression of a cases. Second, it represents an example where the poor interpretation was uncovered. Shulman notes that inaccuracies are not uncommon and that rather the unusual aspect of this case was that the error was actually caught (Shulman, 1993).

In terms of signed language interpreting specifically, additional challenges arise for interpreters. As noted above, interpreters may not have appropriate training for legal interpreting. Brennan and Brown detail how signed language interpreters can experience major obstacles while working in courts, such as inaccessible language or a lack of preparatory materials (M. Brennan *et al.*, 2004). Recent research has shown that ISL interpreters in Ireland are also poorly paid for legal interpreting and so it is an undesirable job to accept (McEvoy, 2025a). Signed language interpreters must also work between two modalities of language, spoken and signed. Napier and Spencer state that this

> presents further challenges for interpreters as they need to visually encode information into sign language that may be critical to a case, for example, did the murderer walk on the left or right hand side of the victim? (Napier & Spencer, 2008: 80)

Russell also notes that the type of interpretation used can greatly impact the accuracy of interpretation. Recall that simultaneous interpretation is where the interpreter speaks or signs at the same time as the speaker or signer, whereas consecutive interpretation waits for the speaker or signer to finish a point before the interpreter takes a turn to render the interpretation (Napier & Spencer, 2008). Russell's study notes that for signed language interpretation, simultaneous interpretation yielded 87% accuracy whereas consecutive interpretation yielded 95% accuracy (Russell, 2000).

There may also be problems in interpretation when police are tasked with sourcing interpreters for deaf people because 'not all officers appreciate the need to source an interpreter or know how to source one who is appropriately trained' (Skinner, 2024). In fact recent research has shown that this failure to appreciate the need for an interpreter has been part of the Irish legal system since early moder times (Leonard, 2023). It has also been confirmed by a recent Irish study that police officers do not investigate the relevant qualifications of interpreters and assume that this duty lies with the agency who has provided the interpreter (Leeson *et al.*, 2020). Poor quality signed interpretation is unlikely to be caught by a police officer and it will be up to the deaf person to accommodate for this (Brunson, 2007). In fact, this precise issue arose in the data with Deaf3's experience, as discussed below.

Interpretation that is unskilled can pose a significant barrier to an accused's participation in the process against them. If they are prevented from understanding, or misunderstand based on the poor interpretation, then they cannot be said to effectively participate. We will now move to discussing the case law from the UN HRC and the ECtHR on the matter of interpreter standards.

5.3.1 UN Human Rights Committee

The impact which unskilled interpretation can have on procedural access can be seen in *Hill and Hill v. Spain* (*Michael and Brian Hill v. Spain*, 1997). In this case it was alleged that during the trial, inaccurate interpretation caused the trial judge to draw inferences that the defendants were lying because of a miscommunication about whether a campervan owned by the Hill brothers ran on petrol or diesel. Nevertheless, it was submitted by the State party that the interpreters who was provided to the Hill brothers, were not:

> ...selected ad hoc by the local police but a person designated by the Instituto Nacional de Empleo (INEM) upon agreement with the Ministry of Interior. Interpreters must have satisfied professional criteria before being employed by INEM. (para 9.2)

In spite of this claim from the State party, the Hill brothers claimed that the interpreters were insufficient. They further attested to relying on the aid of 'two bilingual inmates' in order to prepare themselves for trial. Brian and Michael Hill also requested the services of a 'consular representative who could assist as an independent interpreter' from the British Consulate.[6] Had the Hill brothers been provided with adequate interpreters and access to adequate interpreters, they would not have needed to resort to such measures. The person who was made available during the police interview of the Hill brothers was described as a 'young, unqualified...student interpreter'. The HRC did not address this alleged violation of Article 14.3(f), however. This is disappointing as it misses an opportunity to shed light on the calibre of interpreter required to satisfy the right. Nevertheless, the Hill brothers complained of a violation of the right to an interpreter because of the multiple instances where the felt interpretation was poor and unsatisfactory. These allegations suggest a lack of procedural access. As a result of the limited and poor interpretation, the Hill brothers were arguably prevented from fully participating in the proceedings against them (including consulting with their counsel and forming a defence).

Where an interpreter is provided, but that interpreter lacks the skill necessary to actually facilitate interpretation, then the right has been executed in name only. An accused cannot effectively engage in proceedings where their interpreter is not facilitating communication.

Figure 5.1 depicts the judgments made by the HRC regarding both the entitlement to an interpreter and interpreting standards, as well as the HRC's general commentary on the right to an interpreter. It may be helpful to visualise how the jurisprudence on the right to an interpreter has progressed over time.

As can be seen, the jurisprudence of the HRC has not engaged in the specifics of interpreter provision, nor has it connected the right to an interpreter with the right to effective interpretation. In the following section, I explore how the ECtHR has engaged with these issues regarding the right to an interpreter.

5.3.2 The European Court of Human Rights

The issue of unskilled interpreters has arisen in the ECtHR also. In *Kamasinski v. Austria*, the accused was assisted by individuals who were not trained interpreters:

> During the [police] questioning on 15 October interpretation was provided by a prisoner who, however, had only a limited knowledge of English. The person who interpreted on 6 November, [date of subsequent police interrogation] whilst not a registered interpreter, was

Figure 5.1 HRC jurisprudence on the right to an interpreter timeline

> someone regularly asked to assist at police interviews when no registered interpreter was available. It cannot be established from the evidence adduced whether the person who provided interpretation on 16 December 1980 was a registered interpreter or not. (*Kamasinski v Austria*, 1989: 11)

Not only did authorities make use of an unregistered interpreter, but there was also a prisoner who had only 'limited knowledge' of English used as an interpreter. In addressing this, the ECtHR held that it was not at liberty to adjudicate on the interpretation system in place in a Member State. If the right to an interpreter is to have any meaning and ensure procedural access, then a competent interpreter must be provided, who can actually carry out the job of interpretation. Otherwise the accused is not guaranteed procedural access and denied the ability to effectively participate. The Court went to hold that during the pre-trial investigations the requirements under Article 6.3(e) had been met:

> ...the Court, like the Commission, finds no indication in the evidence before it that the requirements of this provision were not met during Mr Kamasinski's pre-trial questioning by the police and the investigating judges. An interpreter was present on each occasion. It does not appear that Mr Kamasinski was unable to comprehend the questions put to him or to make himself understood in his replies. (para 77)

The Court essentially noted that the prisoner in custody, with limited English who acted as Mr Kamasinski's interpreter was an effective execution of the right to an interpretation. The mere fact an 'interpreter' – irrespective of skill or professionalism – was provided has satisfied the requirement under Article 6.3(e) in the eyes of the Court. As discussed, the profession of interpreters is complex and highly skilled. There was no interrogation in this case of whether the provision of a prisoner in custody to act as an interpreter actually satisfy the complex and professional role of interpreter.

The issue of competency of interpreters arose again in *Hermi v. Italy*. In this case the Court appeared to update its jurisprudence from *Kamasinski* by suggesting that States might be under some duty to assure the quality of interpreters in terms of assuring that the right to interpretation remains practical and effective:

> In view of the need for that right to be practical and effective, the obligation of the competent authorities is not limited to the appointment of an interpreter but, if they are put on notice in the particular circumstances, may also extend to a degree of subsequent control over the adequacy of the interpretation provided...(*Hermi v. Italy*, 2006: 70)

The Court included the proviso that the right to an interpreter must be 'practical and effective', which is a step towards procedural access in that an interpreter is practical and effective when they allow an accused to effectively participate in the proceedings against them. The Court added the qualification that the need for a state to be concerned about the quality of interpretation was related to 'particular circumstances' and being 'put on notice'. They did not go as far as reading the right to an interpreter as including a general provision of competency or effectiveness.

Of particular concern relating to interpreter competency is the use of family members as interpreters for accused persons. In *Baytar v. Turkey*, the interpreter provided at trial was 'simply a member of the applicant's family waiting in the corridor' (*Baytar v Turkey*, 2014). While it was not stated whether or not the family member used was competent or capable to act as interpreter, it was pointed out that the court 'failed to verify [their] skills'. A family member as an interpreter was also at issue in *Cuscani v. UK* (*Cuscani v The United Kingdom*, 2002). However, in both cases the Court failed to address the matter in its judgment.

Additionally, and perhaps most worryingly, the issue itself that a family member was sought to provide interpretive aid was not addressed in either case. There was no indication given of concern for bias or a conflict of interest when a family member is charged with interpreting at court (Pawlosky, 1996). Interpreting for a family member who is being investigated by the police or standing trial and is no doubt an incredibly stressful situation. As Pawlosky notes, even where the family member is trying to interpret proceedings in 'good faith' there is a risk that they could 'subconsciously misrepresent certain testimony in an effort to shelter [a] loved one' (1996). This can undoubtedly impact procedural access: if a family member is subconsciously shielding a loved one from procedures, then the accused is barred from effectively participating in proceedings. However, the ECtHR's decision in *Vizgirda v. Slovenia* possibly holds a silver lining. As noted above the ECtHR positively cited the EU Directive 2010/64/EU in its decision. In considering the quality of interpretation, the Directive mandates that interpretation must be of:

> ...quality sufficient to safeguard the fairness of the proceedings, in particular by ensuring that suspected or accused persons have knowledge of the case against them and are able to exercise their right of defence. (Article 2.8)

This can be read in terms of procedural access: That interpretation must provide the accused with an opportunity to effectively participate in the proceedings against them. This could mean that going forward the ECtHR could require interpreters to be of sufficient quality to safeguard

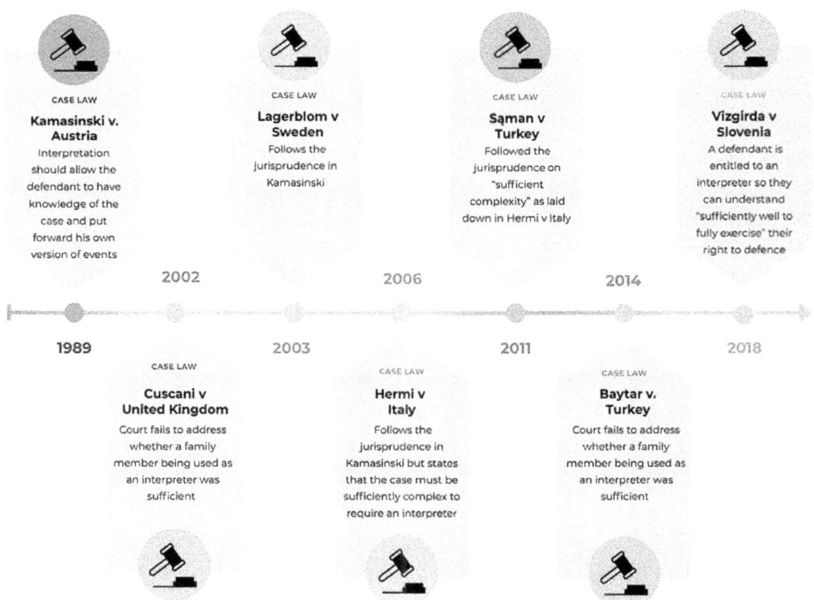

Figure 5.2 ECtHR jurisprudence on the right to an interpreter timeline

the fairness of proceedings, as an inherent part of the right to an interpreter.

The effect that incompetent and unqualified interpreters can have on the realisation of a fair trial cannot be understated. Where a defendant is given an unskilled interpreter who cannot effectively follow proceedings, the accused is deprived of the realisation of their right to interpretation. They are not ensured procedural access to justice. Largely neither the ECtHR nor the HRC have addressed quality of interpretation as an aspect of the right to a fair trial and the right to an interpreter. Both institutions have stopped short of reading the right to an interpreter as imposing a duty on states to ensure quality and skilled interpretation.

As above with the HRC, Figure 5.2 depicts the progress of the ECtHR's jurisprudence over time in relation to both entitlement to an interpreter and the standard of interpreting.

5.4 Interpreters in the Data

It is perhaps unsurprising that the issue of interpreters was a major point of contention in interview. Here I present the data collected which coincides with the right to an interpreter during interactions with the CJS.

5.4.1 Access to interpreters

Access to interpreters was a major concern in the data. People repeatedly experienced either no interpreter, or they were delayed in accessing an interpreter, or they were provided with an individual who was either not an interpreter or was a poorly or underqualified interpreter. This was a particular problem in police stations as all of the interviewees had experiences with police, but not everyone interviewed had their interactions go forwards to court.

It should be noted that while there are limited numbers of interpreters working in the field in Ireland, that is not to say in all the cases in Table 5.1, an interpreter was sought, and none was able to be found and that is why there was no interpreter. Briefly, it may have been that police attitudes about minority language users, or othered people generally prevented the Garda in charge from actually perceiving the need for an interpreter. From Table 5.1 we can observe that no person in this study who interacted directly with the CJS as a suspect was provided with an interpreter in a police station setting. Certainly, Lawyer1 and Lawyer2 had experienced their deaf clients having interpreters, but it is not possible to glean information about the quality of interpretation from their perspectives. Dlíodóir1 and Dlíodóir2 are both Irish speaking and therefore there was no need for interpreters to mediate their interactions with Irish speaking clients. But there is no evidence to show whether their clients experienced having an appropriate interpreter in the Garda station prior to their

Table 5.1 Interpreter usage with Gardaí

Use of Interpreters in interactions between Criminal Justice Subjects and Gardaí			
Name	**No Interpreter**	**Garda as interpreter**	**Other**
Gael1		✓	
Gael2	✓		
Gael3	✓		
Gael4			Garda spoke some phrases in Irish
Gael5		Garda tried to speak English when left alone	
Gael6	✓		
Gael7	✓		
Gael8	✓		
Deaf1	✓		
Deaf2	✓		
Deaf3			Interpreter provided after arrangement but was unskilled
Deaf4	✓		
Deaf5	✓		

engagement with their legal representation. At the time of interviews, suspects in police detention were prohibited from having their interviews with police mediated by legal representation. As such none of the lawyers would have had first-hand experience of whether the interview was appropriately interpreted.

Availability of interpreters can also mean that an accused is left without an interpreter entirely. As such, it is important to discuss the availability of interpreters in the context of the right to an interpreter itself.

Prof. Leeson in her interview referred to the estimated number of legal ISL interpreters:

> LL: '...of a pool of maybe 100 interpreters who are operating, maybe ten were working in legal settings.'

Not all who work as interpreters work in legal context, which intensifies availability issues. Availability and barriers to accessing interpreters was noted also by Deaf3, Gael7 and AGS2.

Interpreter availability and its impact on proper procedure was a concern for Lawyer2 in respect of their client's access to court:

> Lawyer2: 'Just if the matter had went to trial, the realities – I don't know if they would have been able to proceed because I don't know if they would have found a second set of interpreters. They would have needed three sets of interpreters in an ideal world – and [client] would have had to give, in order to proceed, [they] would have had to compromise. I am sure [client] probably would have compromised but [they] shouldn't have to compromise. [Client] would have said "We'll do it with two sets or one"'

Lawyer2 recounted their worry and doubt about how feasible it would have been to actually go forward to trial with their deaf client who needed both a hearing and deaf interpreter. Note that for some deaf people, it is necessary to have two interpreters, one who is hearing and one who is deaf, working together to offer chain interpretation. Deaf people can often experience language deprivation which can result in what Glickman and Hall call 'dysfluent language', which they explain as 'language that native users would easily recognize to be unclear, poorly developed, and substandard for everyday conversational purposes...' (Glickman & Hall, 2018a: 2). Wattman explains that deaf interpreters can act to bridge the gap that might exist in deaf people with dysfluent language and hearing interpreters who use standardised American Sign Language (ASL):

> As native users of ASL steeped in Deaf culture, but also widely experienced in the hearing world, Deaf interpreters can often intuit what a deaf client is attempting to say and understand what obstacles are preventing clear receptive or expressive communication. ASL-English interpreters may lack this 'gut sense' of the deaf client's worldview, frame of reference, and linguistic style. (Wattman, 2018: 220)

As such, deaf and hearing interpreters can work together to provide a better interpretation service for deaf people with dysfluent language. The deaf person's signs are understood by the native Sign Language using deaf interpreter. The deaf interpreter interprets into standardised Sign Language for the hearing interpreter, who then renders the content into spoken language. Prof. Leeson noted in her interviews that there is an extremely limited number of deaf interpreters working in Ireland, which affects availability then for deaf people like Lawyer2's client. While they did not end up on trial in the end, Lawyer2 nevertheless acknowledged that it would have inevitably meant 'compromise' for their client. Had they gone forward to trial, their client would have had to accept a lesser standard of interpretation service, because of the limited number of deaf interpreters available.

5.4.2 Interpreter ethics and confidentiality

Confidentiality and privilege are major aspects of lawyer/client relationships, and concern about these issues in interpreter mediated interactions arose in the data. If effective communication with counsel is to be facilitated, a client ought to feel safe in their disclosures (A Guide to Good Professional Conduct for Solicitors, 3rd edn, 2013). Assurance of privacy constitutes well founded practice that defines the lawyer/client relationship. In the context of this research, these practices do not extend to interpreters in the same way.[7] The interpreter used in Garda interviews or in court can often be the same interpreter used in client consultations (Waterhouse, 2014), which may be particularly problematic given that the interpreter is not bound by a requirement to assure confidentiality when they are facilitating a privilege communication. At present there is no legislation dealing with the issue and thus no legal requirements or express rights to privilege extended to interpreters.

Lawyer2 expressed their concern about this risk. They had met with their client and the interpreter in the Garda station prior to the client being interviewed by the Garda in their absence, but with the interpreter:

> Lawyer2: 'But I do know the last time I was in an interview I know I was sent away and the interpreter was kept inside in the Garda station for a chat for half an hour afterwards. So I don't know does that meant that all my advices are relayed to the Gardaí?...So you have to be very careful what you say in front of the interpreter.'
>
> GM: 'Which must be difficult then to relay advice to your client.'
>
> Lawyer2: 'Now we are only thinking they shouldn't be [discussing with the Gardaí] They are not bound by confidentiality. What's stopping them telling the Gardaí what we have discussed?'

Lawyer2 did not have confidence that confidentiality could be maintained which is extremely worrying in the context of the right to a fair trial. Their worry was compounded by the relationship that an interpreter appeared to have with Gardaí (the interpreter stayed back after the interview to chat with Gardaí).

Lawyer1 was also concerned with the use of the same interpreter for their consultation and for the Garda interview with their client:

> Lawyer1: 'One thing that strikes me as I go, is that there was one interpreter brought by the state, which is fine – but when it came to me having a consultation with the client, there was still one interpreter, and I am pretty sure it was the same one'
>
> GM: 'Yeah, I was about to ask'
>
> Lawyer1: 'Rightly there should be a separate independent person, and I think it's obvious why – you should be allowed to consult with someone in private, go to an interview with the guards and have a different interpreter, and then go back to your private setting. That was an obvious flaw in the process'

The concern here was about confidentiality. Lawyer1 worried that the interpreter used in the 'private setting' where privileged communication could occur would contaminate the confidentiality (an 'obvious flaw').

There is no way to know for certain whether the interpreters in Lawyer2 and Lawyer1's accounts did disclose content from the lawyer/client consultations Gardaí. Yet the fear and worry that it is a possibility is important in terms of ensuring the client believes they are being treated fairly and justly. This fear may also exist for the client and impact their ability to speak freely with their counsel if there is a concern about confidentiality and the interpreter. Both lawyers expressed a worry about the safety of their communication with their client. The examples demonstrate that lawyers exercise caution when communicating with clients, possibly impacting on the right to communicate with counsel. This poses a procedural access concern in that it can impede the accused person from effectively engaging with the process.

It should also be noted that this issue represents a lack of substantive access. Lack of regulation or legislation in the field of interpretation means that there is nothing to prevent an interpreter being called as a witness or sharing information with Gardaí (ATII, 2009; Waterhouse, 2014).

5.4.3 Working conditions for interpreters

Interpreters' working conditions may contribute to the low number of interpreters and thus the vindication of the right to an interpreter. Remuneration for legal interpreters can be incredibly low. The Irish Translators and Interpreters Association reports that interpreters can sometimes be paid as little as €5.50 per hour for their work (Irish Translators' and Interpreters' Association, 2013), which was far below minimum wage in Ireland.[7]

Remuneration of interpreters was a concern raised by Lawyer2. Lawyer2 had been appointed as free legal aid and had used an interpreter with their deaf client. They had struggled to have the cost of the interpreter covered by the payments system for free legal aid:

> Lawyer2: '[Trying to recuperate interpreter's pay was] absolutely shocking. I did an awful lot of appealing the decisions with the Legal Aid Board to pay their fees – that would have been a worry. I know the interpreters said from the start 'we'll take whatever they give us, try your best, we'll take whatever, we are not going to come after the client for the money'. We would be worried that we could be found liable – if someone wasn't willing to waive the fees and take whatever. But they did get their full fees, we managed to sort that'.

Here, Lawyer2 recounted an expectation on the part of the interpreters of uncertainty of pay. This suggests that poor or uncertain pay is a common occurrence for these interpreters, and it would concur with some of the interview data collected from experts (Heyerick, 2025).[9] Additionally, Lawyer2 commented on the difficulty they had in securing payment for interpreters. The interpreter must be reimbursed for their services through the Legal Aid Board (because the client is entitled to free interpretation and does not pay for the service). Nevertheless, the process was extremely difficult, and one that Lawyer2 worried could result in liability on their part for non-payment of interpreter fees.

Lawyer2 went on to note the disparity in payment for interpreters who work with the defence and those who work for the prosecution:

> Lawyer2: '...if they are employed by the court, they get a higher rate, but if we as solicitors employ them, they don't. There is huge differences between what the Court Service will pay and what they get paid if they are employed by the solicitors'

This concern mirrors what the ATII stated in 2013, that when working through private interpreter agencies, interpreters are paid significantly less than those contracted by the Court's Service (Irish Translators' and Interpreters' Association, 2013). Offering a significantly lowered rate of pay for working with defence may well impact on the already scarce availability of interpreters who perhaps couldn't or wouldn't accept such poor remuneration.

The work of a legal interpreter itself can be extremely stressful, (Knodel, 2018) beyond concerns about pay. Professor Leeson commented on the work environments that legal ISL interpreters must often face:

> LL: 'You know [an ISL interpreter would say] 'I'm trying to do my best, I'm here on my own, it's three in the morning and this isn't a dialect that I'm particularly comfortable with but they [the Gardaí] are not letting me go because they're saying that we have somebody here and the clock is ticking' so you've got so many competing demands'.

Leeson shows that the pressure put on interpreters to work in difficult situations is compounded by the interest of Gardaí in avoiding undue delay. It is also notable that in this instance, Leeson is describing an interpreter who is struggling to carry out their duties. The interpreter can find themselves in an impossible situation, unable to leave on account of pressure from Gardaí, but cognisant of their own shortcomings and the potential to negatively impact the fairness of procedure. From the perspective of a deaf suspect reliant on such an interpreter, these circumstances have the potential to jeopardise the fairness of procedure. An interpreter ill-equipped to facilitate a police interview has the potential to prejudice or misinterpret the deaf person's intent, which may have disastrous consequences (Shepard, 2007).

In terms of court interpretation, Dr Mary Phelan noted in her interview that there is no practice of interpreters working in pairs, or being afforded breaks:

> MP: 'Well there's no relief for interpreters in the Irish legal system. No. Zero. So an interpreter's expected to interpret all day, basically. Yeah. Which is crazy.'

Interpreters are under intense pressure, sometimes working hours on end without relief. It is unsurprising then that burnout is common among interpreters, affecting their availability (Heyerick, 2025; Knodel, 2018).

Keeping the right to interpretation in mind, an overworked and underpaid interpreter is likely to impact on the standard of interpretation. Interpreters who suffer from burnout are unlikely to maintain high standards in performance. There are reasons to be concerned that this is happening in Ireland. Ultimately, this puts the accused who is reliant on interpretation for access to justice at risk of being denied procedural access and the opportunity to effectively engage with the proceedings. Where an interpreter underperforms, buckles to pressure or where none can be located, the accused is denied a right to participate in the proceedings and ultimately, denied procedural access.

5.4.4 Interpreter training

Competency in language is in no way equivalent to being an interpreter. It should be noted that this is not meant as a criticism of those who are working as interpreters without training. Globally, there are little to no interpreter training courses or professional qualifications available. There are little to no requirements for qualifications for people to act as interpreters.[10] In Ireland, individual interpretation companies may indeed provide training days for staff, but there is no requirement to do so. In a recent request for tenders for spoken language court interpreters from the Courts Service, three levels of interpreter skill were sought from competing interpretation agencies:

> **Level 1**: There is objectively verifiable evidence that the person is competent to interpret spoken words…fully accurate so as to meet the standard of quality necessary to satisfy the requirements of due process…
>
> **Level 2**: The person is a Native Speaker of the language concerned and can be shown meet the above Level 1 competency standard regarding English, OR is a Native Speaker of English and can be shown to be competent in the language concerned.
>
> **Level 3**: The person is a Native Speaker of English with a Third Level Qualification in the language concerned, OR a Native Speaker of the language concerned with a Third Level Qualification in English (Irish Translators' and Interpreters' Association, 2013).

Notably, none of the three levels of spoken interpreters requested require specific third level/professional qualification in interpretation. While the lowest level, Level 1 is qualified by the need for 'objectively verifiable evidence' that an interpreter 'is competent to interpret spoken words', without a testing or quality control system in place, it is not possible to ascertain such evidence in the absence of testing, as noted by the ATII (2013).

Some interviewees reported problems with poorly trained or untrained interpreters. Although the *Irish Sign Language Act, 2017* (ISL Act) now mandates that all ISL interpreters be trained, all participants were interviewed before the entry into force of the ISL Act. As such, Deaf3's experience here was not overshadowed by any legislative requirements for trained interpreters:

> Deaf3: 'I was called in just to make a statement...And there was an interpreter for that and I was surprised. I had never seen the interpreter before. I asked who [interpreter was] and [they told me their name]. I had never heard of [them] before, I had never seen [them] before...So we went through the interview with the Gardaí. And the interpreting was ok. There was some signs that were wrong, some confused numbers like 17 and 12. For me, that put extra pressure on me to be alert to the communication. Because this is a statement in relation to the [incident]. And then this was obviously through the interpreter, the Garda asked me 'do you want to read back through the statement through the interpreter or do you want to read it yourself?' And I said I'd read it myself. And luckily enough I can read. But what about other deaf people who don't have good literacy skills? I was lucky. I was able to read it over myself. And to be fair, most of it was ok. I still wasn't comfortable with the idea of having an interpreter I wasn't sure of. Their qualifications and who they were, and I thought about it more [and Deaf3 subsequently found out that the interpreter] never finished the course [at the Centre for Deaf Studies] [They weren't] qualified, [they] had only done one year and left. And I am horrified to think that [they are] interpreting in a Garda station.'

It was evident that this was a distressing experience for Deaf3. Their role switched from interviewee to quality control for an untrained interpreter. And while the interpretation was 'ok' in the end, there were still fundamental mistakes, impacting the quality of evidence being secured in an investigation.[11] Deaf3 was aware of the gravity of the situation and took it upon themselves to ensure accuracy. It is relevant that they noted their own literacy skills too, and the commonality of a lack of literacy among deaf people (Cradden, 2016). They acknowledged that they were 'lucky' to be literate and to be able to correct mistakes. This 'luck' is not guaranteed for all deaf people. Deaf3 was 'horrified' at the thought of an unqualified interpreter working in a Garda station, because of the potential negative impact they could have on an 'unlucky' deaf person.

It is worth noting that while the ISL Act mandates that all ISL interpreters be trained and maintain their position on the Register of Irish Sign Language Interpreters (RISLI) there is no specific training given to interpreters around legal or medical interpreting (McEvoy, 2025a). As such, while interpreters typically have a degree qualification, they do not have any mandated training for legal interpreting. There are many interpreters working in the field who have no experience in this kind of work and who will refuse such assignments (McEvoy, 2025a). This means that while it is unlikely that an interpreter will struggle with basic numbers, there is still a risk that the interpreter booked for a police station interview will lack appropriate skills to carry out the job.

Deaf3's experienced was mirrored by Dr Phelan in respect of spoken language interpreters:

> MP: 'the people who are working as interpreters in Garda stations or in the courts, I guess they're doing their best, but they haven't actually been trained, they haven't been tested in any way to ensure they're competent, so I think they're in a very difficult position…I am convinced that there are cases where everybody believes that the interpreter is doing a good job and they're not doing a good job. It has to be happening. It has to be happening. And they're the ones that are just missed basically, you know everybody assumes that they're doing a good job because everybody's checking is one party speaking for really long and the other party is just saying very little, you know, what is going on. They're the obvious things that jump out in every situation but there have to be others where it looks as if the interpreter is interpreting and doing a good job but they're not.'

Phelan here connected the lack of training to the grave potential for miscarriages of justice to occur (*R v MR*, 2020). Shulman also held a similar view, stating that interpreter errors were common and actually identifying those errors was rare (Shulman, 1993).

Because interpreters lack training and the process lacks oversight mechanisms, there is a real danger that poor interpretation is producing unfairness or potentially giving rise to miscarriages of justice.

Dr Phelan also raised an alarming concern that where interpreters are untrained, they may also be unfamiliar with what their role is in the CJS:

> MP: 'But you don't know I mean when people aren't trained, they may well feel that their job is to ensure that there is conviction.'

This issue mirrors the fears from lawyers that interpreters could be relaying their advices to Gardaí as discussed above. Those fears are realised where the interpreter believes they are 'on the same side' as the police or judiciary, and that they possibly have a role in securing confessions or convictions.

An interpreter is there to facilitate communication between parties who do not share a language. They ought to bridge the gap and level the inequality experienced because of language. When interpreters are untrained and ill-equipped to deal with the technical or ethical considerations of the job of a legal interpreter, the gap in communication is not bridged. Whether through lack of linguistic competency or misconceptions about ethical considerations, untrained interpreters risk blocking an accused from participating fairly in the trial against them.

5.4.5 Interpreter entitlement

Finally, it is important to address interpreter entitlement. Judges or the Gardaí can act as gatekeepers for accessing a free interpreter (M. Brennan *et al.*, 2004). If either is in doubt about the need for an interpreter, they may block access and refuse to sanction or call an interpreter (Shulman, 1993). I have already noted that this may have been a contributing factor to the lack of interpreters provided to any participant illustrated in Table 5.1.

In respect of interpreters in court, Dr Mary Phelan noted that judges have denied requests for interpreters on many occasions:

> MP: 'So that happens quite a bit in the courts, some of the courts, in a district court level for example some judges will say, you know, how long have you been living here, you've been living here, it might be 3 years, 5 years, 10 years, you've had plenty of time to learn English, you know, what do you mean you need an interpreter? I'm not going to sanction one.'

This discourse directly connects entitlement to merit and shows bias against those who do not meet this arbitrary sense of merit. This attitude is a fundamental misunderstanding of the intricacies involved in language learning, as noted by Pillar. There is no standard time associated with learning a language (Piller, 2016). Language acquisition depends on a multitude of factors, including race, gender, socioeconomic status, age and sheer luck (Piller, 2016).

Nevertheless, this expectation is common, as Phelan notes in research on this subject:

> The misconception that a person who can reply to simple questions is also able to understand complex language, is still prevalent among some members of the Garda, lawyers and judiciary and is probably associated with the absence of training in this area… (Phelan, 2011: 81)

Not only does this attitude fundamentally oversimplify the process of language acquisition, it also shows an expectation of assimilation: immigrants are expected to learn the language of the state, and learn it quickly (Piller, 2016).

Gael4 recounted getting permission from the judge to have an Irish language interpreter. They recalled their satisfaction having been granted an interpreter 'both ways'. Gael4 was aware of several Irish speakers who had previously appeared in court and been granted only 'one way' interpretation. The 'one-way' interpreter they referred to was where an interpreter was only allowed to interpret Irish speech into English and not render English speech to Irish for the Irish-speaking accused. To Gael4's satisfaction, the judge had given permission for an interpreter to appear in court and interpret Irish speech to English and also English speech to Irish. This is how standard court interpretation works. Effectively, Gael4 was led to believe that they had been given special allowances, when in fact they have been granted a standard court interpreter. Irish speakers who appeared before Gael4 were possibly offered 'one-way' interpretation as lip-service, or a tick-box execution of their right to an interpreter based off of assumptions about their 'need' for an interpreter. The issues in granting interpreters to Irish speakers were evident from Gael4's interview, particularly in how relieved they had been to be given proper interpretation. Similar to Phelan's comments above, this experience could also point to problems of integration for Irish speakers who are not deemed to need interpreters.

Language competency is highly situational (Berk-Seligson, 1998). Where the gatekeepers of interpreter access do not believe that an accused needs or should need an interpreter, the accused may be denied procedural access. An accused who needs an interpreter but is perceived to not need one is at an immediate disadvantage in that they are prevented from fully participating in the proceedings against them.

5.5 Chapter Summary

The right to an interpreter is an integral part of the right to a fair trial. When considering language and minority language users, the right is the most evidently relevant minimum standard under the right to a fair trial. However, as this chapter has shown, the right to an interpreter is not always straightforward. The two major issues which I have addressed look at entitlement to an interpreter and the competency of an interpreter. Both of these issues are connected to procedural access to justice. Where an interpreter is needed and one is denied, the accused's ability to effectively participate in the proceedings against them is blocked. Similarly, if the accused is provided with an interpreter, but that interpreter is not sufficiently skilled to carry out their function, then the ability to effectively participate is again blocked. Procedural access is not guaranteed where either of these issues arise.

Under much of the jurisprudence of both the HRC and the ECtHR, the right to an interpreter is limited, and does not take into account the specific and individual needs of the accused. An accused is not entitled to an interpreter where they have an 'adequate' understanding of the language of the CJS, 'simple but adequate' command of the language of the CJS, or where the language of the CJS is not 'sufficiently complex' to warrant an interpreter. This of course shows a shift in the scope of the right to an interpreter under both institutions as of late. The ECtHR has made a shift towards a more accused centric approach to interpreter entitlement, with the accused's individual needs at the centre. These approaches are positive steps towards ensuring procedural access for an accused under the ECtHR.

In assessing interpreter entitlement, if the bar to being denied an interpreter in court is 'understanding' the language of court, there must be clarity on what it means to understand a language in this context. As the literature on language and domain shows, understanding a language is situational. Merely because a person can use a language in one domain or in many domains, does not mean that they will be capable of using that language in a court domain, which is particularly complex. Denying an interpreter to an accused who cannot understand the language of court interferes with their access to justice and is contrary to the purpose of the right to an interpreter itself.

In this chapter, I have also shown that interpretation is a highly skilled profession. Even the slightest deviation or mistranslation can have a grave impact on the course of proceedings in the CJS. And so it is essential that the interpreter is skilled and, where possible, trained and qualified. However, neither the ECtHR nor the HRC has made any movements to acknowledge this. Neither body has connected the right to an interpreter with the right to a *quality* interpreter, and a duty on states to ensure that the interpreters provided and available to work in the CJS are skilled. In fact, the HRC and the ECtHR have repeatedly tolerated instances where the interpretation was clearly poor quality. There has been no attempt to imply that poor quality interpretation risks impacting the fairness of trial. Nor has there been finding that the right to an interpreter cannot be truly vindicated where the interpretation is poor or the interpreter unskilled.

We can see from the data that access to an interpreter is in no way guaranteed, and this can be due to attitudes about the need for an interpreter by those in power, the number of working interpreters, or the availability of trained interpreters. Interpreters themselves face barriers in the CJS with little regulation around required training, pay structures or the limits to their confidentiality or their stated role in the maintenance of privacy for suspects. This collectively points to a failure to adequately provide for the right to an interpreter, and a failure to ensure access to justice for minority language using accused persons.

Notes

(1) It should also be noted that there is no definition provided for what is understood by 'mother tongue'. One would assume it is used here to refer to the language an accused acquired first, or their home language, but this classification is not a hard and fast rule. For Deaf people, for example, their home language is unlikely to be an SL, given that approximately 90% of Deaf people are born into hearing families and therefore can often grow up without their SL used in the home.

(2) Note that all the EU members states are also members of the Council of Europe, although not all members states of the Council of Europe are part of the EU.

(3) While the UK had adopted the Directive, it is no longer part of the EU, but remains, at the time of writing, part of the Council of Europe. Denmark, an EU Member State, did not adopt the Directive.

(4) Keeping in mind that it is possible to argue that if an accused person engages in criminal activity, then they are inviting engagement with the state, but also recalling that not all accused persons have actually engaged in criminal activity.

(5) Note that the ATII was formerly known as the Irish Translators and Interpreters Association and many of the documents cited here were published under that name and have not been updated. While their code of ethics was published in 2009 under the older name, it has been relaunched under the ATII name, although the date of publication remains the same. See https://www.atii.ie/wp-content/uploads/2024/04/ATII-Code-of-Ethics-for-Community-Interpreters-v02.pdf [Date accessed: 9 January 2025]

(6) Although this request was denied, it also raises questions as to the type of interpreters which can be deemed acceptable. There is no further information available in respect of the person who was requested to help from the British Consulate, but it is notable that they are described as a 'consular representative' who might 'assist' in interpretation, rather than as 'an interpreter'.

(7) In Ireland, there is no mandated code of ethics for interpreters, monitoring or professional body, no oversight mechanisms, no required oath of office, etc. Only ISL interpreters, as addressed earlier are mandated to have professional training under the ISL Act.

(8) In 2013, when this report was published, the minimum wage in Ireland was €8.65 per hour. See https://www.eurofound.europa.eu/publications/report/2016/eu-member-states/statutory-minimum-wages-in-the-eu-2016 [Date accessed: 9 April 2020].

(9) Note that although payment was offered, none of the interpreters who facilitated the interviews for this research would accept payment, due to their understanding of the importance of research for the Deaf community and because of their dedication to the community.

(10) Under Article 2.8 of the EU Directive on the Right to Interpretation and Translation in Criminal Proceedings interpreters in criminal justice contexts 'shall be of a quality sufficient to safeguard the fairness of the proceedings, in particular by ensuring that suspected or accused persons have knowledge of the case against them and are able to exercise their right of defence'. However, this requirement has not necessarily altered or introduced national legislation or regulation for interpreters. For example, Ireland is party to this Directive and complies with Article 2.8 without any introduction of regulated training for legal interpreters.

(11) Note that the handshapes for 12 and 17 are formulated in a similar way, but numbers are a very basic level part of ISL learning. Learning to count is covered in the beginner ISL classes offered by the Irish Deaf Society (Quality and Qualifications Ireland Level 3).

6 Minimum Standards of the Right to a Fair Trial and Procedural Access

6.1 Introduction

This chapter analyses the minimum standards of the right to a fair trial under Articles 6 and 14 of the ECHR and the ICCPR, respectively. I focus on those rights, other than the right to an interpreter, which are impacted by language. Underpinning almost all these rights for the other language or minority language user is access to an interpreter. Where language is at issue, without an interpreter it is impossible to fully realise the provisions under the right to a fair trial. As such, the content of the previous section must be borne in mind. The rights under the right to a fair are distinct, but also connected. Where one right is not vindicated, it can have a knock-on effect on other rights. For example, if an accused is not provided with an interpreter where they need one, they could be unable to communicate with counsel. Where they are unable to communicate with counsel, they will likely be unable to adequately prepare a defence, and so on.

When considering the scope of the right to a fair trial, we must address them in light of access to justice, and once again, in terms of procedural access. If there are barriers to effective engagement which are not removed, then there is no procedural access to justice (Flynn, 2015). In addition to the right to an interpreter, other minimum standards are impacted by language. It is necessary to consider these minimum standards in their own right, through this lens of access to justice. In this chapter, I interrogate how individual minority language using accused persons effectively engage with the CJS, where the engagement is theoretical or ineffective, procedural access is blocked.

Section 3 of both Article 14 and Article 6 refers to the minimum guarantees afforded to accused persons when they stand trial. It is those minimum guarantees which are most impacted by language and which most affect the minority language user that are being analysed herein. I address three minimum standards: the right to adequate time in contrast to the right to trial without undue delay; the right to communicate with counsel; and the right to be present at one's own trial in the context of language. First, however, I explain the reasoning behind the selection of these minimum standards, and their relevance to language usage.

6.2 Justifying the Selection of Minimum Standards

It is reasonable to question why I have curated a discussion around some minimum standards, but not others. Primarily, I discuss the specific minimum standards which arose in the data, and which have a linguistic element. Each of these minimum standards poses particular linguistic issues and therefore warrants discussion. In many cases, the minimum standard is made available or accessible through the provision of an interpreter. As such, they must be understood in light of the discussion in the previous section.

There are minimum standards which will not be addressed, such as the right to be informed of the charge in a language the accused speaks (Article 14.3(a) of the ICCPR and Article 6.3(a) of the ECHR), the right of the accused not to be compelled to testify (Article 14.3(g) of the ICCPR), and the right to counsel of one's own choosing (Article 14.3(b) of the ICCPR and Article 6.3(c) of the ECHR). There may indeed be linguistic elements which could conceivably arise in respect of these other minimum standards. These minimum standards did not arise as part of the empirical research. As such, I have omitted them from discussion.

As with the previous chapter, two timelines are included as a useful reference guide for the reader. Figures 6.1 and 6.2 show the development of jurisprudence from the HRC and the ECtHR respectively around the minimum standards on the right to a fair trial, covering delay, communication with counsel and presence at trial under each institution.

6.3 Trial Without Undue Delay

Articles 14.3(b) of the ICCPR and Articles 6.3(b) of the ECHR protect the right to adequate time and facilities to prepare a defence. The protections under the two instruments are worded similarly, ensuring the right to have adequate time and facilities for the preparation of his defence (Article 14.3(b) of the ICCPR and Article 6.3(b) of the ECHR). Directly connected to the right to adequate time and facilities is the right to trial without undue delay. This right is contained in Article 14.3(c) of the ICCPR, where the accused is guaranteed the right to 'trial without undue delay'. The corresponding right under the ECHR is present in Article 6.1 where it is stated that 'everyone is entitled to a fair and public hearing within a reasonable time'. If the accused is to effectively engage with the process of a fair trial, that effectiveness must include adequate time. But it must not be so drawn out so as to encroach onto undue delay. Procedural access mandates effective participation in proceedings and the removal of barriers to

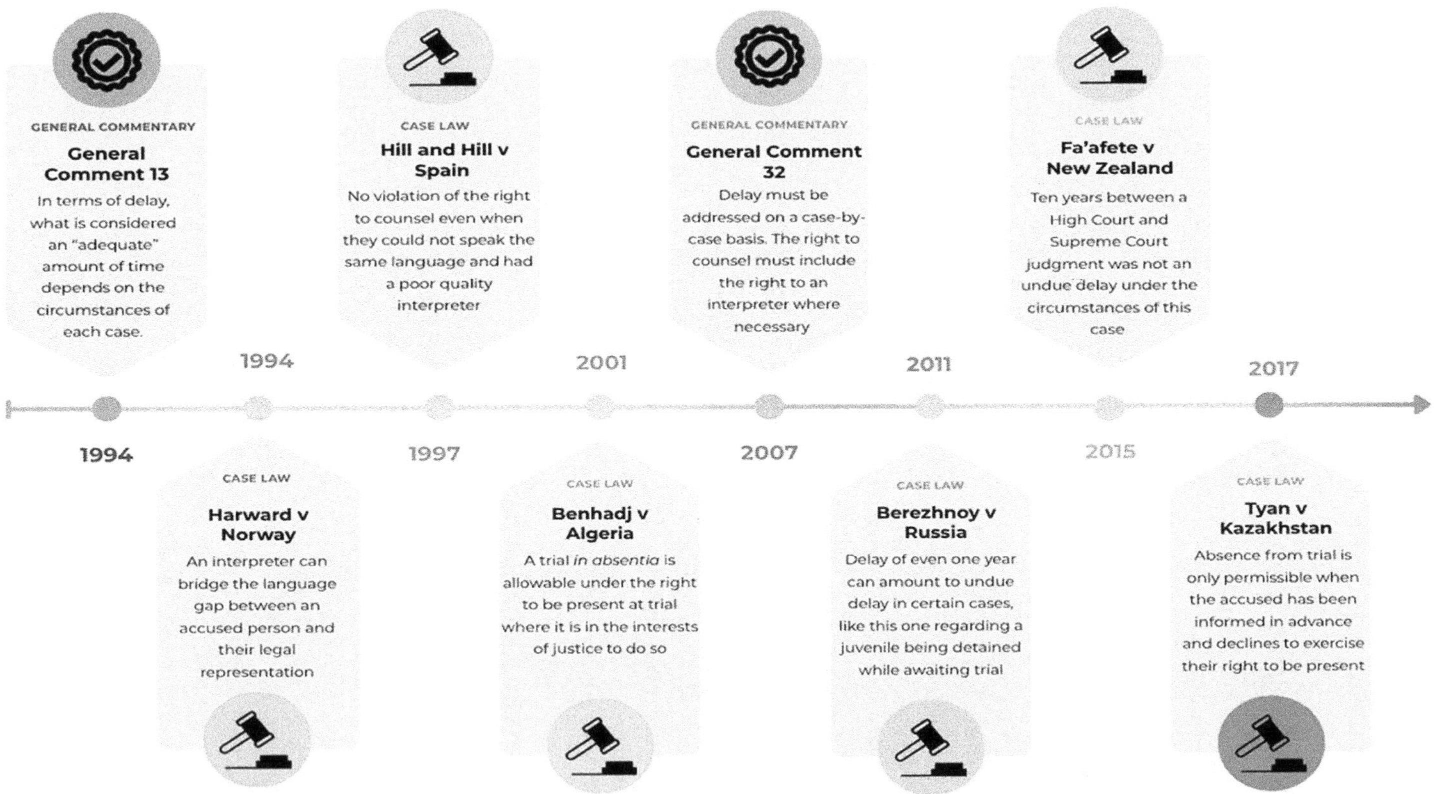

Figure 6.1 HRC jurisprudence on the minimum standards of the right to a fair trial timeline

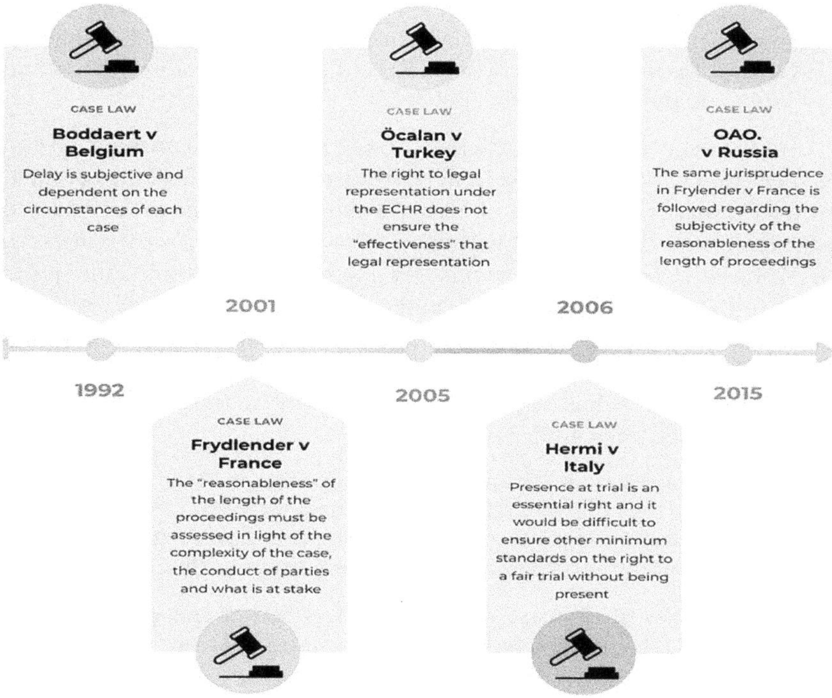

Figure 6.2 ECtHR jurisprudence on the minimum standards of the right to a fair trial timeline

that participation. Where an accused faces delay because of their language, and they are encouraged (either directly or indirectly) to forgo certain facilitations (such as interpreters) to avoid the delay, then the barriers to participation have not been removed.

6.3.1 Jurisprudence on delay

Language usage can impact on the time it takes to prepare a defence for an accused. Use of another language can warrant more time and facilities through the procurement of an interpreter (Leeson & Venturi, 2017), the translation of documents and evidence (Cao, 2007), the use of an appropriate environment (such as a police interview room capable of video recording an SL interpreter).[1] The HRC has concluded that what is considered 'adequate' 'depends on the circumstances of each case' (General Comment 13: 1994: 9). Similarly, it has also been held by the HRC that there is no standard time limit for what constitutes an undue delay:

> What is reasonable has to be assessed in the circumstances of each case, taking into account mainly the complexity of the case, the conduct of the

> accused, and the manner in which the matter was dealt with by the administrative and judicial authorities. (Human Rights Committee, General Comment 32, Article 14, Right to Equality before Courts and Tribunals and to a Fair Trial, 2007: 35)

Undue delay in one instance may be adequate time in another, as can be seen from various case law. In *Berezhnoy v. Russia*, a juvenile detained for over a year from the time of arrest to the time of trial was considered a breach of the right to trial without undue delay (*Berezhnoy v. Russia*, 2011). In *Fa'afete v. New Zealand*, a delay between a High Court judgment and a final Supreme Court judgment of almost 10 years was not considered a breach of this right, based on the circumstances of the case (*Fa'afete v. New Zealand*, 2015). The ECtHR has taken a similar stance to this. The ECtHR has held that the concept of '"reasonableness" of the length of proceedings' under Article 6.1:

> ...must be assessed in the light of the circumstances of the case and with reference to the following criteria: the complexity of the case, the conduct of the applicant and of the relevant authorities and what was at stake for the applicant in the dispute... (*Frydlender v France*, 2001: 26)

The specifics of the case will determine whether there has been an undue delay. Delay is subjective and dependent on the circumstances of each case (*Boddaert v. Belgium*, 1992). From this we can see that there is no standard time where 'adequate' crosses the threshold to 'delay'. A subjective view of time, reasonableness and delay is necessary to determine fairness of individual cases.

To relate it back to the research at hand, there is to be a certain level of delay associated with translation or interpretation (Cao, 2007; Gaiba, 1998). Namakula highlights the effect that language may have on the progression of a criminal trial: 'The linguistic requirements of a trial contribute to how long it takes' (Namakula, 2012: 84). The process of interpretation consists of one person or a rotating team of persons who repeat the words of another in the target language (Gaiba, 1998). It is oral or signed. It may be consecutive, where the interpreter waits until the speaker has finished speaking to interpret; whispering, where the interpreter sits close to a person and whispers interpretation into their ear while the speaker speaks; or simultaneous, where the interpreter sits in a soundproof booth and their words are heard via headsets.[2]

As such, the method of interpretation used may have an effect on time. Where consecutive interpretation is used, the case effectively takes 'twice as long' (*US v. Mayans*, 1999). The court must hear the speaker first and then wait for the interpreter to repeat and it is a process described as 'appallingly slow' (Gaiba, 1998: 29). It could be considered that consecutive interpretation is considered part of the adequate time to be allocated to the accused, depending on the specifics of the case. Additional aspects to consider relate to domestic laws on arrest and detention periods. Under domestic legislation, there may be a time limit on the length of time an accused person can be detained after arrest.[3] When considering language elements, extra strain can be put on these limits. If there are limited interpreters for a specific language and a user is arrested in a rural or isolated area, it may not be possible to procure an interpreter under the time frame. This can be particularly true for minority languages where there are a limited number of interpreters working, as noted in the previous chapter (Leeson & Venturi, 2017). Additionally, some available interpreters may be unwilling or unable to interpret during a police interview setting (Bacik, 2007). If the interview is taking place late at night or in a remote location, there may be no interpreter available within the timeframe for detention.

It is not possible or desirable to have a standard time frame that each case can be concluded in a criminal matter – the facts and circumstances of each case are different and so what is too long a delay in one case may well be adequate time in another. In keeping with the underlying principle of access to justice, the goal of providing minimum rights under the right to a fair trial is to ensure that fairness is achieved. An individual's specific needs must be considered in the pursuit of access to justice. In the case of a minority language user, a balance must be found between ensuring they have appropriate facilities but that they are not subjected to unreasonable delay in awaiting facilitation of their linguistic needs.

6.3.2 Delay in the data

Availability of interpreters and access to an interpreter when interacting with the CJS arose for participants in the data. At the time of the data collection, there were about 111 trained ISL interpreters working in Ireland (Leeson & Venturi, 2017). At the time of writing, there are 120 registered ISL interpreters on the Register of Irish Sign Language Interpreters (*'Find an Interpreter'*, 2025). This is for an estimated population of about 5000 deaf and hard of hearing (HoH) people in Ireland, although not all deaf and HoH people are ISL users (*Fact: Information on Irish Sign Language*, 2024). By comparison, Australia has a population of approximately 6500 Deaf Auslan (Sign Language of Australia) users and over 1000 registered Auslan interpreters (Leeson & Venturi, 2017). When a deaf ISL user is party to criminal proceedings, delays will be exacerbated by the lack of availability of appropriate interpreters.

Prof Lorraine Leeson and AGS2 both highlighted that the 100 or so available ISL interpreters are unevenly distributed across the country, which affects availability:

> LL: '...to my knowledge there might be maybe one or two interpreters in Donegal, in that general area. I think there is maybe one in Sligo, in that general area, there's maybe two in Galway, there's a cluster down in Kerry [redacted], there's a little cluster down in Cork for sure. I think there's one in Waterford, there's loads in Dublin – most of them are in Dublin. And

then there's like a sprinkling across here [midlands] and then there's a couple up around Drogheda. But you know when you look at it there really is this whole gap. Like Monaghan? Best of luck. Cavan? Best of luck. Westmeath or somewhere like that? Best of luck. So those [counties] are very poorly serviced. Sort of midlands and Wicklow, there's very few people. So you do tend to get the clustering around the cities but also around where the deaf communities are heavily based. But that leaves huge gaps'.

Leeson is highlighting the lack of ISL interpreters in rural areas (with the exception of Kerry) and noting that interpreters tend to be localised in cities and towns. At the time of writing, there are now 119 registered ISL interpreters in Ireland, including 24 deaf interpreters ('RISLI,' 2025).

AGS2: 'That's the biggest difficulty, as we all know, in the deaf community, there can be a scarcity of interpreters in certain parts of the country'.

Both Leeson and AGS2 suggested that access to interpreters is a postcode lottery for deaf people who need an interpreter. While Lesson did note that the distribution of ISL interpreters can correspond with a density of the deaf population (e.g. there is an active deaf community in Kerry and Cabra in Dublin, where the Irish Deaf Society is located and deaf people have congregated), not all deaf people are facilitated. Deaf people are not necessarily born into or reside in areas where other deaf people live and as such, can be isolated from ISL interpreters. This is even more concerning when not all interpreters necessarily work in legal settings. This has an impact on the delay. If a deaf person is arrested in certain rural areas, as Leeson suggests, they will necessarily have to wait for an appropriate, available interpreter to arrive, which could mean hours of travel time. This has an impact on the custody rights, as AGS2 noted:

AGS2: 'Geographically, it's impossible sometimes to get [an ISL interpreter] to arrive in the station within the timeframe. And you are looking at the clock...It doesn't say anything in Section 4 of the Criminal Justice Act [about interpreters arriving in the detention timeframe] If you couldn't, that's your fault. The solicitor is going to make mincemeat of you if you took six hours for the interpreter to come and your first six hours has gone, you are detaining this person – that's your fault. That's the criminal justice system's fault. That's not the suspect's fault, if you couldn't get the person in.

Here, AGS2 refers to regulations on the length of time a suspect can be detained at a Garda Station under the *Criminal Justice Act, 1984*. The fear of delay here was depicted as a solicitor making 'mincemeat' of a Garda later on when the issue gets to court if there is a delay in accessing interpreters. AGS2 noted that such a delay is seen as the Garda's 'fault'. While they did go on to note how this can impact on the individual deaf person in custody, their immediate concern was how this would affect

Gardaí and their ability to secure a conviction at trial. The primary concern was not the realisation of the detainees' rights.

A consequence of this delay is that while it may be possible to organise interpreters in advance for certain aspects of the trial process, acquiring an interpreter for a last-minute situation may be an impossibility. This was described by Deaf3:

> Deaf3: 'And there is not – in terms of interpreting, there's not a lot of interpreters. It's very hard to gain access, you know, you have to book in in advance and that can be quite difficult. To get an emergency interpreter last minute is very difficult.'

Deaf3 pointed out that there is delay associated with acquiring an interpreter. Even when 'booking in advance' is done, it can still be 'difficult'. There is a concern that instead of enduring such difficulty, Gardaí may decide to go ahead with an interview without an interpreter, possibly in an attempt to satisfy custody time limits. Time constraints may override a detainee's rights in the making of such a decision. This concern was raised by AGS2, Prof Leeson and Lawyer2 in their interviews. In circumventing the risk of delay because of lack of interpreters, authorities may forego interpreters altogether, as happened in the McGrotty case described in Chapter 1 (Cradden, 2016). The human rights implications of this failure to provide an interpreter were raised by AGS2:

> AGS2: 'We have both seen the chronicle of the issue last year with that poor deaf man who was arrested, charged and brought before the court without an interpreter. Again, that's a breach of human rights, no matter what way anyone looks at that.'

AGS2 was referring to the McGrotty case, where the suspect was not given access to an interpreter. AGS2 demonstrated the consequences of avoiding delay: violating the human rights of a person entitled to an interpreter. This was experienced by participants: only two deaf people (Deaf3 and Lawyer1's client) were provided with an interpreter in their interactions with Gardaí. In both of those cases, the interview was prearranged in order to organise an interpreter because of the knowledge that sourcing an interpreter would cause a delay. This raises a question as to whether, this concern about delay in accessing an interpreter was a reason why all the other deaf participants were not provided with an interpreter.

Delay in accessing interpreters was also experienced by some Irish-speaking participants. While Gael7 acknowledged multiple causes for their delay, they were clear that the repeated rescheduling of court dates was impacted by the availability of an Irish language interpreter:

> Gael7: 'I think, if I remember correctly, some of it [delay], there wouldn't have been an interpreter available, there wouldn't have been, it was after being said to the court clerk that the case would be held, and then we would be waiting around and then suddenly the judge that we were

> supposed to have for the day wouldn't have Irish. It took a long while actually to get everything correct on the day'

Gael7 described needing an interpreter, a court clerk and a judge all with Irish and the difficulty in aligning their schedules. While it is acknowledged that delay is a common aspect of the criminal process, (Waterhouse, 2014) it must also be noted that Gael7 saw Irish – and the court's unpreparedness to cope with Irish language cases – as a cause of the delay they experienced. Their attempt to assert their minority language right actively slowed down the process considerably, bringing with it all of the negative consequences of delay which have been identified in previous research such as anxiety, (Fielding, 2013) stress and apprehension (Ezendam & Wheldon, 2014), as well as the risk of violating the right against undue delay itself.

6.4 Communication with Counsel

Access to a lawyer is an essential aspect of the right to a fair trial. The right to counsel is contained in Article 14.3(d) of the ICCPR which reads that an accused has the right to:

> ...be tried in his presence, and to defend himself in person or through legal assistance of his own choosing; to be informed, if he does not have legal assistance, of this right; and to have legal assistance assigned to him, in any case where the interests of justice so require, and without payment by him in any such case if he does not have sufficient means to pay for it...

Under Article 6.3(c) of the ECHR the accused has a right to:

> ...to defend himself in person or through legal assistance of his own choosing or, if he has not sufficient means to pay for legal assistance, to be given it free when the interests of justice so require...

The importance of this right has been recognised by the Council of Europe in respect of the ECHR:

> The opportunity for an accused to confer with his defence counsel is fundamental to the preparation of his defence (Council of Europe, Guide on Article 6 of the European Convention on Human Rights: Right to a Fair Trial. (Criminal Limb, 2019)

The right to counsel needs to include the opportunity to prepare a defence and actually communicate with counsel.

6.4.1 Jurisprudence on communication with counsel

When considering the right to legal assistance for a minority language user, particular consideration must be paid to communication and language. If an accused is represented by counsel with whom they do not share a language, it will pose a barrier to their ability to communicate and therefore to construct an adequate defence. In respect of access to justice, an accused cannot be said to have effectively engaged in the process if they cannot discuss their defence or communicate with the person representing them. In addition, part of procedural access involves identifying and removing barriers to the mechanisms of the justice system. Where this barrier is not removed, an accused is not guaranteed procedural access to justice.

Under its jurisprudence, the ECtHR has held that the mere provision of legal assistance does not alone satisfy the right to communicate with counsel:

> [The] Convention is designed to 'guarantee not rights that are theoretical or illusory but rights that are practical and effective' and that assigning a counsel does not in itself ensure the effectiveness of the assistance he may afford an accused… (*Öcalan v. Turkey*, 2005: 135)

Merely appointing counsel in no way shirks the responsibility to provide for the right to legal representation. If it is to be practical and effective, then the right surely ought to include assurances that the accused and their counsel can understand each other and communicate.

In *Harward v. Norway,* the HRC demonstrate how interpretation can effectively realise the right to communicate with counsel and ensure access to justice. In that case, it was:

> …undisputed that an interpreter was available to the defence for all meetings between counsel and Mr. Harward and that simultaneous interpretation was provided during the court hearings. (*Harward v. Norway*, 1994: 92)

There existed no break in understanding, and there were no complaints made as to the quality of the interpretation provided. The barriers to access that existed through the accused and counsel not sharing a language were removed by the provision of an interpreter.

The HRC changed its position on this issue after *Harward*. In *Hill and Hill v. Spain* the applicants were appointed counsel with whom they did not share a language and were provided with an inadequate and poor-quality interpreter, as discussed in the previous chapter (*Michael and Brian Hill v. Spain*, 1997). The Hill brothers argued that 'confusion and misunderstandings were common' with their first lawyer. They complained that legal aid later appointed to them did not speak English. They stated that this lawyer came to consult with them either in the presence of a poor interpreter or without any interpreter at all. The brothers claimed *inter alia* that this unsatisfactory communication with their lawyer amounted to a violation of Article 14.3(b). In spite of the arguments made by the Hill brothers, the Committee held that there was no violation of the right to communicate with a lawyer.

There is an inconsistency in the jurisprudence visible here from the HRC. Where the accused does not share a language with their counsel, the right under Article 14.3(d) is not violated when an interpreter facilitates their communication, as occurred in *Harward*. But neither is the right under Article 14.3(d) violated when the accused does not share a language with their counsel and they are not facilitated by interpretation. That being said, in its General Comment 32, after *Harward* and *Hill and Hill*, the HRC stated in analysing the right to communicate with counsel that it must include access to an interpreter. Reading the right in light of this development suggests a return to the *Harward* reasoning that the right to communicate with counsel must include an interpreter where necessary. This reasoning would align with the procedural access. At the centre of the right to communicate with counsel must be the ability of the accused to effectively participate in proceedings against them.

6.4.2 Communication with counsel in the data

Formulating the best possible defence for their client is the role of defence counsel. Under their professional guidelines, they are duty bound to put forward 'every technical defence which is available to the defendant' (*A Guide to Good Professional Conduct for Solicitors*, 3rd edn, 2013: 43). The ability to do so is hindered where there is a barrier to communication and this barrier is not overcome. This was a concern raised by some of the lawyers interviewed for this research. Both the lawyers dealing with deaf clients spoke of communication barriers with their clients. The Irish-speaking solicitors did not share this experience, as they both spoke Irish and were likely hired by clients because of their dedication to the language in their work.

Lawyer1 expressed concern for a deaf client who appeared to have trouble appreciating the gravity of the situation when they were being interviewed by Gardaí. The client had presented themselves at a Garda station for a voluntary interview, rather than under arrest and so Lawyer1 was allowed to be present for the interview. In this case, the client was an ISL user, and there was an interpreter present:

> Lawyer1: 'I had advised [my client] to say nothing...But I don't think [they] appreciated at the time what a culture shock it was. [My client] didn't know what [they were] facing...But the client simply didn't appreciate the seriousness of what [they were] facing. Maybe it's because of [their] marginalisation from society...[They] didn't expect this and [they] didn't know how to deal with it. Me being there helped [the client], but only to a certain extent. What happened was – as the interview progressed, [my client] began to very much incriminate [themselves] – in spite of me telling [them] very clearly, "If this comes up, you say nothing – you're entitled to say nothing, you exercise your entitlement to say nothing"'.

There are a number of issues of concern in this extract. First, Lawyer1 alluded to a difficulty in communicating vital information and legal advice to their client, even in the presence of an interpreter. Second, they suggested that the breakdown in communication could be related to the marginalisation experienced by their client (Glickman & Hall, 2018b). This could raise issues about competency and the vulnerability of the client. It is impossible to say for certain what was the cause for the breakdown in communication. It may have been that the client struggled to comprehend the concepts; it may have been poor communication skills on the part of the lawyer; it may have been the fault of the interpreter. It may have been a combination of all three. In this instance, the client may have benefited from a team of interpreters, one deaf and one hearing to better facilitate communication and ensure the client understood the situation given their social marginalisation (Boudreault, 2005). As noted above, the lack of available professionals may well have deemed this an impossibility ('RISLI,' 2025; Leeson & Venturi, 2017). There was an apparent barrier in accessing the right to communicate with counsel for the accused.

Lawyer2 noted the difficulty in communicating with their deaf client during consultation in preparation for court. They described how the use of a relative as an interpreter complicated their ability to communicate with their client directly:

> Lawyer2: '[My client] found it very stressful – the length of time it took to be able to consult with [my client] properly – now we were doing it properly, but we were consulting with [my client] with the aid of [their sibling]. They have a typical [sibling] relationship. [The sibling] is the older [one] and we'd even find when we'd be saying something to [the sibling] and [they'd] be doing the interpreting, if [the sibling] didn't think [my client] needed to know, [the sibling] didn't interpret it. Not on purpose. [The sibling] didn't know [they were] doing it. And [my client] might be trying to say something to us – and it would be pretty obvious that [my client] would be trying to say something to us – but [their sibling] might turn and continue talking. And [the sibling] didn't know [they were] doing it. But for our purposes, we would have to say "what is [my client] saying to you?"'[4]

For Lawyer2 the lack of availability of interpreters meant that there was no other option for interpretation in during consultations. Using a relative who is not an interpreter to act as one is clearly problematic (Pawlosky, 1996).

These clients experienced limited access to their counsel. In Lawyer2's case, a team of trained interpreters were eventually sourced and made available before and during court and so the client was eventually given access. But in Lawyer1's instance, there was no improvement in communication reported, although charges were later dropped and the client did not have to attend trial. Participants thus experienced limited communication with their counsel, impacting on the ability to build a defence. this is a procedural access concern. Where there is a lack of communication or limited and stunted communication between a client and their legal representative, accused persons cannot effectively engage with the proceedings against them. They are barred from participating effectively in proceedings designed to administer justice and therefore denied procedural access.

6.5 Presence at Trial

Under both the ICCPR and the HRC, there is a right of an accused to be present at their own trial. First, as seen above, the right to legal assistance includes the right of the accused to be 'tried in his presence' under Article 14.3(d) of the ICCPR and 'to defend himself in person' under Article 6.3(c) of the ECHR. Additionally, there is also a right of an accused to examine witnesses against him under Article 6.3(d) of the ECHR and 14.3(e) of the ICCPR. The right to be present at trial is fundamental to the fairness of trial.[5] An accused cannot be expected to highlight to the court or their counsel to inconsistent evidence, points of information, or generally have knowledge of the case against them when they are not permitted to be present. This is also relevant to procedural access in that if an accused is denied the right to be present at trial, then they are denied an opportunity to effectively engage in the proceedings.

The ECtHR stated in the case of *Hermi v. Italy* that:

> Although this is not expressly mentioned in paragraph 1 of Article 6, the object and purpose of the Article taken as a whole show that a person 'charged with a criminal offence' is entitled to take part in the hearing. Moreover, sub-paragraphs (c), (d) and (e) of paragraph 3 guarantee to 'everyone charged with a criminal offence' the right 'to defend himself in person', 'to examine or have examined witnesses' and 'to have the free assistance of an interpreter if he cannot understand or speak the language used in court', and it is difficult to see how he could exercise these rights without being present. (para 59)

This shows that the accused should be present in order to exercise their other rights under the minimum standards to fair trial. It also shows a dedication to procedural access, as explained by Flynn (2015), by stating that the accused has the right to 'take part' in proceedings. The ECtHR held that 'in the interests of a fair and just criminal process it is of capital importance that the accused should appear at his trial' and that presence at one's trial 'ranks as one of the essential requirements of Article 6' (*Hermi v. Italy*, 2006). The ECtHR recognised here the central role that presence has on the vindication of other minimum standards in the right to a fair trial.

6.5.1 Jurisprudence on presence at trial

The HRC has shared this point of view and positioned the right to be present as an essential element. The Committee stated that:

> ...accused persons are entitled to be present during their trial and that proceedings in the absence of the accused are only permissible if this

is in the interest of the proper administration of justice or when accused persons, although informed of the proceedings sufficiently in advance, decline to exercise their right to be present...(*Tyan v. Kazakhstan*, 2017)

In this vein, the right to be present at trial is not an absolute right and departures can be made under certain circumstances. The HRC has made allowances for trials *in absentia* where they are in the interests of justice (*Benhadj v. Algeria*, 2001).

In connecting this to the research at hand, we must consider what it means to be 'present at trial' and what the purpose of that right it. If it meant to afford the accused the right to 'take part' (*Hermi v. Italy*, 2006: para 59), then there is an active element. I understand being present at trial in this active sense. In ensuring procedural access, the accused needs to be given the opportunity to effectively engage, to participate and to take part. The right to be present is an active presence, not a passive one. A person can be physically present but have no access to the benefits of presence because of language barriers. If language is a barrier to taking part, and that barrier is not removed via an interpreter, then procedural access is not assured. Therefore, the right to be present is not vindicated based on an understanding of procedural access. This argument is demonstrated the US case *Negron v. New York* (*US ex rel Negron v. New York*, 1970).

In that case, it was held that Mr Negron was denied the right to be present at his own trial and to confront adverse witnesses because no interpreter was provided during his case. Mr Negron testified that 'I knew that I would have liked to [have known] what was happening but I did not know that they were supposed to tell me'. Because of the lack of interpretation given to Mr Negron, he was totally unaware of his rights and could not effectively engage in the trial process. The Court held that it is:

...imperative that every criminal defendant – if the right to be present [at trial] is to have meaning – possess 'sufficient present ability to consult with his lawyer with a reasonable degree of rational understanding'. (1970: 389)

The Court deemed that in order for the right to be present at trial to be actually meaningful and in order to ensure basic 'humaneness', the accused 'deserved more than to sit in total incomprehension as the trial proceeded' (1970: 390). Mr Negron had no access to the case against him. He could not 'take part' in a meaningful way, which the court deemed infringed on his right to be present and to confront the evidence against him (Del Valle, 2003; Salinas & Martinez, 2010). The circumstances had caused him to be a passive, oblivious on-looker in the trial against him.

In the absence of an interpreter where one is needed, an accused cannot 'take part' in the trial. As such, the right to an interpreter – and an effective interpreter – necessarily facilitates the right to be present at trial. Without an interpreter where one is needed, the minority language user is rendered an observer to the trial against them. They are a passive onlooker, rather than an active participant. If procedural access is to be ensured, the accused must be given the opportunity to effectively participate or take part in the proceedings against them, should they so wish.

The line of reasoning used in *Negron* (*US Ex Rel Negron v. New York*, 1970), as described, constitutes the lens through which the right to be present is analysed. That is, if the accused is present in body, but has no access to the court by virtue of language, they cannot be said to have been present. A language barrier poses a barrier for an accused in accessing their right to be present, therefore impacting procedural access. I have presented presence at trial therefore as being inherently linked to language and access to the language of the court.

6.5.2 Presence at trial in the data

In facilitating the right to be present physically, it is essential to ensure that the accused can be present cognitively and linguistically. Lawyer2 spoke of the delay in acquiring interpreters and how this had a grave impact on their deaf client's access to their case:

> Lawyer2: 'It's just that it took so long for [my client] to be able to sit down with people who were able to communicate properly with [them]. So when [they] did understand, [they] broke down. It wasn't that [they] had a level of – it wasn't – it was that nobody had been capable before the interpreters to explain it to [my client]...'

The client here had limited access to the details of their case and as a result did not comprehend the gravity of the situation until an interpreter was provided. Through this, they were not given the opportunity to effectively participate in the proceedings against them, and therefore procedural access was interrupted. The delay here was a delay in access for the client. Proceedings progressed, but the client was not accompanying that progression in any reasonable, cognitive way. They were delayed in accessing their right to be present.

Deaf4 also recalled issues with the right to be present at trial:

> Deaf4: On the day of their court hearing, Deaf4's solicitor never told them when their case was heard – Deaf4 had arrived early to the court, at 9am and sat all day until 4pm. It wasn't until then that someone came to tell them that their case had been heard that morning at around 9:15am.

Deaf4 had no access to the court They were not provided with an interpreter and so they could not access the language of the court. As such, they were completely unaware that their case was heard in their presence, but without their knowledge. They were present in body only, much like the experiences of Maolra Seoighe, (Ó Cuirreáin, 2017) John McGrotty (Cradden, 2016) or Rogelio Nieves Negron (*US ex rel Negron v. New York*, 1970). Based on their account, Deaf4 was barred from accessing their right to be present at trial, by virtue of the lack of an interpreter.

In the following extract, Gael5 expressed their doubt about whether the judge was capable of following the case in Irish and therefore, whether they could be actually heard at their court hearing:

> Gael5: 'Anyway, the judge, the judge with Irish, I was in great doubt about whether he had enough Irish. It's certain that if he were listening to what I have been saying here, that there would be loads and loads of words that he would not understand. And this isn't a technical conversation. It's a general legal conversation. He wouldn't be so good in a general conversation even. I'd say that he would have a basic understanding. Sure he had some level of Irish – but [counsel] spoke in Irish only. It's certain that the judge didn't understand exactly what was going on.'

Gael5 showed a doubt about whether they were even heard and understood by the judge. If the purpose of the right to be present is to participate in the trial, then the right must include the opportunity to be heard by a judge. Where a judge is unable to understand the case before them, then the right to be present is not fully vindicated, because that presence is ignored. While the interviewee was physically present and capable of communicating with their counsel, Gael5 alleged that the judge could not be communicated with, and so their case could not be heard.

Dr Mary Phelan acknowledged the impact that access and being present at trial can have on an accused and on the vindication of human rights in her interview:

> MP: 'Well I think it's really, really important because for people to understand what's going on. I mean it's a bit Kafkaesque if people are standing there and they don't know what's being said and they don't understand what the other, what the charge is, they don't understand what the solicitors are saying, what the judge is saying what witnesses are saying. It's really, really, it's vital for them to understand what's being said in court and also if they're being questioned it's really, really important that the information is conveyed correctly. So yeah, it's essential…I think that it's essential that anybody on trial should understand what's being said in court. You can't get more basic than that. So I don't see how it can possibly be a fair trial if the person doesn't understand what's being said in court. Because that's the whole point, isn't it? To hear the evidence against you and to be able to refute it if necessary. And for your own voice to be heard, if you are speaking'.

Dr Phelan highlighted the fundamental nature of the right as an underlying principle of the right to be present. She pointed out the essential aspect: access to the court. The right to be present includes being heard, but also a judge or jury who can listen and carry out their function in the facilitation of justice.

The right to be present ensures the right to communicate a defence. If a person is present at their trial and incapable of, or prevented from communicating, their presence is pointless and purely physical. Thus, they are denied procedural access. As shown, there were instances in the data where people experienced this lack of procedural access by being denied the benefits associated with the right to be present. As a consequence, they are barred from effectively engaging in the proceedings against them. Communication cannot be one-sided. An accused must be able to communicate with the court (either firsthand or via their counsel) in order to actually benefit from the right to be present. If no interpreter is provided when one is needed, the accused cannot communicate; the accused can neither listen nor be listened to.

6.6 Chapter Summary

A defendant faces a particular risk when they appear before the CJS; the loss of their liberty; loss of their freedom; damage to their reputation and so on. Ensuring access to justice can ensure that these risks are mitigated by a fair procedure. When barriers remain in place, blocking fairness of procure for the accused, procedural access to justice is not guaranteed.

Each of the above sections demonstrate how language can intersect and interfere with the minimum standards under the right to a fair trial. In Chapters 2 and 3, I explored identity and the innate connection that people can have between their language and their identity. The content of this section must not be considered in isolation. An accused who is a minority language user has specific concerns related to their identity when they interact with the CJS. Already minoritised by their identity, they are further marginalised as a weakened player in the CJS. Procedural access must remove the barriers that exist for these marginalised people, so that they may also effectively engage in the proceedings against them. When 'freedom [is] hanging in the balance' (Del Valle, 2003: 172), when an accused's reputation and connection to the community in which they live is placed in jeopardy, when they must put their whole life on hold for the outcome of a trial, the necessity for access to justice is vital to the proper execution of the right to a fair trial for minority language user.

I addressed the issue of undue delay as it relates to language usage. There is a balancing act to be done in any fair trial, between adequate time and undue delay. As shown, language will inevitably impact the length of time it takes to conduct proceedings. Accessing interpreters, awaiting interpretation itself, the procurement of translated materials (where allowed) will necessarily cause delays. Whether or not this delay is appropriate must be addressed on a case by case basis. However, it is possible that for minority language users, interpreters will be unavailable within the detention timeframe. This is problematic for the fairness of trial: if police go ahead with interviewing the suspect without an interpreter, they have been denied their right to an interpreter. If police wait until they can avail of an interpreter, there is the potential to infringe on the accused's right to trial without undue delay.

With respect to the right to communicate with counsel, I argue that the requirement that the appointment of counsel be practical and effective under the ECHR must include the opportunity to communicate with counsel. This approach aligns with procedural access to justice. It is a right to active presence, not only to passive presence. This right has a specific language element. Where an accused is denied linguistic access to the trial, they cannot effectively access their right to partake. Therefore, their presence remains illusory and physical only. In *Negron,* we can see how an active presence is required for the accused to make full and actual use of their right to be present, and this can be facilitated through appropriate interpretation.

The takeaway from this chapter is that language has an effect on the right to a fair trial, beyond just the right to an interpreter. The language used by a minority language user can and does interact with the right to a fair trial. Language can act as a barrier to access to justice when it is left unchecked. This potential to impact and obstruct the fairness of trial and access to justice is often not seen by the ECtHR or the HRC in determining the rights under Articles 6 and 14 of the ECHR and ICCPR, respectively. The result has the potential to infringe on fairness and obstruct access to justice for the minority language users.

Notes

(1) As was garnered from interviews, however, this is not always facilitated and there is no mandate under the ICCPR or the ECHR to do so.

(2) This is the method first used at Nuremberg and used at the ICTY. The delay in this case is minimal. The interpreter is 'only a few second behind the speaker' at http://www.icty.org/en/about/registry/translation-and-interpretation [Date accessed: 17 January 2025].

(3) See, for example, Ireland's *Criminal Justice Act, 1984,* Section 4 where the standard detention period is six hours.

(4) Use of relatives as interpreters is somewhat common in interactions with Deaf suspects, as described in Brennan, M., Brown, R.K., MacKay, B., University of Durham, & Deaf Studies Research Unit (2004) *Equality before the law: Deaf people's access to justice.* D. McLean: 83

(5) This acknowledges that in some jurisdictions, such as France and Italy, trial *in absentia* is permissible.

7 Substantive Access and Legislation, Training and Inclusion

7.1 Introduction

In the previous two chapters, I explored how procedural access arose in the data in respect of the right to a fair trial. In this chapter, I explore the instances of substantive access which arose in the data. In doing so, I will be focusing on the laws and the policies which address Irish and ISL usage in the CJS and how these laws impacted the interviewees.

To reiterate, substantive access aims to ensure that the realities of marginalised groups are taken into account in the laws and policies that impact those groups (Bahdi, 2007). A key aim of substantive access is participation from affected groups in the creation of those laws and policies (Flynn & Lawson, 2013). It arises when the specific needs of a group are included in policy or legislation from the start where there has been involvement from that group in policymaking or the legislative process. In that vein, substantive access also ensures equitable and beneficial judicial outcomes for marginalised people (Beqiraj *et al.*, 2017). Substantive access measures ensure that when interacting with the legal system, the structures in place have been created with consideration of the lived realities of marginalised people and this is reflected in the ability to obtain fair outcomes.

In this chapter, I discuss the specific substantive access issues which arose in the data, and the effectiveness of these measures in reality. In doing so, I focus on two areas. First, I address legislation, specifically the *Irish Sign Language Act, 2017* and the *Official Languages Act, 2003*. I present data which both directly and indirectly demonstrates the limitations of these acts and how ultimately, they have lacked substantive access. Second, I discuss policy and training, focusing on the training given to Gardaí and to judges in respect of Irish speakers and deaf people. I show that through the training in place, substantive access has not been ensured and the specific needs of Irish speakers and deaf people are not created and carried out with their needs in mind.

7.2 Legislation

Two major pieces of legislation must be considered in addressing substantive access for Irish speakers and ISL-users: The *Official Languages Act, 2003* (OLA) and the *Irish Sign Language Act, 2017* (ISL Act). Both pieces of legislation operate to provide regulations and laws surrounding the rights of minority language users to use their specific languages with the State. In both, there is specific reference to the right to use Irish or ISL respectively before the courts and within the CJS. Now I examine how participants discussed the legislation, taking them in turn.

7.2.1 *The Irish Sign Language Act, 2017*

The ISL Act came into force in December 2020 (*SI 658/2020 Irish Sign Language Act, 2017 (Commencement) Order*, 2020). Interviews with deaf participants took place after it was signed into law in December 2017, but before that law came into force in December 2020. As such, no interviewee's experience was directly impacted by that law. Therefore, it is difficult to assess whether the ISL Act has brought about equitable and beneficial outcomes. Nevertheless, participants were aware of the ISL Act and it is possible to discuss substantive access from the perspective of deaf involvement in the creation of the ISL Act.

The Act itself formally recognises

> the right of Irish Sign Language users to use Irish Sign Language as their native language and the corresponding duty on all public bodies to provide Irish Sign Language users with free interpretation when availing of or seeking to access statutory entitlements and services. (Section 3)

The ISL Act also provides specifically for ISL usage in legal proceedings (Section 4). The right to use ISL in court is qualified under Section 4(2) which states that:

> Every court has, in any proceedings before it, the duty to do all that is reasonable to ensure that any person competent in Irish Sign Language and who cannot hear or understand English or Irish appearing in or giving evidence before it may be heard in that language, if that is his or her choice, and that in being so heard the person will not be placed at any disadvantage.

This provision qualifies the right to use ISL in court by mandating courts 'do all that is reasonable', particularly when considering the socioeconomic realities of deaf people in Ireland as alluded to throughout this work, and the likelihood of social disadvantage that deaf people experience. The construction leaves space to wonder what are the limits of reasonableness, and why this qualification was necessary, particularly when the outcome would place a deaf person at a disadvantage.

The ISL Act came into being after 30 years of activism from the deaf community (Conama, 2019). The deaf community collaborated with Senator Mark Daly in the first major moves to introduce an ISL Act. Conama notes that 'Senator Daly engaged a legislative draftsman to draw up the Bill, in consultation with [Irish Deaf Society] representatives'. This step shows the positive inclusion of concerned parties in the creation of laws which govern their affairs: it exemplifies substantive access. However, this substantive access was maintained only during initial drafting, and the Bill which was subsequently passed into law lacked the initial elements of positive inclusion (Conama, 2019). In her interview, Professor Leeson noted that significant compromise on the initial needs of the deaf community needed to be made in order to pass the legislation:

> LL: 'Well, [the passing of the legislation] was very hard won. And definitely there was a great deal of compromise that had to go in – it doesn't reflect all of the issues that the Irish Deaf Society and all others that were involved in proposals wanted to see in there for sure... [the Act] should be stronger, it should be stronger. It really did become about "what can we get over the line?"'

Leeson is saying that ultimately, the ISL Act needed to be scaled back significantly in order for it to be passed into law. Conama also refers to this in his work, stating that the initial inclusive measures were 'severely curtailed' in the final legislative process (Conama, 2019: 25). In fact, the ISL Act is significantly less detailed than the initial Irish Sign Language Bill, with the Bill containing 30 sections and the ISL Act containing only 11 sections (The Recognition of Irish Sign Language for the Deaf Community Bill, 2016). As an example of the dilution of the content of what would eventually become the ISL Act, in the early version of the Bill there were details on the specific entitlements to ISL interpretation. The Bill stated that by 2016, a person would be entitled to up to 120 hours of interpretation per year. Section 7.2 detailed the maximum allocation of ISL interpretation in education. These provisions would be in addition to the provision of ISL interpretation for members of the deaf community in accessing medical services, education and legal proceedings (Section 7.3). The Bill also aimed to establish an Irish Sign Language Council (Section 12), with the purpose of promoting and developing ISL (Section 13(a)); regulate teaching of ISL (Section 13(b)); regulate the provision of ISL interpretation (Section 13(c)); regulate the provision of deaf interpretation services (Section 13(d)) and; to promote the continued education and professional development of ISL teachers (Section 13(e)). In the final ISL Act the establishment of the Irish Sign Language Council is not provided and there is no corresponding detail on the entitlement to ISL interpreter hours, reflecting what Leeson and Conama both stated above that the ISL Act represents a dilution of the substantive access measures secured in the initial drafting process.

In discussing the specific problems with the ISL Act, Professor Leeson highlighted the overemphasis on disability:

> LL: 'But, I think fundamentally there are problems around Irish Sign Language – even though it's called the Irish Sign Language Act – Irish Sign Language being seen as a tool used to support a disability'.

Professor Leeson is pointing out here a particular problem whereby ISL (and sign languages generally) are often not seen as languages, but rather as tools to aid the disabled in communication. As noted earlier, this can be problematic for the deaf community when disability discourse is understood in context of the medical model and their identity as deaf people becomes paternalised (Ladd, 2003). This can be seen in the parliamentary debates discussing the ISL Bill. While the debates are generally positive, there is a significant emphasis on disability in the language used. While this in itself is not negative, it is not always clear what is meant by the term 'disability' when it was used. There was more emphasis on disability than on culture in the debates: during a Seanad debate on 19th October 2016, there were 37 references to 'disability' or 'disabled' and only five references to 'culture' or 'cultural' (*Recognition of Irish Sign Language for the Deaf Community Bill 2016: Second Stage*, 2016a; *Recognition of Irish Sign Language for the Deaf Community Bill 2016: Second Stage*, 2016b). In a Seanad debate on 17th October 2017, there were significantly more references to 'culture' in respect of the Bill, but these references mostly related to an amendment to actually remove reference to 'deaf culture' from the Bill as it was deemed inappropriate for the legislator to have any say over what does or does not constitute a culture (*Recognition of Irish Sign Language for the Deaf Community Bill 2016*, 2017). Throughout the process, there is repeated use of the term 'hearing impaired', including from the then Minister of State for Disability Issues, Finian McGrath.[1] This term is generally viewed negatively in the deaf community and is indicative of a medicalisation of deafness, through a focus on the 'impairment' that is being deaf or hard of hearing. While many deaf people welcome the disability identity, this is not the only identity to be considered, as discussed in Chapter 3. It also undermines the substantive access measures initially shown: in spite of the involvement of deaf Organisations, harmful stereotypes persisted and found their way into the finalised ISL Act, according to Leeson. This is demonstrative of a lack of substantive access, as the specific needs of deaf people and their identity as deaf people have been overshadowed by the dominance of a paternalised view of deafness as a medicalised disability.

The use of this language in the drafting of legislation to provide rights and recognition for ISL and the deaf community shows the importance of symbolic access as well. Where there has been a lack of symbolic access and a failure to tackle the societal barriers that obstruct the empowerment of deaf people, these attitudes can seep into the legislative process.

Ultimately, the result is as Leeson described above: the ISL Act views ISL as a tool for disability, or through a medical model lens.

7.2.2 *The Official Languages Act, 2003*

As for Irish speakers, the *Official Languages Act, 2003* (OLA) regulates the states obligations to use Irish and codifies the entitlements of Irish speakers. The OLA sets out the duties of public bodies to *inter alia*; engage with individuals in Irish (Section 11); to publish certain documents in Irish (Section 10); and to display the Irish language on official signage and stationery (Section 9). Included in 'public bodies' is An Garda Síochána and the Courts Service (First Schedule of the OLA). Specific to this research, the OLA also states that a 'person may use either of the official languages in, or in any pleading in or document issuing from, any court' (Section 8.1).

It also states that:

> Every court has, in any proceedings before it, the duty to ensure that any person appearing in or giving evidence before it may be heard in the official language of his or her choice, and that in being so heard the person will not be placed at a disadvantage by not being heard in the other official language.

Specifically, this section ensures that there will be equality in the treatment of Irish language users in the courts, that individuals will not be disadvantaged by their use of Irish. The OLA itself was brought into force under then Minister for Community, Rural and Gaeltacht Affairs Éamon Ó Cuív. Ó Cuív is a longstanding, notable member of the Irish language community (Ó Cuív, 2015). There was also involvement from Irish language organisations in the legislative process suggesting substantive access. However, just as can be seen with the ISL Act, some of the comments from legislators during the drafting of the OLA show that stereotypes about Irish speakers persisted in the legislative process.

One senator stated that 'it would be a good idea if those who spoke Irish were more friendly to those who try to speak it' (*Seanad Debate*, 2002), displaying a perception of Irish speakers as rude or unwelcoming. Again, I would compare this attitude to a problem of integration, whereby Irish speakers should alter their behaviour (deemed as rude) in order to appease an English-speaking majority. That same senator, Dr Henry, began her Seanad remarks in Irish, (*Seanad Debate*, 2002) stating 'Níl mé ábalta caint as Gaeilge anois ach fadó, fadó bhí fáinne agam' which translates to '*I am not able to speak Irish now, but long, long ago, I had a fáinne*'[2] before delivering the rest of her lengthy speech in English. This is an example of the tokenism of Irish described by Brennan and O'Rourke, whereby Irish is only used for niceties at the beginning of a speech, before switching to English for the actual content (S. Brennan & O'Rourke,

2019). Dr Henry's remarks tell us two things: Irish speakers can be perceived as rude and unwelcoming; and that Irish is a decorative flourish, rather than a functional language. This discourse featured throughout the legislative process. The inclusion of the community in the legislative process (right up to the role of the governing Minister) was not sufficient to prevent the persistence of harmful stereotypes about Irish speakers and Irish during the drafting of legislation intended to protect and promote the language and its users.

The OLA set out the provision for creating an Irish language Commissioner (Coimisinéir Teanga) to act as an Ombudsman of sorts over issues related to the provision under the OLA (Section 20). There has been controversy in the operation of the Office of the Coimisinéir Teanga. The first Commissioner stepped down from the role because of a failure by the government to provide Irish language services (Ó Caollaí, 2013). This controversy shows a failure to take seriously the concerns of Irish speakers and a minimisation of their identity, in spite of constitutional and legislative requirements. Dr Seán Ó Conaill referenced the issue of the Coimisinéir Teanga stepping down and the overall the effectiveness of the OLA:

> SÓC: 'I suppose the Official Languages Act was a great idea. And it still is – to be honest, I support the vast majority of it. Again, it goes down to the actual implementation of it. There is the theory and the practice. It's unbelievable. When someone as astute, as learned as Seán Ó Cuirréain [first Coimisinéir Teanga] steps down from the office because he says he's not getting anywhere – you know you've a problem. And the problem he had is getting government departments to respond to actual issues that he was highlighting with the Act. And they just ignored him. Which is unbelievable'.

Dr Ó Conaill's comments here show that there is a disconnect between the provisions of the OLA and how those provisions are actually implemented. And this is mirrored in the experiences of other participants: there was a disconnect between what the OLA should provide and what participants experienced when trying to use their language with state bodies. Gael1, Gael2, Gael3 and Gael5 all experienced being penalised for using Irish with Gardaí, even though the OLA mandates that An Garda Síochána must engage with people in Irish:

> Gael1: [Gael1 offered a witness account of a fight in Irish to a Garda on the scene] 'And he said "none of that now". And I said '*Well I am not willing to give you an account of the fight if you are not willing to hear it in Irish*'. And the thing he accused me of was "*obstructing the course of justice*" or "*perverting the course of justice*" or something like that because he know that I was not willing to share it with him [in English], or "*withholding*" or one of those crimes. Disrupting the legal process in a way. I can't remember exactly what he charged me with. But he became angry as well – which then made me angry. And he put me, we went down

to [the station] and I spent the rest of the night [in the station] He put me in a cell'.

Note that italicised text denotes the interviewee quoting the Garda speaking in English, while the interview was conducted in Irish.

Gael1 connected the penalty the received with their use of Irish. Gael2 encountered even more abrupt hostility:

Gael2: '...he [Garda] said something like "*I don't have the time to be dealing with your leprechaun bullshit. Can you just give me your address [in English]?*"'

Gael2 was subsequently arrested and connected that arrest to their use of Irish.

Gael3: 'Because he [Garda] said that line that was just bad, "*I was going to caution you at the side of the road but you seem to be playing a bit with me [by speaking Irish] so I'm just going to send a ticket out to you*"'

Gael3 stated that they were fined because their use of Irish annoyed the on-scene Garda.

Gael5: '[Gardaí were saying] insulting things like "*who does he think he is, he's absolutely stupid speaking Irish. He's going to get put off the road for years now*". Things like that'

Gael5 recalled being arrested and intimidated by Gardaí because of their use of Irish. These examples all demonstrate how the provisions of the OLA are not effectively translating to how Irish speakers experience using Irish with An Garda Síochána. They show that in spite of legislative requirements to provide services in Irish, not only are those services unavailable, but interviewees were penalised for seeking them. In these circumstances, there was a lack of beneficial outcomes flowing from the OLA. This is also in spite of the existence of an information card for Gardaí with useful Irish language phrases. The card is produced by An Garda Síochána (see Figure 7.1). On the front page of the wallet-sized card, it states that

An Garda Síochána recognises the right of citizens to conduct their business in Irish and is committed to the full implementation of the *Official Languages Act, 2003*

These information cards are supposed to be made available to members of the service to improve their engagement with Irish speakers. In spite of the reminder of An Garda Síochána's obligations and dedication under the OLA, interviewees still experienced discriminatory attitudes from Gardaí as shown.

Dr Seán Ó Conaill, in addressing this disconnect between 'theory and practice' of the OLA stated:

SÓC: 'Maybe that's the ultimate flaw in the Act...You know, if you look at it, there's a criminal offence in the Official Languages Act of not cooperating with an investigation, when the Commissioner has started an investigation. So there is one criminal offence, and there's a few others connected to that. But actually, ignoring the provisions of the Act has no criminal penalty! [laughing] As long as you cooperate when we're doing it. Ok, that's that then! The Minister can set a fine, but it's the government that you are fining. It's a bit silly. There is nothing to say that you couldn't be fined a euro for not cooperating. As long as you cooperate, but tell the Coimisinéir "well we're not going to do any of that, sorry we don't have time or resources, or we just couldn't be bothered" so be it. It's a bit of a farce in that sense'.

Ultimately, from Dr Ó Conaill's assessment, we can see that the OLA lacks teeth to actually be enforceable or impactful on organisations. The needs of Irish speakers have not been translated into concrete action, and this is evidenced by the stepping down of the Commissioner, and the data from Gael1, Gael2, Gael3 and Dr Ó Conaill.

There is a disconnect between what the OLA can provide in theory and what it can provide in practice. What this tells us is that even where there has been an engagement with concerned parties, substantive access is not guaranteed. The experiences from the data do not point towards beneficial outcomes for Irish speakers when they engage with the state using their language.

Further, the attitudes about Irish language users shown in the Dáil debates while drafting the OLA, suggest that there is also a lack of symbolic access. Attitudes towards Irish speakers can often be hostile in Irish society, as explained by Ní Raifertaigh J in *Ó Cadhla v. The Minister for Justice* (2019). Media reports about Irish regularly position Irish as limited in its function, a waste of time or a waste of state resources (Boland, 2016; Cooper, 2019; De Barra, 2017; Delaney, 2019; Fitzpatrick, 2014; Gilligan, 2019; Holden, 2007; Irish Examiner, 2020; Rousseau, 2019; Walshe, 2003).

In spite of substantive access measures, the negative societal perceptions of Irish speakers persist, and these attitudes become pervasive among state bodies (including the CJS). The data collected shows that even where there has been substantive access, the associated benefits can be undermined by a lack of symbolic access. This will be discussed in greater detail in the next two chapters. Where there has been no effort to tackle the harmful stereotypes which hinder progress for marginalised communities, substantive access measures can be undermined and rendered obsolete. For access to justice to be achieved, all three aspects of access to justice must be ensured.

7.3 Training

Training and training policies for CJS operatives is another area where substantive access can make a difference. As Bahdi notes, 'policies and programmes – through which rights are implemented' (2007: 25) must be designed in a way that considers the lived reality of those affected in order to pursue substantive access. Maintaining substantive access in the creation of policy and training will ensure that the needs of concerned parties are factored into that policy and training. Where this has happened, the outcomes of these policies will be equitable and beneficial to those marginalised groups.

In this section, I discuss the training of Gardaí and judges in turn. All Garda recruits are trained at the Garda Training College before they become Gardaí. Similarly, solicitors and barristers must complete professional training at the Law Society of Ireland and Kings Inns respectively,[3] a requisite qualification for appointment as a judge. Part of the training for both includes mandatory Irish language training, where the facilitation of Irish-speaking members of the public or clients is the aim. In both instances, it is uncertain who has been involved in the creation of the syllabi and so it is not possible to say with certainty whether substantive access measures were taken. However, it is possible to look at the syllabi or teaching models and examine them to see if they show substantive access measures in their construction.

At present, there is no mandatory training in any other languages for Gardaí recruits, trainee solicitors or barristers.[4] As such, there is limited data from interviews pertaining to ISL training of or usage by Gardaí or judges: most of the data relates to Irish usage. Nevertheless, this data still speaks to how minority languages and minority language users can be treated when they engage with the CJS in respect of substantive access.

7.3.1 Garda training practices

Training for all Gardaí in Ireland involves three phases of training, the first of which mandates recruits attend and reside at the Garda Training College in Templemore for a period of 34 weeks (*FAQs*, 2024). In that time, they attended classes, of which 'Irish language and Physical Fitness are mandatory parts of the various modules and programme'. It is no longer a requirement that recruits hold a qualification in Irish or English to join An Garda Síochána, pursuant to efforts to increase ethnic diversity in the service ('Irish No Longer a Requirement to Join An Garda', 2005). Included in the list of modules studied by Garda recruits is 'Foundations of Policing including Irish' (*FAQs*, 2024). The training is underpinned by the requirements under the OLA as described above. An Garda Síochána provides mandatory basic Irish language training to all recruits in order to facilitate their legislative and constitutional obligations.

AGS1 discussed the Irish language training mandated at the Garda Training College:

> AGS1: 'At the moment [trainee Gardaí] do Irish in two different modules which is Foundations and Traffic...Obviously dates, ages, numbers, times

and stuff like that are hugely important. That would be done in the Foundations. And then in the Traffic the two modules or roleplays are focused on checkpoint and drink driving...'

The emphasis on traffic is not surprising, as traffic-related incidents provide frequent interactions between Gardaí and the public.[5] AGS1 went on to justify the emphasis on traffic-related terminology as follows:

AGS1: 'And the reality is that anybody who is engaging with An Garda Síochána and especially if they are trying to report a missing person – they are not going to stand on the language right. They are going to communicate in the language that is best going to help the organisation and help themselves. So in that case, we can kind of – and I am not saying limit what we cover – but be more realistic about what we cover so that we cover it better...We say in worst case scenario, if somebody is charged with murder and they are trying to defend themselves – if it were me am I going "I can be principled and I have the right to do this through Irish, I might. But I think maybe they'll understand me better" – I think if the nature of something is so serious, you are going to go with the language that best defends you, best puts your case forward. I don't know if that's a personal decision or if that's – because I want to use Irish with the Gardaí doesn't mean I have to either. The important thing is that it's my choice. And that the choice is mine – not because of inefficiency on behalf of the organisation.'

There are a number of issues to consider here. First, limiting focus to traffic terminology can possibly create a perception that it is only in these circumstances that a person would use Irish. Encountering a speaker outside of these scenarios (such as in reporting a missing person) is not likely to be anticipated. Second, this outlook mirrors Brennan and O'Rourke's work (2019), as outlined above in that Irish is tokenistic and used for the less serious instances of road checkpoints or drunk driving, but not for serious crimes such as 'murder' or 'missing persons', the individual will undoubtedly resort to English. Third, while traffic concerns can undoubtedly be serious, AGS1 makes a note that for 'serious' issues (such as murder or missing persons), people are unlikely to resort to using Irish: 'I think if the nature of something is so serious, you are going to go with the language that best defends you, best puts your case forward'. This implies that Irish is for use in less serious interactions, that using it in serious instances is not putting one's best case forward. It implies that English is the language one ought to use if they wish to effectively engage with An Garda Síochána, directly contravening the provisions of the OLA.[6] Fourth, AGS1 directly linked the use of Irish to a choice. As will be discussed in greater detail in the following section, this binary of choice of language is not how language usage was experienced by interviewees. To describe interviewees' language usage as a mere choice is to trivialise their experiences and their identities.

An emphasis on traffic was also evident from an information card given to Gardaí, which AGS1 kindly provided. The card (see Figure 7.1) was developed over 10 years ago and contains statutory wording such as

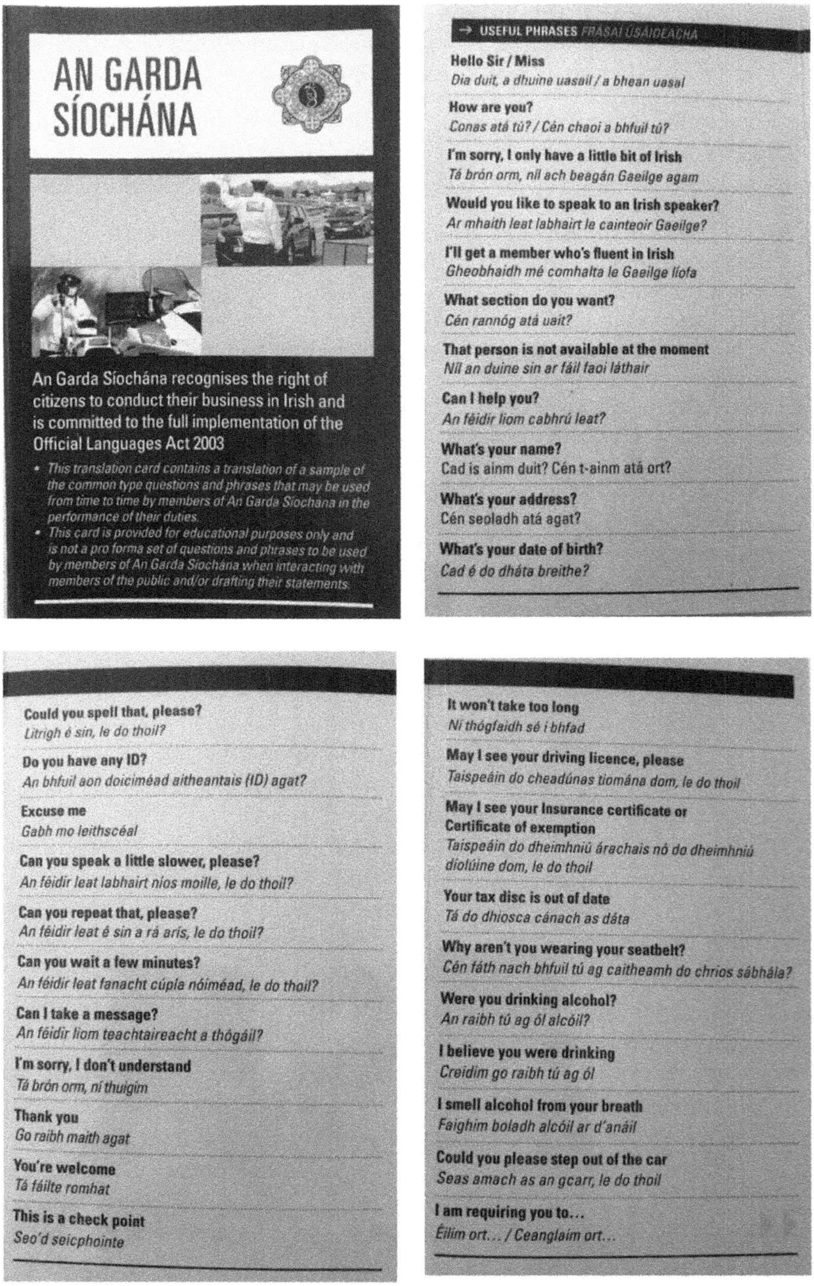

Figure 7.1 Garda Síochána Irish Card. Reproduced with permission

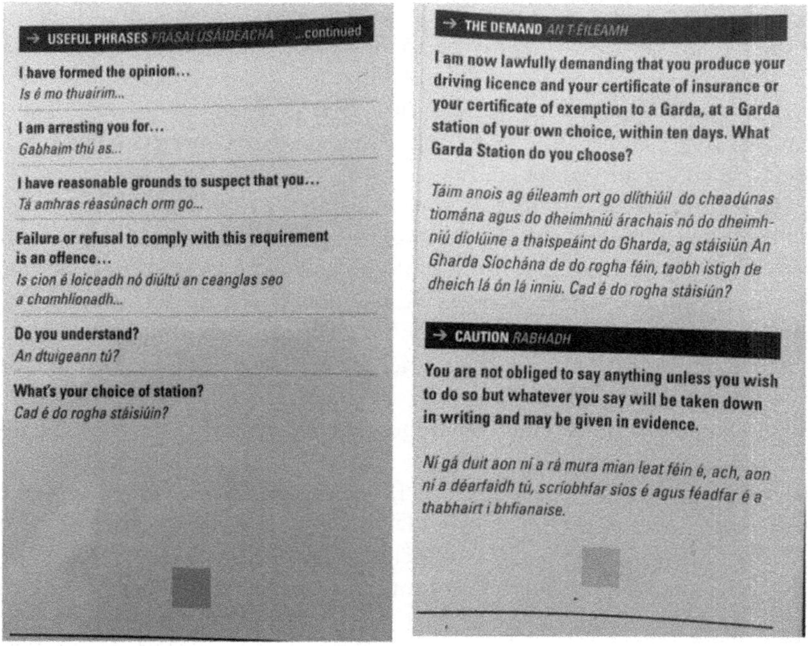

→ USEFUL PHRASES *FRÁSAÍ ÚSÁIDEACHA* ...continued

I have formed the opinion...
Is é mo thuairim...

I am arresting you for...
Gabhaim thú as...

I have reasonable grounds to suspect that you...
Tá amhras réasúnach orm go...

Failure or refusal to comply with this requirement is an offence...
Is cion é loiceadh nó diúltú an ceanglas seo a chomhlíonadh...

Do you understand?
An dtuigeann tú?

What's your choice of station?
Cad é do rogha stáisiúin?

→ THE DEMAND *AN TÉILEAMH*

I am now lawfully demanding that you produce your driving licence and your certificate of insurance or your certificate of exemption to a Garda, at a Garda station of your own choice, within ten days. What Garda Station do you choose?

Táim anois ag éileamh ort go dlíthiúil do cheadúnas tiomána agus do dheimhniú árachais nó do dheimhniú díolúine a thaispeáint do Gharda, ag stáisiún An Gharda Síochána de do rogha féin, taobh istigh de dheich lá ón lá inniu. Cad é do rogha stáisiún?

→ CAUTION *RABHADH*

You are not obliged to say anything unless you wish to do so but whatever you say will be taken down in writing and may be given in evidence.

Ní gá duit aon ní a rá mura mian leat féin é, ach, aon ní a déarfaidh tú, scríobhfar síos é agus féadfar é a thabhairt i bhfianaise.

Figure 7.1 (*Continued*)

the demand and the caution. It should be noted that this card is not in operational use today. It is a historical document and is not used in current Garda guidance or training. The card lists translations of useful phrases, many of which are related to traffic incidents. It is worth noting that Gael1, Gael3, Gael5, Gael6 and Gael7 all interacted with Garda on issues related to traffic. Interviewees recalled a general unpreparedness and hostility from Gardaí when Irish was used at traffic stops.

In their interview, AGS1 shed light on attitudes to the mandatory Irish language training that many recruits hold when at the Garda Training College, which might explain why Gael3 and Gael5 experienced negativity when they used Irish:

> AGS1: 'they didn't join the Gardaí to study Irish. It's a great source of angst for some of them.'

AGS1 made this statement in the context that trainees are generally not enthusiastic about taking Irish classes, and that it was understandable because learning Irish was not the reason why they joined the Gardaí. Irish language training is put in place to ensure Gardaí can fulfil their duties and facilitate an Irish-speaking public. It has both a legislative and constitutional basis. In the same way that carrying out powers of arrest or interviewing suspects is part of the job, so too is dealing with people in

Irish. Irish being a source of angst does not nullify the fact that it is part of the job, and indeed, ought to be an anticipated part of the job. To recall Reiner's cop culture as discussed in Chapter 2, it is possible that learning Irish is counter to the sense of action that is a feature of cop culture (Reiner, 2010), and manifests as 'angst', such as that experienced by Gael1, Gael2, Gael3, Gael5 and Gael7.

In terms of access to justice, the description of the way Irish is taught to Garda recruits, and the experiences interviewees have had when using Irish with Gardaí point to a lack of substantive access. From the data shown, the policies for training Gardaí do not take into account the 'patterns of disadvantage and oppression' of Irish speakers and have not been 'designed in ways that take [their] socially constructed disadvantage into account.' (Bahdi, 2007: 27)

In respect of ISL or Deaf Awareness training, no specific or dedicated training could be found. In recent years there have been instances of members of An Garda Síochána learning ISL and there have been initiatives to ensure the deaf people are provided better access to Garda services ('Collaboration with An Garda Síochána and Trinity College Dublin to Pilot New Service for Deaf Community', 2019; 'Deaf People Can Deal with Police Using Sign Language,' 2019; Irish Deaf Society, 2018; Kiernan, 2019). However, this training is *ad hoc* and so the potential effectiveness of these measures is limited to those who have received training. AGS2 highlighted that there is a lack of general awareness within the service about deaf issues. They went on to note that there was a lack of any formalised policy for engaging with deaf people within the organisation:

> AGS2: 'I do believe An Garda Síochána is sadly lacking in its disability awareness and that's not through lack of effort of the members, but just having concrete, written policies and learning practice'.

Here, while AGS2 expresses it from a disability perspective, they are stating that An Garda Síochána is not adequately prepared to interact with deaf people. This could be garnered from the testimony of many deaf interviewees. As will be explored shortly, Deaf4 stated that in their experience, Gardaí perceive deaf people as 'stupid' and did not interact with deaf people. It is possible that the lack of training and policies which AGS2 mentions has enabled the treatment that Deaf4 recounted.

In terms of substantive access, there is an interesting point to be raised from AGS2's words here. AGS2 is engaged in the creation of policies and practices for deaf people interacting with An Garda Síochána. AGS2 favoured disability language to refer to the deaf community. They explained their choice of wording as follows:

> AGS2: 'The deaf community – it's about definition. Is it disabled, is it a different culture? Well, that's up to the deaf community to decide. The deaf community would probably get better access to human rights if it was defined as disabled'.

AGS2 generally conflated being deaf with being disabled throughout their interview and then justified this use of language this way. They favoured this language because they believed that disability constituted a more robust way for the deaf community to get rights. This point of view is of course held within the deaf community: that the language of disability is better for accessing human rights (Darach Ó Séaghdha, 2021). As discussed, many deaf people identify as disabled. Yet a disability narrative is not favoured by all members of the deaf community, and it is not the only identity that deaf people have. No deaf participant in this research identified as disabled, for example. For the police to suggest that a group should define their culture strategically, rather than in terms of expressing their internal identity, compounds rather than resolving the issue of misunderstanding identity. The overrepresentation of only one deaf identity among those charged with creating policy has the potential to filter down and manifest in the paternalism experienced by Deaf3 and Deaf4:

> Deaf3: 'When the Garda arrived and realised that I was deaf, there was no communication at all. He was chatting with the car in front and the people who had run into the back of me. He just gave me a pen and a piece of paper and said write down your name and address and never asked me what happened. He spoke to the people on either end but didn't speak to me at all. And for me, on that day, I was upset'.
>
> Deaf4: Gardaí think [deaf people] are stupid, they see through you. They don't see you as an individual – they will speak to the hearing person that is with you.

Both Deaf3 and Deaf4 experienced being paternalised when their identity as deaf was made known. I explore these instances of paternalism in greater detail in the next chapter, but for now it is notable to connect the emphasis from AGS2 on disability discourses and the paternalism that both Deaf3 and Deaf4 recounted. When there is a dominant disability narrative used to describe deaf people within An Garda Síochána, there is the potential that 'disability' will be understood in the medical model context, resulting in a paternalised view of deaf people among members of the service (Degener, 2017b). AGS2 acknowledged in their interview that they have encountered outdated and harmful perceptions of deaf people within An Garda Síochána. However an emphasis on disability language – even when that language is using a social or human rights model of disability (Charlton, 2004) – can medicalise deaf people according to Ladd (2003), bringing their identity back to a lack of hearing (Delaney, 2019), rather than a culture (Ladd, 2003). This has an effect on substantive access. While the Centre for Deaf Studies has been engaged with An Garda Síochána in developing policy, ultimately those in charge of policies are Gardaí. Deaf people are not permitted to become Gardaí.[7] And so there is no possibility of deaf people actually being decision-makers in this context.

Prof Lorraine Leeson spoke of this work that the Centre for Deaf Studies at Trinity College Dublin has done in her interview:

> LL: 'We spent a full day down in [Garda Training College] with senior detectives and people from their law and policy unit, going through a mock witness statement, using their new protocols...They were so open. It's not the first time that we've done something like that with Guards. But it's about how do you – they were very senior people, they were very experienced interviewers, they were very open to feedback. But how do you get it from that elite cohort if you like to your average person in a police station in...Donegal or West Cork. These are actually the places where you're more likely to see these stories [of ill-treatment of deaf people] coming out'.[8]

Here Leeson touches on a particular point of interest as it relates to police culture, as discussed in Chapter 2. In Reiner's assessment, pragmatism governs how police perceive innovation and changes to laws and policies. Among 'rank and file' offers, there is a 'pragmatic, concrete, down-to-earth, anti-theoretical' (Reiner, 2010: 131) approach to policing. In this approach, Reiner notes that there is commonly a reluctance to 'contemplate innovation, experimentation or research'. He references the 'gulf' between 'management cops' and 'street wise' officers in terms of the isolation and solidarity as a feature of cop culture (Reiner, 2010). While upper levels of management may introduce or encourage policy changes, the belief in these changes does not always filter through to police on the ground. This is precisely the point Leeson makes – while upper management – the 'elite cohort' – at the Garda Training College were extremely receptive to their work, there is a disconnect with what is understood in 'rural stations' where the 'average person' interacts with police most often.

It is possible to map the literature on access to justice onto Leeson's assessment and cop culture literature. Substantive access measures among upper management, which might include input from deaf organisations is met with reluctance from police pragmatism. That pragmatism is fuelled by a failure to tackle the societal perceptions of deaf people as something deeper than 'disabled' because of the predisposition to stereotyping and the prevailing societal power structures which support this view including those coming from Gardaí themselves (see AGS2) (Reiner, 2010). For deaf people then, the attempts to achieve substantive access measures among the 'elite cohort' are rendered obsolete when they do not filter down to field officers who are most likely to encounter deaf people in society.

7.3.2 Judicial training practices

In continuing this discussion of substantive access in training practices, I am now addressing how judges are trained to interact with minority language users, and Irish speakers and deaf people in particular.

The Judicial Appointments Commission Act, 2023 (Judicial Appointments Commission Act, 2023) recently set up the Judicial Appointments Commission (JAC) in Ireland, which follows 'best practices from across Europe' for the implementation of 'improved procedures and requirements for judicial office selection through a streamlined and transparent process' (*Judicial Appointment Commission – About*, 2025). The act calls for the judicial appointment recommendations to include a 'sufficient number of judges with a proficiency in the Irish language', based on an understanding of the amount needed after consultation with the Courts Service (Sections 39.2(c) and 56.4). The Courts Service is the organisation which operates and administers courts in Ireland and is responsible, among many other things, for procuring and providing interpreters or Irish-speaking judges where they have been requested. A shortage of capable judges would be known to the Courts Service. However, there is the potential that a lack of judges who speak Irish is, in itself, a deterrent to people who would otherwise seek to use Irish in courts. It may be that there are those who seek an Irish-speaking judge, and are delayed or must use English because none are available. Many of those interviewed for this work who ended up going to court and having Irish-speaking proceedings knew that they would encounter delay and were willing to do so in order to assert their rights. But there also may be those who wish to avoid delay and opt for English, even when they would prefer to have their proceedings held in Irish. It is unlikely that these people would be included in any report from the Courts Service about the need for Irish-speaking judges.

In fact, there is no specific training that is provided to people who are appointed as judges in Ireland beyond annual, one-day conferences ('Judicial Education,' 2024). As such, there is no specific language training that is provided to new judges. Judges are appointed from the legal profession, either solicitors or barristers. During training to become a solicitor or a barrister, trainees complete mandatory Irish language classes (Forde *et al.*, 2013), just as with Garda recruits. Similarly, there is no other mandatory training provided in any other language. Those appointed as judges in Ireland must have worked for at least ten years as either a barrister or a solicitor ('Appointment to Judicial Office,' 2024). Therefore, the only mandated language training received by judges is that which is carried out at Kings Inns or the Law Society of Ireland when training as a barrister or solicitor, and this training will have occurred at least 10 years prior to judicial appointment. The training in both institutions is explained as follows:

> The course in each case has the aim of enabling the identification through the medium of Irish of a legal service that is required and where appropriate facilitating the referral to a practitioner who is competent to conduct the case through the Irish language. The course provided by each body is not to be subject to examination. (Forde *et al.*, 2013: para. 3.30)

Two points emerge here. First, these courses are not subject to examination. There is no way to ensure that the training has resulted in any level of competency in the absence of assessment and it shows that the training represents lip service, or box ticking, rather than actually ensuring that lawyers (and subsequent judges) actually have Irish. Although it requires for the recommendation of Irish-speaking judges for appointment when needed, the Judicial Appointments Commission Act 2023 also does not specify how competency in Irish will be assessed or reported. It may be that there are judges who profess to be able to speak Irish, but in fact, are not capable of conducting legal proceedings in Irish. Recall from Chapter 5 that language domain means that fluency can be highly situational (Berk-Seligson, 2017). Gael5 noted their doubt about whether the judge appointed to their case actually spoke sufficient Irish to understand what was happening in the court, and this was reiterated by Dlíodóir2. Due to a lack of any assessment procedures, it may be that the Courts Service is recording such judges as being competent to conduct proceedings in Irish.

Second, there is an acknowledgement that part of the training includes facilitating a referral to a more capable practitioner. This may be a useful skill, but there is also the possibility that it is preparing trainee lawyers to 'pass off' or not deal with Irish-speaking clients. It does not instil a requirement that they be prepared to deal with cases in Irish.

This concern is compounded in the Law Society of Ireland Professional Practice Course I 2019: Legal Practice Irish Handbook.9 This handbook is no longer in use at the Law Society of Ireland at the time of writing. Via this course, trainee solicitors learned basic terms and phrases to facilitate menial converin Irish. Legal Practice Irish is compulsory for all Professional Practice Course 1 (PPC 1) trainees (Legal Practitioners (Irish Language) Act, 2008), irrespective of prior knowledge of Irish or lack thereof (Law Society of Ireland, 2019). In the Law Society of Ireland Professional Practice Course I 2019: Legal Practice Irish Handbook, there were six specific sce focused on a different area of law. In each scenario, trainees were presented with facts and a script detailing an interaction with a client who seeks to conduct their business in Irish. Of particular interest is the scein week one (see Figure 7.2)

In the Week 1 Scenario depicted in Figure 7.2, a client who is a Jehovah's Witness (Ms K) attends a solicitor's (aturnae) office. The client was given an emergency blood transfusion during childbirth and is seeking a remedy: 'I mí Mheán Fómhair 2006, tar éis ordú cúirte, tugadh aistriú fola do Ms K/*In September 2006, after a court order, Ms K was given a blood transfusion*'. In the script, Ms K wishes to use Irish with the aturnae (solicitor). The aturnae is unable to provide a service in Irish: 'Tá faitíos orm nach ndéanann an oifig seo aon obair trí Gaeilge/*I am afraid that this office does not do any work in Irish*'. Of particular interest is the line from Ms K in response to the aturnae stating that their office does not

Creatlach Scéil Seachtaine 1 (Week 1 Scenario)
Cás Choimhlint Cearta (A Rights Dispute Case)

I mí Mheán Fómhair 2006, tar éis ordú cúirte, tugadh aistriú fola do Ms. K, tar éis di thart ar 80% dá cuid fola a chailleadh i mbreith a páiste in Ospidéal na mBan sa Chom i mBaile Átha Cliath. Tamall roimhe sin chuir sí in aghaidh aistriú fola a fháil ó tharla go raibh sé in aghaidh a creidimh mar Fhinné Iáivé. Mar sin féin, d'éirigh leis an Ospidéal ordú cúirte éigeandála a fháil, a cheadaigh dóibh aistriú fola a thabhairt don bhean seo. Chuir said an argóint chun tosaigh go bhfaigheadh an bhean bás mura dtabharfaí aistriú fola di.

Sa chás seo, deir an t-ospidéal go bhfuil sé de chúram orthu cearta saoil na mná a chosaint, i ngeall ar an gcosaint a thugtar do chearta saoil sa Bhunreacht. Tá an argóint á dhéanamh freisin go bhfuil sé de chúram ar an Stát cearta saoil theaghlaigh na mná agus a páiste a chosaint.

Deir Ms. K go ndeachaigh an t-aistriú fola in aghaidh a cuid cearta faoin ECHR agus nár ghlac an t-ospidéal lena cearta chun diúltú do leigheas. Ar an ábhar sin creideann sí go ndearna an t-ospidéal ionsaí agus foghail ar a cuid cearta agus dá bhrí sin tá sí i dteideal cúitimh. Tagann Ms. K chuig do ghnólacht agus tugann do rúnaí isteach chuig d'oifig í.

Script:

Aturnae: Dia duit, tá an-fháilte romhat.

Ms. K: Go raibh maith agat as mé a fheiceáil chomh luath seo

Aturnae: Ná habair é. Fuair mé do litir ag tagairt do gach a tharla san Ospidéal Máithreachais. Céard ba mhaith leat a dhéanfainn?

Ms. K: Ba mhaith liom go gcuirfeá an dlí orthu as ionsaí agus foghail a dhéanamh orm agus táim ag iarraidh go gcloisfear an cás i nGaeilge.

Aturnae: Tá faitíos orm nach ndéanann an oifig seo aon obair trí Ghaeilge.

Ms K: Nach bhfuil ceart bunreachtúil agam mo chás a chur i nGaeilge?

Aturnae: Tá go deimhin! Ar mhaith leat go gcuirfinn i dteagmháil thú le haturnae atá in ann cás a dhéanamh i nGaeilge.

Ms. K: Ba mhaith go deimhin. Brón orm as mo ghlór a ardú – tá an-strus orm faoi láthair agus ní fhaigheann an páiste mórán codlata.

Aturnae: Ceart go leor. Tabharfaidh mé sonraí Kevin O'Hara & Co. duit Tá a chárta gnó agam anseo.

Ms. K: Go raibh míle maith agat.

Aturnae: Fáilte romhat. Tá súil agam go n-éireoidh leat. Go raibh maith agat as teacht.

Ms. K: Slán.

Aturnae: Slán.

Figure 7.2 Law Society legal practice Irish training. Reproduced with permission

provide Irish language services: 'Nach bhfuil ceart bunreachtúil agam mo chás a chur i nGaeilge?/*Don't I have a constitutional right to pursue my case in Irish?*'. Ms K then says 'Brón orm as mo ghlór a ardú/*I am sorry for raising my voice*' indicating anger about not being provided with an Irish-language service. Ms K arrives at the offices of the aturnae, demanding to have her constitutional right to speak Irish ahead of a serious infringement on their bodily autonomy and religious freedom. She is 'standing on the language right' as AGS1 noted above.

She begins to shout for her rights when the aturnae simply admits their inability to conduct a case in Irish. This particular interaction creates a picture of a cantankerous Gael who stubbornly demands service in their language. The only antidote to this cantankerous Irish speaker in this scenario is to pass them off onto a more capable colleague, but only where the passing-off is done *in* Irish. In fact, the major focus in this curriculum is on referral in Irish to another, more fitting colleague. Of the six weekly scenarios in the LPI Handbook 2019, five involve a referral to another colleague or law firm better suited to the case.[10] These referrals are done in Irish. This fulfils one element of S.2(d) of the *Legal Practitioners (Irish Language) Act 2008*. The Law Society interpreted this requirement to train students to refer clients to more suitable lawyers as an obligation to provide a referral *in* Irish, even when the solicitor does not actually speak Irish, rather than just facilitate a referral in English. I argue that this training furthers a negative perception of Irish speakers: Trainees must learn how to refer a client to an Irish-speaking colleague in Irish – even when they do not speak Irish or practice in it – because the angry, cantankerous Irish speaker will not accept being spoken to in English.

There is a more in-depth Irish language training course available at the Law Society: Advanced Legal Practice Irish. This course is not compulsory and is available for trainees who wish to be certified to practice in Irish (*Law Society of Ireland*, 2021). Qualified solicitors are then added to the Irish Language Register (Lowney, 2023). There is no requirement that judges, or that any judge, appointed in Ireland come from this list, or the corresponding list of barristers competent to conduct business in Irish (*Find a Barrister*, 2025). Thus, between the distance since language training and the lack of additional training, there is no guarantee that judges will be competent to conduct proceedings in Irish.

In respect of the level of competency in Irish among judges, there were conflicting attitudes from Dlíodóir1 and Dlíodóir2. Dlíodóir1 was confident that Irish usage was commonplace within the Courts:

> Dlíodóir1: 'Every day that I am in the court, I meet people, and I speak in Irish - maybe there is not a lot of cases happening through Irish, but every day I meet with practitioners, lawyers, barristers, judges. It would surprise you. Every day in the court, I speak in Irish.'

By comparison, Dlíodóir2 was more pessimistic about the availability of judges with Irish:

> Dlíodóir2: 'There is a lack of judges available anyway. There used to be a time where maybe six of the judges in the High Court had Irish. Now, only three of them speak it. Including the President. And one of them, the [judge] is involved in matters of family law for the most part.'

It is unclear from these two accounts whether there is availability of judges competent in Irish or not. As noted above, Gael5 was confident that the judge appointed to oversee their case could not speak Irish. This example shows that in spite of laws compelling the courts to provide for an accused to be heard in Irish, the practical application of that right is lacking. This was the reason that the first Coimisinéir Teanga stepped down from his role (Caollaí, 2013). As argued above, the basic Irish language training for solicitors presents Irish speakers in a negative, cantankerous light. The training cannot be said to take the interests of Irish speakers into account effectively, and so there is a lack of substantive access.

As for other languages or Deaf Awareness, no information could be found about specific and mandated training for other language or minority groups for legal practitioners, or judges. There is no such legislative requirement for training in ISL or Deaf Awareness. That being said, the Law Society of Ireland recently provided pilot training of basic ISL to trainees ('Sign Language Course a First for Law School', 2020), as well as a Continuous Professional Development (CPD) training course on 'Irish Sign Language in a Legal Setting' (*An Introduction to Irish Sign Language (ISL) in the Legal Setting*, 2021), both on an optional basis. This training appears to operate in conjunction with the deaf community, and so there has been an effort to meet substantive access measures. For the CPD course, it is stated that in addition to learning basic ISL, participants will also learn 'about the deaf community, deaf culture and deaf people as a linguistic minority group' (*An Introduction to Irish Sign Language (ISL) in the Legal Setting*, 2021). It would seem that there is potentially a symbolic access element here, to at least equip availing solicitors with an understanding of the socioeconomic realities of deaf people and the societal barriers which they face.

7.4 Chapter Summary

Substantive access must ensure that laws and policies which affect marginalised people are mindful of the realities of those people. As such, a key goal of substantive access measures is that marginalised people be involved in the creation of laws and policies which affect them. From this chapter, I have found that legislative and training and policy measures, designed to serve the Irish-speaking and deaf communities do not effectively reflect the needs of those communities. Again, the research presented in this chapter represents a new contribution to the field of access to justice scholarship, in expanding its application to minority language users and their experiences of substantive access in the CJS and the right to a fair trial.

The ISL Act appears to lack substantive access. Although there was initial involvement from the deaf community, the final version of the Act was 'severely curtailed' (Conama, 2019: 25) and constituted 'a great deal of compromise' according to Professor Leeson above, on the measures that were initially important to the deaf community. Similarly, the OLA lacks teeth to actually hold effective and enforceable rights for Irish speakers. This has played out in the resignation of the Coimisinéir Teanga and the failure of the OLA to actually impact the experiences with Gardaí which Gael participants relayed.

In terms of teaching policies, again, the inclusion of affected groups has either not been sought in the creation of syllabi or diluted to such a degree that it has not resulted in substantive access. I have found that this has allowed for the perpetration of harmful stereotypes – such as a medicalised deaf person or a cantankerous Gael – which will be explored further in the next two chapters.

Ultimately, the failure of substantive access measures to actually deliver substantive access can be rooted back to a lack of symbolic access. I argue that law and policymakers cannot provide effective substantive access when they lack the understanding of the realities of marginalised people which accompanies symbolic access. Substantive access examples herein, such as including organisations in law and policymaking have all been diluted down and eventually been rendered ineffective and tokenistic. I will discuss this reality in the next two chapters. The first of these considers how participants experienced their perceived or external identity as they went through the CJS and the second considers how this fit with their internal identity. Through this analysis the issues of symbolic access will be addressed.

Notes

(1) During the 19 October 2016 Seanad debate, the term 'hearing impaired' was used by Senator John O'Mahony, Senator Gabrielle McFadden and Deputy Finian McGrath. The term was also used by Senator Trevor Ó Clochartaigh, Senator Colette Kelleher and Deputy Finian McGrath during the 17 October 2017 Seanad debate. It was used also in the lower house during the Dáil Debate 14 December 2017, vol 963, no 3 by Deputy Michéal Martin.

(2) Wherein a 'fáinne' is a small ring-shaped pin often worn by Irish speakers to indicate to others that they can speak Irish. The pins are available to purchase and are supposed to depict the level of Irish a wearer has, where silver (fáinne airgid) shows a basic level of spoken Irish and gold (fáinne óir) shows fluency in Irish.

(3) Note that in order to be appointed as a judge in Ireland, a person must have been a practicing solicitor or barrister for at minimum, 10 years. See https://aji.ie/

the-judiciary/appointment-to-judicial-office/ [date accessed: 17 January 2025]. There is no additional training mandated for work as a judge.

(4) Note that an entry requirement for An Garda Síochána includes competency in two languages, one of which is English or Irish.

(5) Checkpoints on roads to carry out spot checks of tax and insurance or to breathalyse drivers are common. Garda will also carry out speed checks on roads, direct traffic following a collision or for traffic management purposes.

(6) Where 'public bodies' are required to respond to requests in Irish in that language and An Garda Síochána constitutes a public body under the provisions of the OLA.

(7) Part of the entry requirements for An Garda Síochána includes a physical fitness test, which entail potential recruits listening for various sounds and conducting corresponding actions to those sounds.

(8) Note that Leeson is referring to the Justisigns project, an EU research project aimed to explore issues related to Sign Language usage in legal settings. See http://www.justisigns.com/JUSTISIGNS_Project/About.html [date accessed: 15 January 2021].

(9) Cited with permission from the Law Society of Ireland. Note that Gearóidín McEvoy has been an LPI teacher with the Law Society of Ireland since 2017.

(10) Week 1 Scenario (cited above), Week 2 Scenario (related to civil/criminal law), Week 3 Scenario (a family law and conveyance issue), Week 4 Scenario (a business and EU law issue) and Week 6 Scenario (an employment law issue).

8 Symbolic Access and the External Identity: The Slíbhín and the Créatúr

8.1 Introduction

In the previous chapters, I explored how Irish-speaking and deaf participants experienced procedural and substantive access in the CJS (Bahdi, 2007; Flynn, 2015). I discussed participants' experiences under the minimum standards of the right to a fair trial. These experiences are of concern and affected the participants in their interactions with the CJS.

It was clear from the research that a strict view of how participants experienced the minimum standards of the right to a fair trial would ineffectively tell their stories. In most cases, the issues of contention for participants went beyond the right to a fair trial. The major concerns went beyond substantive access and procedural access. As such, in this chapter and the next, I discuss how participants' experiences related to symbolic access (Flynn, 2015). Such was the volume of instances which related to symbolic access, that it has been necessary to divide the discussion into two chapters. To reiterate, symbolic access, according to Flynn, includes a:

> ...society in which, due in part at least to its laws and justice system, individuals from marginalised communities are fully included and empowered to participate as equal citizens...(2015: 16)

In this chapter, I explore the external identity of the research participants (Goffman, 1969), as it was made known to them by operatives in the CJS. This external perception of identity adds a layer of understanding to how minority language users can be perceived in the CJS, how they experience the CJS and how their identities and language impact their experiences.

I have identified two tropes from the data experienced by participants which fundamentally shape their experiences, as alluded to in

Chapter 3. I present these tropes in this section. Exploring these tropes provides context for how participants interacted with the CJS. These tropes are the 'créatúr' and the 'slíbhín', both of which are explained in detail in this chapter. The créatúr is applicable to deaf people and represents an outdated, paternalistic view of deaf people when they appear before the CJS. The slíbhín is applicable both to Irish speakers and deaf people and represents a view of a minority language user as a malicious troublemaker. I identified and named two further sub-tropes to provide a context for Irish speakers under the slíbhín trope: the 'Good Gael', the 'Bad Gael'. They show how minority language users can be viewed when they interact with the CJS and how this view can impact access to justice.

The tropes are barriers to symbolic access. In viewing deaf people or Irish speakers as only a créatúr or a slíbhín, they cannot be viewed as their true, internal identity, which will be explored in the next chapter. Therefore, they are met with the negative and patronising stereotypes associated with these external tropes and are prevented from being seen as empowered participants in society.

In this chapter and the next, I return to the concepts of the 'créatúr' and the 'slíbhín' tropes first introduced in Chapter 3. I present the tropes as they appeared in interviews with participants and show how these tropes impacted their engagement with the CJS. In turn, I then explore how these tropes relate to and interact with existing scholarship on identity, cop culture and judicial bias. Combining these strands of literature deepens the understanding of how those subject to these tropes can face barriers to accessing justice. Finally, I position these tropes in the context of access to justice and show how their existence in the interactions interviewees had with the CJS is indicative of a lack of symbolic access.

8.2 Defining the 'Créatúr' Trope

Créatúr is an Irish term but also appears in Hiberno-English. The *Ó Dónaill Foclóir Gaeilge-Béarla* Irish to English dictionary lists créatúr as the following:

> **créatúr**, *m*, (*gs*.& *npl*. **úir**, *gpl*. ~).Creature. **1.** Created thing. **Guí ar gach ~**, to pray for all creatures. **Mar atá Dia lena chréatúir**, as God is to His creatures. **2.** (As expression of sympathy) **An ~, an ~ bocht**, the poor thing. **Na créatúir atá inamhuinín**, the unfortunate people who depend on him. **Ba mhaith é, an ~**, he was good, the poor fellow. **3.** (Contemptuously) **Níl ann ach ~(gan mhaith)**, he is only a(good-for-nothing) creature. (*Var*:**créatúir** *m, pl*. **créatúireacha**). (*Foclóir Gaeilge–Béarla (Ó Dónaill)*, 2024)

The term is inherently paternalistic in its usage. That same paternalism can be seen on the online dictionary search engine focloir.ie, where the entry for créatúr includes the following definitions: bleeder; bugger;

creature; critter; lamb; thing; unfortunate; wretch (*Créatúr – Translation to Irish Gaelic with Audio Pronunciation of Translations for Créatúr by New English-Irish Dictionary*, n.d.). The phrase 'créatúr bocht soineanta é' is translated as 'he is only a babe' on focloir.ie, but it might be more directly translated to 'he is a poor innocent creature/wretch'. The term is also found in Hiberno-English, where it is used to similar effect. *A Dictionary of Hiberno-English: The Irish Use of English* has entries for both 'créatúr' and 'creature'. Both are defined as 'a term of endearment', with 'Come here you poor little créatúr, who did that to you?' and 'The poor creature, she's all alone now' used as example sentences in both instances (Dolan, 1999: 66).

There is a distinct element of pity and paternalism present in the term 'créatúr'. In a sense, the medical model of disability is effectively captured by 'créatúr' because it is inherently paternalistic. 'Créatúr' has not had the same evolution or reclamation that 'disabled' has had in English: instead it remains rooted in paternalistic notions of some poor wretch and the medical model of disability. For this research, I have developed and defined 'créatúr' as follows:

Definition:
Créatúr, *noun, singular*/créatúir, *noun, plural*: a description referring to individuals who are seen as pitiful because of their apparent affliction. They are viewed through a paternalistic lens. They are observed as lacking capacity, childlike and cannot be held accountable for their actions.

Aspects of the créatúr trope can be seen in literature on Deaf Studies, as alluded to in Chapter 3. Lane writes specifically about the perception of deafness as a disability or an infirmity: 'In the hearing stereotype, deafness is the lack of something, not the presence of anything. Silence is emptiness' (Lane, 1999). Here, he is noting that for most hearing people, being deaf is seen as an affliction, rather than a cultural identity (Ladd, 2003). A sense of pride in being deaf is inconsistent with this trope, as deafness is a stigma to be overcome. As discussed, not all deaf people perceive themselves and their community in light of disability discourse. However, the more dominant hearing world views deaf people as créatúir. The trope is more visible than deaf internal identities. Charlton refers to this dominant paternalism in his work on disability:

> Paternalism lies at the center of the oppression of people with disabilities. Paternalism starts with the notion of superiority: We must and can take control of these 'subjects' in spite of themselves, in spite of their individual will, or culture and tradition, or their sovereignty. The savages need to be civilized (for their own good). The cripples need to be cared for (for their own good). The pagans need to be saved (for their own good).

> Paternalism is often subtle in that it casts the oppressor as benign, as protector. The relation between ideology and power is expressed as natural to justify relations of oppression (Charlton, 2004: 53).

The subject to be saved and cared for here is the poor, deaf créatúr, underpinned by a sense of paternalism. It should also be noted that there is evidence of Irish speakers themselves being seen as créatúir in the past, where they were viewed as pitiful and uneducated under colonial rule (Phelan, 2019). However, the perception of Irish speakers in this light did not arise in this data.

8.2.1 The 'Créatúr' trope in operation

While generally describing the experiences of deaf people, Deaf4 stated that harmful perceptions of deafness still exist in society. In demonstrating the existence of the créatúr trope in the CJS, Deaf4 reference how deaf people are generally perceived by police:

> Deaf4: Gardaí think [deaf people] are stupid, they see through you. They don't see you as an individual – they will speak to the hearing person that is with you...You can see it in their [Gardaí] body language – deaf people are really good at reading body language. They [Gardaí] talk about you like you are not in the room. There is a lack of common decency.

There are two issues which point towards the créatúr trope here. Firstly, Deaf4 was adamant that Gardaí think deaf people are 'stupid'. They perceived that for police, deafness was connected to intelligence, or lack thereof. Secondly, Deaf4 perceived that Gardaí devalue deaf people's autonomy, preferring to ignore them or defer to a hearing person present. Deaf4 presented both of these issues as a 'lack of common decency'. They felt that because they are deaf, they have been paternalised in interactions with police, indicating the créatúr trope. The lack of symbolic access that Deaf4 experienced was evident when interacting with Gardaí. They felt that they were treated as lesser and denied the empowerment and inclusion which are necessary in ensuring symbolic access.

Deaf3 recalled a distressing road traffic incident where the créatúr trope can be applied. When a Garda arrived on the scene, the interviewee was upset by the limited communication:

> Deaf3: 'When the Garda arrived and realised that I was deaf, there was no communication at all. He was chatting with the car in front and the people who had run into the back of me. He just gave me a pen and a piece of paper and said write down your name and address and never asked me what happened. He spoke to the people on either end but didn't speak to me at all. And for me, on that day, I was upset'.

From their account, Deaf3 was viewed as someone who could not be communicated with, and whose witness account was not valued – again, amounting to a lack of symbolic access. Additionally, the differential treatment which Deaf3 received was jarring and evident and left them feeling upset. The Garda did not treat them the same as the other participants to the incident. The realisation that Deaf3 was deaf was what triggered the lack of communication (*'When the Garda arrived and realised that I was deaf, there was no communication at all'*). Deaf3 connected the negative experience they had to the communication of their identity, and how that identity was subsequently perceived externally by the Garda.

The créatúr trope is also present in Deaf5's experience. For Deaf5, rather than being ignored they were granted discretion which they suspected was connected to paternalism:

> Deaf5: '...but he [Garda] turned around and said 'Do you realise your engine doesn't sound good?!' And I said 'No, I am deaf, I wear two hearing aids!' [Laughter] And so he said 'Oh! Ok!' So I don't know if he felt sorry for me and he didn't process [the fine] – I don't know! But I do know, at the time, I was – I knew I was wrong [knew they were evidently breaking the law]'
>
> *Fieldnotes:* In imitating the Garda, Deaf5 initially showed that the Garda was serious and solemn in their words: 'Do you realise your engine doesn't sound good?!' However, their tone changed to surprise, losing that seriousness when imitating the realisation that Deaf5 was deaf: 'Oh! Ok!'

Here, Deaf5 reported that the Garda used their discretion and did not issue a fine. It was alluded to that the Garda's tone and mood changed once they realised that Deaf5 was deaf. The use of discretion may well be an exercise in paternalism as Deaf5 suggested, that the Garda took pity on them and did not pursue a fine. Deaf5 was of course pleased with this outcome as they did not incur a fine or penalty. But if the Garda used his discretion because they pitied Deaf5, or did not see them as an autonomous person capable of committing crime, then they have undermined Deaf5's autonomy. Again, this shows a lack of empowerment for deaf people, pointing to a lack of symbolic access. The view of Deaf5 as créatúr and worthy of pity hindered their ability to fairly police a situation which would have warranted a penalty were Deaf5 hearing/not a créatúr.

As shown in the previous chapter, in discussing the deaf community AGS2 repeatedly referred to the deaf people in terms of disability and 'special needs', favouring this language over that of culture and identity. This view is shared by some members of the deaf community (Darach Ó Séaghdha, 2021). It shows the necessity to compromise the internal, culturally deaf identity as discussed in Chapter 3 (Leigh *et al.*, 2018), in favour of the external identity. In addition, this language can have a negative impact on those who are only familiar with a medical model of disability (Degener, 2017b). AGS2 was not implying a créatúr trope in their language. In fact, it was clear that AGS2 was inferring empowerment, and possibly the human rights model in their use of 'disability' (Degener, 2017a). However, that this empowered understanding of disability was not necessarily received by other members of the service:

> AGS2: 'I sometimes have come across the misuse of words and poor use of words around deafness and disability [within the Gardaí]'.

AGS2 stated that they had experienced members of An Garda Síochána using the term 'deaf and dumb' to describe deaf people. This language is offensive in the deaf community and harkens to an inherently medicalised view of deaf people, where their deafness is perceived as an impairment to be corrected (Lane, 1999). They showed that the harmful créatúr trope persists among members of An Garda Síochána and is applied to deaf people. When considering symbolic access, if this harmful stereotype persists as a dominant known-about-ness for deaf people, it will inherently limit the empowerment and inclusion necessary to ensure symbolic access.

The créatúr trope appeared frequently in the data. It showed how deaf participants were frequently met with outdated, harmful perceptions, and how those perceptions coloured their interactions with the CJS (specifically with the police). Though there have been developments in disability discourse, those developments were not experienced by participants. The participants' experiences mirrored the literature, which shows that being deaf is seen as a stigma rather than as an empowered identity (Ladd, 2003).

In terms of symbolic access then, the persistence of these perceptions within the CJS shows that there is still progress to be made in terms of access to justice. Where deaf people are paternalised and stigmatised because of their cultural and linguistic identity, they are blocked from being empowered, valued members of society and prevented from fully participating in the process.

8.3 Defining the 'Slíbhín' Trope

The slíbhín trope is rooted in a perception of the other as deviant or malicious, as discussed in the Chapter 2 (Jefferson, 1993). Othered individuals, and people or groups displaying their othered characteristics are often perceived negatively (Leary, 1999). Language usage can constitute this othered behaviour (Chan, 1997).

I am calling this trope the 'slíbhín'. Again, I am using an Irish/Hiberno-English term, which I found more accurately fit the trope inferred. *Ó Dónaill Foclóir Gaeilge-Béarla* defines 'slíbhín' as follows:

> *m.* (*gs.* ~, *pl.* ~í). Sly person.' (*Foclóir Gaeilge–Béarla (Ó Dónaill)*, 2021) Focloir.ie defines "slíbhín" as "serpent" or "sneak" and provides the phrase "the sly dog" as a translation for "an slíbhín" (*Slíbhín*, 2021).

Just as with 'créatúr', 'slíbhín' has entered Hiberno-English lexicon. In *A Dictionary of Hiberno-English: The Irish Use of English*, the anglicised spelling 'sleveen' and 'sleeveen' are provided. 'Slíbhín' is also given. It is defined therein as 'a sly person; a trickster; a smooth-tongued rogue; a toady; a crooked person'. An example sentence is given as 'Keep away from that sleveen!' (Dolan, 1999). The term is distinctively negative, conjuring an image of untrustworthiness, deviance and malice. For this research, I developed and defined the 'slíbhín' as follows:

Definition:

Slíbhín, *noun, singular*/slíbhíní, *noun, plural:* a descriptor which indicates a sneaky, troublemaking and untrustworthy person. The slíbhín is a sly person who delights in causing problems and making mischief. Their behaviour/language use is disingenuous and an attempt to evade justice.

A multitude of reports under the ECRML show that using othered languages is perceived as deviant, or slíbhín behaviour. In a 2001 report from the Committee of Experts for the ECRML, it was noted that Swedish-speaking Finns can experience damaging tropes in their engagement with the justice system:

> [Swedish-speaking Finns who engage with the court] felt constrained to give up using Swedish, or requesting to use Swedish, because it created an atmosphere which is not always very positive in judicial proceedings, the individual having the feeling that he or she may be considered as a 'trouble maker'. (European Charter for Regional or Minority Languages Report of the Committee of Experts on Finland, 2001: 76)

The Committee of Experts has found evidence of this perceived deviance in Germany, Slovenia, Austria, Ukraine, Bulgaria, Croatia, Czech Republic, Romania and Spain (Austria, 2018; Bulgaria, 2016; Croatia, 2019; Czech Republic, 2015; Germany, 2006; Romania, 2012; Slovenia, 2014; Spain, 2012; Ukraine, 2017). García-Sánchez and Nazimova note in their research that a display of multilingualism in a typically monolingual space can give rise to a presumption of deviance (García-Sánchez & Nazimova, 2017). This slíbhín trope can also be seen in discourses where language and a national or regional identity are intertwined, particularly where those national identities represent secessionist views. Irish-speaking in Northern Ireland is inherently connected to Nationalist politics (C.C. O'Reilly, 2014), which is then often demonised (Aodha, 2017). Spanish speakers in the US were repeatedly construed as deviant and dangerous by former President Trump (McIntosh & Mendoza-Denton, 2020). Language is often used in these context as a proxy for other forms of bias: racial, gendered, cultural, socioeconomic, political or ethnic bias, for example (Gillon *et al.*, n.d.). As noted in Chapter 10, both Phelan and Waterhouse have discussed biases from the court in respect of non-traditional language users (Phelan, 2011; Waterhouse,

2014). Recall that in her interview, Dr Phelan referenced non-traditional language users being disbelieved about their need for an interpreter for court, and the assumption that a request for an interpreter was rooted in malice and deviance. Deviance, it would seem, can be the external identity imposed on both traditional and non-traditional language users.

The slíbhín trope is visible in literature on policing too. Chan states that the troublemaker trope is a relatively common practice in policing (Chan, 1997). Police often view othered persons as beyond normal, and therefore, troublesome: 'those who deviate from society's images of middle-class respectability and conformity are often considered by police as "trouble"' (Chan, 1997: 41). In the context of this research, the deviation from what is standard or 'normal' constitutes a person who uses another language. Reiner states that suspicion is another characteristic of policing (Reiner, 2010: 121). It is a constant aspect of a police officer's job and something 'that cannot be readily switched off' (Reiner, 2010: 121). I am arguing that through this suspicion, the slíbhín trope emerges. When police are suspicious of the individual's language usage, having not initially anticipated it (Jefferson, 1993), they perceive it – and the individual using that language – to be deviant or troublesome.

The slíbhín trope can be applied to Irish speakers, ISL users, or other non-English language users (Chan, 1997), which I address now. However, I also have broken down this slíbhín trope further in respect of specific sub-tropes which arose in interviews with Irish speakers. I define the 'Good Gael' and the 'Bad Gael' below. These sub-tropes reflect broader societal attitudes of what it means to speak Irish and how speakers are perceived in different contexts.

8.3.1 The 'slíbhín' trope in operation

Deaf1's experience with Gardaí demonstrates the perception of the 'Slíbhín' in action:

> Deaf1: '[the Garda] took me and put my arms behind my back and I couldn't, I was saying "I'm deaf, I'm deaf!" and he took me and he was kind of [interpreter clarifies if interviewee means they were walking or in the car] So he had me like this, with my arm squeezed behind my back and was going to bring me to the station. And then [he] pushed my head up against a fence as well. And I wasn't saying anything and he started doing this to me [motions lightly tapping the chin, in a condescending way] patronisingly like [he was] saying "come on, talk!" and I was saying "I'm deaf! I'm deaf, I can't talk"...'
>
> *Fieldnotes*: Deaf1 indicates that the Garda was sceptical about their deafness and that they were being mocked in this interaction.

Deaf1's account suggested that the Garda either did not believe they were deaf or did not understand the realities of being deaf. The Garda was patronising and incited Deaf1 to speak. This was a particularly violent encounter, where physical force was used on Deaf1. In addition to the violence itself, this also had the effect of gagging Deaf1, impacting their ability to sign and communicate. Deaf1 was not treated with dignity. Their account shows that the Garda possibly perceived them as a slíbhín, unworthy of respect. The possible perception that Deaf1 was pretending to be deaf was sufficient to allow the Garda to apply the slíbhín trope and use force as a result. This indicates a possible failure of the attitude test (Brown, 1988), mentioned in Chapter 2, whereby Deaf1 did not behave in a way that the Garda anticipated (Chan, 1997), or that was disrespectful (Brown, 1988), and they were duly punished for that behaviour. Police property was also explored as a concept in Chapter 2 and it is suggested that this interaction indicates that the slíbhín may constitute police property (Reiner, 2010). It also suggests again, a lack of symbolic access, where the known-about-ness of the deaf identity lacked equality and empowerment in the hands of this Garda.

Disbelieving deaf people about being deaf arose in other interviews too:

> Deaf5: 'People find that very hard to believe because I speak very well'.

Deaf5 noted generally that they were often disbelieved about being deaf. The connection to speaking 'very well' possibly indicates a known-aboutness of deaf people that anticipates that they do not speak, or at least that they do not speak 'very well'. In contradicting this known-aboutness, Deaf5 is met with disbelief, which has the potential to engage the slíbhín trope as their external identity.

> Lawyer2: '[it was suggested] that "your client understands everything. [The client is] lip reading from across the room" All of this sort of stuff'.

In this instance, there was a suggestion to Lawyer2 that their deaf client was faking being unable to comprehend proceedings in order to game the system. Lawyer2 did note that their client looked like a 'normal' person, with no distinguishing characteristics that might indicate that they were deaf, and that this was likely the cause for such allegations. Again, there is a known-about-ness element here for consideration. Lawyer2 indicated that there was an expectation that being deaf would be visible or evident in some way, and when their client did not match that expectation, their deafness was called into question. This is similar to the experiences described by Phelan (2011) and Waterhouse (2014), in respect of non-English language users in Irish courts.

Deaf people were not believed about being deaf and this gave rise to an assumption that there was malice in their claims about being deaf. The slíbhín trope was applied to them when their external identity did not match the known-about-ness of being deaf. This shows a lack of understanding of deaf identity and a lack of symbolic access. The slíbhín trope, when applied, showed that deaf people were neither valued nor empowered to fully participate in the process.

As shown, deaf participants experienced the slíbhín trope, but it more frequently appeared in interviews with Irish speakers. Such was the volume of the slíbhín trope which arose in interviews with Irish speakers, further sub-categories of the slíbhín trope arose. As such, I developed the 'Good Gael' and 'Bad Gael' sub-tropes.

8.3.2 Defining the 'Good Gael' trope

I have called the first of the Irish speaker sub-tropes the 'Good Gael'. This sub-trope represents the ideal notion of an Irish speaker. It represents an idealised version of an Irish speaker who is good and honest in their use of the language. The 'Good Gael' represents a performance by Irish speakers to avoid being labelled as the troublesome slíbhín.[1]

For this research, the 'Good Gael' is a display of language usage in a non-threatening, non-offensive way. Irish usage is often presented as a performance of culture and heritage for an observer, rather an as a functional language or an internal identity. O'Reilly refers to this phenomenon in her work on language, ethnicity, nationalism and Northern Ireland (C.C. O'Reilly, 2014). In respect of the perception of Irish in the Republic of Ireland:

> Cultural discourse...includes similar phrases such as 'beautiful language', 'heritage' or 'Gaelic/Celtic heritage' and 'tradition'. A connection is sometimes made between a person's interest in the language, and history songs and literature in Irish. There is often a distancing from nationalism or any possible political implications of an interest in the language. Speaking Irish is generally seen as a cultural activity, and may be considered a hobby or a pastime. (C.C. O'Reilly, 2014: 91)

Irish as a 'hobby' rather than a serious and functional language is central to the 'Good Gael' trope. Irish is anticipated in arenas which facilitate culture or performative displays of tradition and heritage, but not in other areas where serious business occurs, as with Brennan and O'Rourke's 'cúpla focal'. Irish is often used as a flavour or garnish for communication, but it is not perceived as the sole means of communication outside of private and familiar interactions. The use of the 'cúpla focal' and the nod towards Irish heritage can be seen throughout Irish society.[2] This was shown in respect of the multitude of Irish language named organisations in Ireland which do not operate in Irish, in spite of a requirement to do so. Irish is relegated to a performance of Irish-ness, rather than a functional language in this context.

The 'Good Gael' then reflects this perfomativeness. I developed and defined the 'Good Gael' as follows:

Definition:

Good Gael, *noun, singular*/Good Gaels, *noun, plural:* a person who used Irish in private, among friends, in a non-invasive manner. They switch to English in the presence of English speakers to ensure their comfort. They use Irish, or a 'cúpla focal' [translation: a couple of words] for ceremonial purposes, such as in greetings and at the beginning of speeches but they conduct business in English. They do not use their language to insult, demean or evade culpability.

They are 'good' because they neither impose a language or ideology on others. They do not expose a lack of Irish in those who are required to have some working knowledge of the language, nor do they utilise the language strategically or to achieve some personal advantage.

Below I show how this sub-trope manifested itself in interviews, and how many Irish-speaking participants showed a consciousness of this trope and internalised the behaviour of the 'Good Gael' in interactions with the CJS.

8.3.3 The 'Good Gael' trope in operation

Many participants described actively trying to be perceived as the amenable 'Good Gael', to circumvent any risk of being perceived negatively, as the slíbhín or 'Bad Gael'. Gael4 made a point to note that they never used Irish to be 'rude' to people:

> Gael 4: 'But one of the basic rules I have is not to ever be rude when using Irish. Because I don't think that helps anybody at all...[to persist in using Irish where it is known that the other person doesn't have Irish] would be bad mannered...And life is difficult enough – everyday life is difficult enough – without bringing more trouble down upon yourself'.

> Gael4: 'I never use Irish to be rude or bad mannered to people around me'.

Gael4 endeavoured to ensure politeness and good behaviour in their use of Irish. They also alluded to the use of Irish as being troublesome and that its use might incite trouble. They were aware that negativity could be attached to the use of Irish, with the inference of the 'Bad Gael' (as is addressed below) and so they made a conscious effort to counter this, to be the 'Good Gael'.

Gael8 and Gael7 also alluded to the 'Good Gael' in identifying themselves as well-mannered and amenable:

> Gael8: 'The thing is, I am a polite person. I don't like to argue or to be rude to people and I was very nice to the Garda...I suppose for me it would have been easier to say 'I want a doctor who speaks Irish' because if I'd have said that, they would have had to go and get a doctor with Irish and maybe the drink would have been gone [out of my system] by then...'

Gael8 connected their refusal to use Irish with politeness, even in the belief that it would have benefited them in the scenario.

> Gael8: 'I am not the type of person who if the service isn't available in Irish, that I am going to give out about it, or that I am going to argue about it because in my experience when the service isn't there, I want the less complicated life'.

Here, Gael8 noted that pursuing the use of Irish would be detrimental and 'complicated'.

> Gael7: 'I am not one of those people who is negative without a reason. It's not that I would be discussing things with the Gardaí or with an office of government or whatever, and I would refuse, it's not that I have the decision made 'I am not going to speak any English to the legal profession or to the state service"'.

Gael7 referred to 'those people' who would seek to be difficult in their use of Irish, making a point to differentiate themselves from such people.

> Gael7: 'I am not the sort of person who forces Irish on people who do not have Irish'.

Gael7 here went further, indicating their distinction from people who 'force' Irish on those who do not have it.

These extracts show an awareness of how Irish is perceived generally, and in the CJS. These participants made an effort to distance themselves from deviant or 'rude' behaviour, or from 'forcing' Irish on people, by adhering to the 'Good Gael' sub-trope. It must be noted that Gael4, Gael7 and Gael8 all recalled being penalised or discriminated against because of their use of Irish in the CJS. What this shows is that even after a conscious attempt to appear as the amiable 'Good Gael', they were nevertheless penalised for their use of Irish.

It should be noted that there was no evidence of the 'Good Gael' sub-trope being specifically applied to the participants by outsiders. Rather their experiences reflect an understanding of the negative associations and stereotypes attached to Irish speakers' external identities and a performance to navigate that stigma. Nevertheless, there was an evident belief that in revealing more of their identity back seeking to interact with the CJS in Irish (as is their right to do so) they would be met with hostility or backlash. This points to a lack of symbolic access again. Their attempt to pass as the more amiable Good Gael was so that they would not be devalued or disempowered in their true identities.

8.3.4 Defining the 'Bad Gael' trope

As a contrast to the 'Good Gael' sub-trope, I identified the 'Bad Gael' sub-trope. These sub-tropes are antagonistic: the 'Good Gael' exists as a counter to the 'Bad Gael'. The 'Bad Gael' sub-trope is rooted in the perception of the other as deviant and malicious. It is closely connected to the slíbhín as defined, but represents a specific perception of Irish speaker.

As discussed in Chapter 3, Irish has a complex position in Irish society, where it is often associated with negative stereotypes, including paramilitary activity. As also noted in Chapter 3, O'Higgins states that Irish has a long, colonial history of being perceived as troublesome (O'Higgins, 2007). Negative perceptions about language, heritage and culture which were enforced by colonialism are, to some degree, internalised in a post-colonial society (Ngugi wa Thiong'o, 2005).

The 'Bad Gael' is not only an externally imposed identity on certain Irish speakers. It also represents a deviant outsider for Irish speakers themselves. 'Bad Gaels' damage the reputation of Irish speakers when they use Irish to annoy authority figures, as will be shown. Members of a community making efforts to disassociate themselves from deviance within their social group like this is not uncommon. Becker explained this phenomenon in *Outsiders,* his influential book on sociology and deviance (Becker, 2018). He stated that disassociation from the deviant, stigma-worthy member of a particular group is a common practice:

> ...social groups create deviance by making the rules whose infraction constitutes deviance, and by applying these rules to particular people and labelling them as outsiders. (2018: 9)

The 'rules' broken here, refer to the 'Bad Gael': the Gael who uses Irish to be troublesome and to irritate the authorities is deviant. They have the potential to damage the reputation of other Gaels and as such they are outsiders to the community (Bradley, 2007).

In terms of defining 'Bad Gael', other than a reference to sports fans (Humphries, 2000; Stafford, 2017), I have been unable to find other instances of 'Bad Gael' as a term, and none which reflect the specific meaning I have attributed to the sub-trope which arose in the data. Thus, I am defining the 'Bad Gael' sub-trope as follows:

Definition:

Bad Gael, *noun, singular*/Bad Gaels, *noun, plural:* a person who uses Irish to be a slíbhín. They choose to use Irish to be an annoyance and to frustrate proceedings. They do not necessarily even speak Irish and will use what little Irish they have to attempt to evade justice. They may use Irish to cover up criminal behaviour. They insist on all services being available in Irish and they continue to drain resources, despite being fully capable of doing business in English. They refuse to switch to English because they are being malicious and deviant.

The 'Bad Gael' represents someone who is overtly behaving in an othered way, by using Irish. Internally in the Irish-speaking community, they are people who use Irish as a means to annoy law enforcement. They are deviant outsiders and 'Good Gaels' do not use their Irish in this way. Externally, they are also viewed by those in law enforcement as deviant. Their use of Irish is malicious and a failure to show respect or deference to authority (Brown, 1988).

8.3.5 The 'Bad Gael' trope in operation

The 'Bad Gael' sub-trope arose for many interviewees in their interactions with the CJS. Gael1, Gael2, Gael3, Gael5 and Gael7 all recalled negative Garda reaction when they used Irish in the CJS. Gael4, Gael6 and Gael8 experienced a negative reaction from the judiciary because of Irish. Irish was perceived as malicious or deviant and they were accordingly punished. In particular, the treatment participants received from Gardaí when they used Irish stood out.

Interviewees recalled Gardaí specifically connecting their use of Irish to elevated punishment:

> Gael1: [Gael1 offered a witness account of a fight in Irish to a Garda on the scene] 'And he said "*none of that now*". And I said "Well I am not willing to give you an account of the fight if you are not willing to hear it in Irish". And the thing he accused me of was "*obstructing the course of justice*" or "*perverting the course of justice*" or something like that because he knew that I was not willing to share it with him [in English], or "*withholding*" or one of those crimes. Disrupting the legal process in a way. I can't remember exactly what he charged me with. But he became angry as well – which then made me angry. And he put me, we went down to [the station] and I spent the rest of the night [in the station] He put me in a cell'.
>
> Note that italicised text denotes the interviewee quoting the Garda speaking in English, while the interview was conducted in Irish.

Gael1 connected their punishment (a night in a police station cell) with the Garda's reaction to their use of Irish, which was categorised as obstructing justice. It must be noted that Gael1 was assisting Gardaí by providing a witness account of a crime and they did not report being initially suspected of crime. The known-about-ness of Irish-speaker identity, however, triggered a negative response from this Garda. The Bad Gael is disempowered and devalued and therefore, lacking in symbolic access.

> Gael2: '...he [Garda] said something like "*I don't have the time to be dealing with your leprechaun bullshit. Can you just give me your address [in English]?*"'

Similar to Gael1, Gael2 reported assisting Gardaí with providing a witness statement for an incident of crime. Gael2 reported that they were not initially a suspect of that crime. They provided Gardaí with their name and address, which were in the Irish language. They reported being intimidated to provide these details in the anglicised versions and when Gael2 refused, they were arrested and spent the night in a Garda station cell.

> Gael3: 'Because he [Garda] said that line that was just bad, "*I was going to caution you at the side of the road but you seem to be playing a bit with me [by speaking Irish] so I'm just going to send a ticket out to you*"'.

Gael3 reported a Garda admitting to elevating their punishment because their use of Irish was perceived as 'playing' where playing here referred to troublemaking.

> Gael5: 'And he said something like "*If you'd just spoken English to us, we just would have said 'Go on your way' but you're trying to be thick" or something*'.

Similarly, Gael5 reported that Gardaí admitted that they had only detained Gael5 because they spoke Irish.

> Gael5: '[Gardaí were saying] insulting things like "*who does [Gael5] think [they are], [they are] absolutely stupid speaking Irish. [They are] going to get put off the road for years now*". Things like that.'

During their detention, Gael5 reported being taunted and insulted for speaking Irish, with Gardaí insinuating they would receive extreme punishment (a lengthy driving ban) if they did not switch to English. This is a clear lack of symbolic access – speaking Irish was a source of taunting and intimidation by the Garda under Gael5's account. Irish-speaking identity was deeply undervalued and disempowered in this instance.

> Gael7: 'He continued to be rude, ignorant, so I made the decision at that point, "Well, I am not going to deal with this man." I spoke Irish to him. If you like, I made the decision to do business in Irish now. At that point, he said to me that he was going to take proceedings against me, basically.'

Gael7 connected their use of Irish with Gardaí with the punishment they received. It should be noted, that Gael7 had been apprehended for the minor crime on multiple occasions prior and they reported speaking English in all of those occasions. It was only after they spoke Irish to a Garda that they were ultimately punished and brought before the courts.

In these examples, the use of Irish was perceived as deviant and criminal; perverting the course of justice; leprechaun bullshit; playing; being thick and an aggravating factor in sentencing. In all of these instances, participants recounted being punished for their use of Irish, ranging from being detained overnight in a Garda station (Gael1, Gael2), fined (Gael3), brought before a court (Gael7) or detained, fined and brought before a court (Gael5). Irish usage was met with hostility initially, and then with further hostility at Garda stations, ultimately impacting the fairness of trail.

Both Gael2 and Gael7 were treated with hostility when they started to use Irish in the interaction with Gardaí, having begun the interaction using English: for Gael2, this was when they gave their name (an Irish language name) and address in Irish, and; for Gael7 this was when they switched to Irish after the Garda had shown mocking and disrespect to the Irish language. All of these instances point to a lack of symbolic access for Irish speakers, and that the deviant Bad Gael represented the general known-about-ness for Irish speaker identity.

There were stark beliefs among interviewees that Garda held negative attitudes about Irish speakers:

> Gael2: 'But I believe that if you were to do a survey among the Gardaí, that 90% of them would say "the only reason people want to speak Irish is to try get out of things or to try and undermine things or this, that or the other"'.

Gael2 was adamant that Gardaí perceived Irish speaking as deviant.

> Gael3: 'With the Gardaí, I'd say there would be a figure of around 20% of my [Irish language] interactions with the Gardaí are positive and 80% are negative. With the first person I meet. But after that, they always provide the service after that and it's a positive experience then. But still, I don't know what they say, yeah but the first person I meet, most of the time it's negative from the Gardaí'.

Gael3 frequently worked with and encountered An Garda Síochána. From those experiences, they were confident of a negativity towards Irish and Irish users from the service. This was even acknowledged by AGS1:

> AGS1: 'In the introductory lecture, I'd very often just have a chat with them [recruits] about do they know why they are doing Irish? And then you'd always get the one answer "In case anybody is trying to be awkward and trying to get out of something"'.

Many participants were certain that they would experience negative reactions to the use of Irish. In addition to Gael2 and Gael3's statements here, Gael1 stated that they had anticipated that their car would be impounded as soon as they encountered Gardaí, knowing they would be using Irish. Gael5 noted that they also anticipated being arrested or taken to a Garda station if they used Irish and would have to evaluate whether they could factor the time delay into their day before using Irish. There was an evident expectation of a negative reaction from Gardaí on using Irish. Clearly, participants believed that they would be perceived as this 'Bad Gael' and accordingly punished.

Additionally, in Gael4's description of being arrested by Gardaí there was an assumption that Gael4 would be presenting themselves as the 'Bad Gael'. Four Gardaí arrived at Gael4's home to carry out the arrest, which Gael4 perceived as excessive. When arresting Gael4, the Garda inquired, 'will you be coming easy?'. Gael4 was known to be an activist for the Irish language, and in fact, the cause of their arrest was connected to Irish language activism. Their arrest was connected to a relatively minor, non-violent crime and was somewhat bureaucratic in nature. This inquiry of 'will you be coming easy', coupled with the fact that four Gardaí were sent to arrest Gael4, suggests an anticipation at least that Gael4 might not be 'coming easy' and that they would be likely to cause trouble. The nature of their crimes represented a protest of the state and the status quo, which Gardaí are designed to protect (Conway, n.d.). Protesting the status quo represents deviant behaviour, which is possibly the reason for the heavy-handedness of the circumstances of the arrest. Such heavy-handed responses to relatively peaceful protests can be a feature of policing (Dodd & Grierson, 2021; *Heavy-Handed Police Response to Hong Kong Protest Unacceptable*, 2019; *Police to Look into Who Gave Order to Pepper Spray Helsinki Protesters*, 2020; McCarthy, 2020). Gardaí had shown that they were prepared for Gael4 to act as the 'Bad Gael', because of their awareness of Gael4's activism. Similarly, Gael5 was handcuffed while being arrested, in spite of an admission from Gardaí that they were behaving 'passively' (An Garda Síochána, 2012). Irrespective of their behaviour, they were treated as troublesome and worthy of the use of force. Like Gael4, the anticipation of trouble or deviance arose out of the display of their identity and the perception of that identity in Gardaí.

It is worth noting that the 'Bad Gael' sub-trope was not exclusively externally held. Insiders to the community also referenced the existence of a 'Bad Gael' whose behaviour damaged the reputation of the Irish-speaking community generally.

> Gael1: '...there are the people, when they are stopped on the road by Gardaí, who speak Irish, like just to annoy the Gardaí.'

> Gael5: 'Sometimes when people are drunk and such, they try to plead [with Gardaí] in Irish. And they [Gardaí] think "These are just chancers" That's a very common thing'.

Both interviewees are alluding to a particular type of person, who possibly fits the descriptor provided by AGS1 above: a person who will use Irish to 'be awkward and [try] to get out of something'. This perception of the 'Bad Gael' from Gael participants can also be seen in the extract above, which discussed the 'Good Gael'. Participants who were adamant not to be 'rude' in their use of Irish are acknowledging that there are those who would be rude in their use of Irish. But although Gael participants acknowledged the 'Bad Gael', no participant actually admitted (or alluded) to being a 'Bad Gael' or to using Irish for malicious purposes.

The 'Bad Gael' sub-trope was prevalent in discussions with Gael participants. While not named as such, it was evident that they felt they were perceived, in particular by Gardaí, as deviant troublemakers when they communicated their identity (Eriksen, 2010). It was also evident that participants made steps not to be seen as the 'Bad Gael', acknowledging the existence of the 'Bad Gael' who would use Irish to be deviant. In terms of access to justice, again, it can be seen that the existence of this trope points to a lack of symbolic access. While being perceived in this light, there is a lack of understanding of the true identity held by Irish speakers (as will be discussed in the following chapter). Participants showed that they were not valued or empowered to participate fully as their true selves in the process, therefore indicating a lack of symbolic access.

8.4 Chapter Summary

In this research, I found that the way participants were perceived when they interacted with the CJS and the way they were treated based on that perception was a major source of concern. The negotiation of a marginalised identity in the CJS was something that affected all participants who engaged as Criminal Justice Subjects. I found that the external perceptions of participant's identity could be seen in light of the créatúr and slíbhín tropes, and the 'Bad Gael' sub-trope, where the 'Good Gael' sub-trope represented a performance to avoid the negative perception of the 'Bad Gael'. These tropes and sub-tropes represent an original concept which can help to add context to how Irish speakers and deaf people experience the CJS.

In respect of access to justice, the appearance of the créatúr and the slíbhín tropes as external identities suggest that there is, at least in the experiences of the research participants, a lack of understanding and value in the true identities held by Irish speakers and deaf people. In the following chapter, I discuss the internal identities of participants as they arose in the data, and why it matters that for the most part, these internal identities were not understood. In light of what has been shown in this chapter, I explore why in order to ensure symbolic access to justice, it is necessary for the internal, true identities of marginalised people to be seen and valued. Where the identities of such people are confined to harmful, stereotypical tropes shown in this chapter, the real needs of marginalised people will go unheard and their experiences in the CJS will be clouded by that reality.

Notes

(1) Note that a reference is made to a 'Good Gael' in an article by McKibben analysing the book *An Béal Bocht*. McKibben writes that the 'good Gael should cleave to his pure Gaelic with undying fervor'. McKibben's reference is more reflective of what I have called a 'True Gael', in the following chapter. See McKibben 'The Poor Mouth: A Parody of (Post)Colonial Irish Manhood' 2003 Vol 34 (4) *Research in African Literatures* 94.

(2) See, for example, reaction to the greeting 'A Uachtaráin agus a chairde' by British Queen Elizabeth at a 2011 State Dinner held in Ireland: Reilly '"A Úachtaráin, agus a chairde" – Queen offers "sincere sympathy" to victims of Anglo-Irish conflict' *TheJournal.ie* (18 May 2011) available at: https://www.thejournal.ie/"a-uachtarain-agus-a-chairde"-–-queen-offers-"sincere-sympathy"-to-victims-of-anglo-irish-conflict-139244-May2011/ [date accessed: 25 February 2020].

9 Symbolic Access and Recognising Internal Identity

9.1 Introduction

In the previous chapter, I looked at how Criminal Justice Subjects were perceived when they interacted with the CJS. This discussion focused on how they were externally perceived by actors in the CJS, such as police and judges. The external perceptions could be catalogued under two main tropes; the créatúr and the slíbhín, where Irish-speaking participants could be further understood in light of two sub-tropes: the 'Good Gael' and the 'Bad Gael'.

In this chapter, I explore what is missed when Irish speakers and deaf people are viewed only in terms of the external, the slíbhín and the créatúr. Relying on literature on identity and stigma management, in this section I explore the internal identity held by participants and how that identity was received by actors in the CJS and in society generally (Goffman, 1969). When we do not understand the true identity of a person, then their true needs are also not understood, and symbolic access cannot be ensured (Flynn, 2015). Therefore, their true needs cannot be served.

This chapter tackles three major issues. First, I explore the true, internal identity of both Irish speakers and deaf people, as it immerged in the interviews, and how that relates to existing literature. I show how these identities appear in literature and how they arose in the data. For deaf people, I will discuss the culturally deaf identity, which has a long-standing basis in Deaf Studies literature. For Irish speakers, I have called the true identity held by participants the 'True Gael'. Second, I highlight the consequences that arose for Irish speakers and deaf people when their internal identity was not perceived. Participants had two main options, to either conceal their identity and pass (Leary, 1999), or to communicate their identity and accept the corresponding punishment (Eriksen, 2010). I connect back to the literature on identity and stigma management to provide context for participants' experiences. Third, I explore the underlying access to justice reasons for why the internal identity is not perceived, and why deaf people and Irish speakers must face a 'passing or punishment' as a consequence of their identities in the CJS. I examine the known-about-ness of the deaf and Irish speaker identity (Goffman, 1986). In doing so, this shows how there is a lack of symbolic access for these two groups, who are still seen societally in terms of the harmful external perceptions. I argue that because of the lack of symbolic access, access to justice cannot be achieved.

9.2 Culturally Deaf

The participants to the research largely exhibited holding a 'culturally deaf' identity, as described in Chapter 3. This identity is established in literature, and to recall, is rooted in the cultural aspects of the deaf community (Leach Scully, 2012), rather than in any medical diagnosis (Ladd, 2003). Again, Leigh *et al.* define the process of being culturally deaf as 'using signed languages, being upfront as a Deaf person, being comfortable with other Deaf people, and wanting to interact with them' (Leigh *et al.*, 2018: 8). This internal identity contrasts then with the external, créatúr trope as I discussed in the previous chapter. The créatúr trope is rooted in external pity for deaf people, where deafness is viewed as a deficit and deaf people are paternalized (Lane, 1999).

This culturally deaf identity was internally held by participants, but clashed/conflicted with the créatúr trope, which was the external view of a medicalised and paternalised view of deaf people. I present these instances of conflict now.

9.2.1 Being culturally deaf

In discussing their identity as deaf people, there was a particular focus on the deaf community and a sense of belonging in that community form participants:

> GM: 'Do you feel that you belong in both communities [deaf and hearing]?'
>
> Deaf2: '[interpreter clarifies] Yes I can – I fit in. The sign for fit is the two arms together, but with the deaf community I am using my own language'.

Here, Deaf2 was referencing that they exist in both the hearing community and the deaf community for various aspects of their life, but that in the deaf community, they are connected by language in a way that they are not in the hearing community (Deaf2 lipreads in the hearing community to communicate which is not always a reliable method of communication) (Vernon *et al.*, 2001). Even though they 'can' fit into the hearing community, it is on a different scale to that of their position in the deaf community. Fitting in in the hearing community is something they are able to do through positive actions – lip-reading and gesturing and facilitating hearing people who only have spoken languages. But the way that they fit into the deaf community is more natural – 'two arms together' – because there they can use their own language.

> Deaf3: 'I have always been involved in the deaf community...I don't have any family members who sign. I don't have any hearing friends as such – I suppose my [siblings] they would have kind of their own hearing friends at home in the hearing community, but my friends would be deaf.'

Deaf3 noted that they existed in the personal and professional life almost entirely within the deaf community. It was evident from their interview that the deaf community was a central part of their life and that they embraced being deaf.

> Deaf4 fieldnotes: Deaf4 noted that there is a resilience in the deaf community – a togetherness through the common struggle. Deaf4 stated that they find the community and the identity of being deaf comforting. There you find people who are the same.

Like Deaf3, it was evident from Deaf4's interview that the deaf community was an extremely important part of their life. Similar to Deaf2, Deaf4 co-existed in hearing communities, but they felt a better sense of belonging in the deaf community. Deaf4 connected their sense of belonging in the deaf community to a unified understanding of the deaf struggle. The sense of togetherness and community among participants with the deaf community is mirrored in the literature on deaf culture above. The deaf culture they possessed was rooted in a sense of belonging in the deaf community. No participant connected their belonging to the deaf community with their level of hearing. Rather, their discussions about the deaf community related to friendships, togetherness and fitting-in.

Diversity in the community was evident from the interviews. Participants referenced their varied upbringings and relationships to the deaf community. Some had arrived at the deaf community as children, whereas some had arrived later in life. Participants had varied views on the deaf community too, where Deaf4 explicitly identified as Big D Deaf, whereas Deaf5 rejected the D/deaf dichotomy discussed in Chapter 3 (Ladd, 2003), as they felt it was exclusionary. Dr John Bosco Conama referenced the varied understandings of the deaf community and deaf identity in his interview:

> JBC: 'There is not just one deaf community per se. There's a lot of different paths that you can talk about in the deaf community'.

Dr Conama explained that it is difficult to define the deaf community, and that there are many different ways to make up that community. This mirrors what both Leach Scully and Leigh *et al* have said in relation to the diverse make-up of the deaf community: there are multiple perceptions of the deaf community (Leach Scully, 2012; Leigh *et al.*, 2018). Ultimately, as noted in Chapter 3, deaf identity can be defined in terms of 'attitudinal deafness', whereby a person identifies as deaf and the deaf community accept them as such and as part of the community (Baker & Padden, 1978).

In terms of internal identity a1nd being culturally deaf, Deaf3 specifically demonstrated a pride in their identity as a deaf person:

> Deaf3: 'I am happy to be deaf – if you were to ask me if I wanted to be hearing tomorrow, I'd tell you no. I am very content with who I am'.

Here, it is evident that for Deaf3, being deaf was more than being not hearing – it is their identity. This contrasts starkly with the commonly held view of deaf people that hearing communities have, as described by Lane and Ladd in particular (Ladd, 2003; Lane, 1999), where being deaf is seen as a pitiful deficit. Being deaf is a central aspect of their sense of self, which they are proud of, which they would not change, even if given a chance. This mirrors what Ladd describes in his work, particularly the dichotomy between what is seen of the deaf community externally, where they are 'forever being condemned to live on the margins of existence' and what is the experience of the deaf community internally where they constitute a 'community of people with their own beautiful languages, their own organisations, history, arts and humour, their own lifelong friends' (Ladd, 2003: 37).

That is not to say that culturally deaf people do not experience struggles:

> Deaf3: 'I suppose in relation to the deaf community specifically, I don't feel like we are on a par with hearing society. I think we are very much still behind the times in terms of equality in that sense'

Deaf3 was clear that deaf people are not treated equally, not just in the CJS, but in society generally. The lack of symbolic access, of empowerment and inclusion in society, was evident and was shared also by Deaf1 and Deaf4 in their interviews. Part of the connection that Deaf4 felt to the deaf community was the collective understanding of struggle. In referencing this struggle, Deaf4 went on to noted that the struggles of the culturally deaf community are not encapsulated by a disability discourse:

> Deaf4: Deaf4 notes that deaf people don't see themselves as disabled. Where there are a percentage of jobs reserved for disabled people, deaf people can face a crisis of identity – they are not disabled but are largely perceived as such. For example, the needs of a wheelchair user are vastly different to the needs of a deaf person. A wheelchair user can hear, they can work in customer service. There are variances between the deaf and hearing. You cannot place deaf people on the same pedestal as hearing people. There are differences: psychologically, emotionally and developmentally. deaf people are not the same as hearing people.

The specific needs of deaf people are not understood when viewed solely in the context of disability. As noted in Chapter 3, this view of disability as being an inappropriate lens through which to solely view deaf culture is mirrored in the literature. Leach Scully states that deaf communities have challenged disability discourses, and that it is ineffective to capture deaf experience and deaf culture (Leach Scully, 2012). Ladd also shares this view (2003). When deaf people are viewed exclusively in terms of disability, even when a social model of disability is used, they are inherently medicalised and viewed through their lack of hearing (Ladd, 2003). Their specific identities as culturally deaf and the corresponding needs of a cultural minority then go unseen. The lack of understanding of the culturally deaf identity can result in deaf people being medicalised and paternalised.

Below, I discuss how the failure to externally perceive the true, internal identity impacts the individual within the CJS. First, however, I explore the true identity of Irish speakers.

9.3 The True Gael

In continuing the discussion of true, internal identities, I am now focusing on the Irish speaker identity which arose in the research. I have called this identity the 'True Gael' identity and it represents the internal identity held by Irish-speaking participants to the research.

The term 'true Gael' has been used on occasion, although there does not seem to be one specific meaning for it. Maume, for example uses it to refer to an idealised version of an Irish person who is pro-independence, exhibiting nationalism (Maume, 1998); Gallagher uses 'true Gael' to reference the impoverished Irish speakers from Corca Dorcha in Flann O'Brien's satirical novel *An Béal Bocht* (M. Gallagher, 1983); and there are instances of the term being used to define a fan of traditional Irish sports, hurling and Gaelic football (Humphries, 2000; Stafford, 2017). However, in my research, I am using 'True Gael' to represent the internally held perception of the self that Gael participants had. Unlike the culturally deaf identity, there is no real established concept for what I have identified as the 'True Gael' within literature. As such, I am defining the term, as it applies to this research, as follows:

Definition:

True Gael, *noun, singular*/True Gaels, *noun, plural:* the linguistic identity held by Irish-speaking participants to this research. Irish and speaking Irish is directly connected to their sense of self. There is no choice made about what language they would use when interacting with the state. It is not a conscious decision that is made in the moment, but the natural way they would respond in any scenario where they could use their language.

Previously, I explored how Irish speaking can be perceived as either a twee 'pastime' (C.C. O'Reilly, 2014) or as a deviance, by way of the 'Good Gael' and the 'Bad Gael' sub-tropes. Importantly, neither represented an internal identity that participants referred to as holding. The 'Good Gael' sub-trope was a performance, and the 'Bad Gael' sub-trope was an external identity imposed on participants, or which they imposed on others. By contrast, the 'True Gael' is an internal identity which participants showed. It is a rejection of the societal perception of Irish.

The 'True Gael' identity is visible in O'Reilly's findings from her research in Northern Ireland in the 1990s (C. O'Reilly, 1996). She found that for many Irish users in Northern Ireland, 'language [was] the single most important element of [their] national identity' (1996: 158). The language was the focal point of their identities. This ownership of a specific identity or characteristic is visible in Pride movements, as discussed in Chapter 2 (Eriksen, 2010).

9.3.1 Being the True Gael

All Gael participants showed signs the 'True Gael' identity in interviews: Irish was more than a language, but rather a deep part of their sense of self.

Gael2 noted that they had a '*spiritual connection*' to the language. This connection was referred to also by Gael1 in a follow-up correspondence, who referred to the language as somewhat of a lifelong commitment, similar to a marriage:

> Gael1: 'A phrase from English came to me which explains my outlook on Irish: to have and to hold in sickness and in health!'

Irish would be the language Gael1 used at all times. Dr Seán Ó Conaill also referred to this deep connection to the language in his interview:

> SÓC: 'As corny as it sounds, it's sort of teanga m'anam – the language of your soul kind of.'

The participants acknowledged a deep connection to Irish, and to their sense of being. Their use of Irish was more than a means of communication, but rather an expression of their identity.

This expression of identity was often counter to what might be considered the best interests of participants. Gael4, Gael6 and Gael7 participated in civil disobedience in the pursuit of Irish language rights, with the knowledge that their participation would likely result in criminal sanctions. Their dedication to Irish superseded their own personal interests. Rather than a willingness to avoid punishment, these participants had a willingness to suffer punishment to further their cause and pursue language rights.

For Gael1, Gael3 and Gael5, though not part of any organised campaign, there was an acknowledgment that their use of Irish exacerbated their situations. If they had used English, then they would have avoided the negative reaction. And yet they all used Irish, irrespective of this knowledge. It was clear from the interviews that the use of Irish was more than a simple binary choice: Irish or English? There was an evident dedication to their language and identity as Irish speakers that was greater than any desire for self-preservation:

> Gael1: 'But I didn't switch to English. I knew when he [Garda] approached "he is going to take the car". But he said "you can speak English now if you want" And I was "no, take the car like" '.

Gael1 reported that the on-scene Garda taunted Gael1 to speak English to avoid punishment (by way of impounding the car) but Gael1 refused to renege on the display of their identity.

> GM: 'And at any time did you think to yourself 'I'm just going to speak English'?'

> Gael5: 'No...Once I had said "I would like you to deal with me in Irish" I wouldn't backpedal on that at all'.

Similarly, Gael5 noted their devotion to the display of their identity and a refusal to 'backpedal' once they made their identity known.

In speaking about their relationship to their identity, Gael1 referred to their dedication to Irish in contrast to those would use Irish only to benefit themselves:

> Gael1: '...do you know the concept of cultural appropriation, cultural appropriation? *Now it's a bit of a roundabout way to it*, but my understanding of it, cultural appropriation is when you make use of an aspect of culture which you personally like without doing anything to benefit that culture that you have taken from. So I think that it's people who speak Irish for beneficial things or to make things easier for themselves, without being happy to speak it in order to help the language. Yeah?'

They noted that their relationship with Irish required taking the good and the bad part of using their language, because it is who they are. Their usage of Irish was not limited to how it might further or benefit them. Such behaviour amounted to cultural appropriation. Cultural appropriation can be understood as:

> Any instance in which a group borrows or imitates the strategies of another—even when the tactic is not intended to deconstruct or distort the other's meanings and experiences—thus would constitute appropriation. (Shugart, 1997: 210–211)

There is also an exploitative aspect of cultural appropriation (Rogers, 2006), and often a connotation of 'borrowing' or 'taking' of strategies from one culture to further the interests of another, who does not belong to that culture or group.[1] Gael1 was suggesting that casual or performative use of Irish, only when it is beneficial to the speaker is appropriating from an Irish-speaking, 'True Gael' identity. The person who would use Irish only when it would reap rewards is taking from the culture, when a 'True Gael' is punished for displaying that identity. Irish was never a matter of choice for Gael1, rather it was the only way they would communicate with the state. A person who culturally appropriates the language chooses the moments to use Irish.

Ultimately, the 'True Gael' was the misunderstood, internal identity held by Gael participants. For the most part, their identities were misconstrued, and participants were seen as deviant for using their language, lacking symbolic access, as is shown in the previous chapter. However, there was one instance where a participant recounted their internal identity being perceived: Gael4 was very struck by an incident where a Garda appeared to understand their internal, 'True Gael' identity. Gael4 was to be taken to prison by a number of Gardaí. When Gardaí arrived to escort Gael4, one Garda explained the process, and this led to a particularly touching moment for Gael4:

> Gael4: '[the Garda said] *"Just remember when you are crossing that prison yard, there will be a statute there of Kevin Barry" and he said "remember", he said "you're in good company"* [pause, Gael4 takes a moment to compose themselves] So he was saying that he understood what I was doing and that I should have courage. So I thought that that was very nice to say'.

> *Fieldnotes:* Gael4 was visibly emotional in recounting this interaction. It was evident that the Garda's words, the compassion and kindness shown had a deep impact on their experience.

It is poignant how impacted Gael4 was by the understanding and compassion they were shown. Kevin Barry was a young man who was executed by the British forces during the struggle for Irish independence in 1920 (McElhatton, 2020). In this context, Barry symbolises the struggle for Irish and a righteous fight for Irish identity. Gael4 recounted that the Garda showed an understanding of their fight for their cultural identity, comparing it to that of Kevin Barry. It was evidently an experience that remained with Gael4 and they showed an appreciation for the understanding that the Garda showed, particularly when there was largely no other instance of understanding of their cause from any other member of the CJS.

Otherwise, most interviewees showed that their identity as 'True Gaels' was not understood externally:

> Gael5: 'There is no understanding – they [Gardaí] did not believe that I was speaking Irish all day. They didn't understand that they were officers of the state, stopping a person who had been speaking Irish all day and telling them to speak English. They don't understand – like a lot of Irish people – that Gaeilgeoirí exist'.

Gael5 believed that Gardaí did not believe that Irish speakers existed. As discussed in the previous chapter, Gael5 reported that they were perceived as the 'Bad Gael' when they used Irish and were punished for doing so. Externally, their identity consisted of the 'Bad Gael' sub-trope while their internal 'True Gael' identity was not perceived at all. In Gael1's experience, as cited above, the Garda on the scene expected them to switch to English once their car had been taken. That account shows a Garda who did not understand that the use of Irish was anything but a performance that would be ended once the threat of punishment was made.

> Gael5: '[the Garda] said something like [whispering] "Go on, just tell me what happened in English" I sort of had pity for him, because it was clear that he didn't understand – [he thought that] when we were left on our own that I would speak English'

Similarly, Gael5 reported that the Garda believed they would speak Irish when not observed by others. Their identity was misunderstood as a performance.

All participants exhibited signs of being 'True Gaels' during interviews. Nevertheless, there was a variation in the way they recounted expressing their identity during interactions with the CJS. The interview with me was a safe space to use Irish. All Irish-speaking CJS participants conducted their interviews in Irish. Yet out in the world, Irish and the 'True Gael' identity were acknowledged stigmas that needed to be managed and navigated, or overcommunicated in spite of the inevitable negative consequences. Some 'True Gaels' were bold and overt in their display of their identity. They acknowledged the negative consequences and duly accepted them, for the greater good of their language, identity and community. When the 'True Gael' identity was understood, it had an extremely positive impact. Those who had experienced compassion and understanding from a member of the CJS found comfort in this approach, probably because of the commonality of negative reactions they had come to anticipate. I address these issues of overcommunication and passing in the next, in respect of the 'True Gael' and the culturally deaf identities.

9.4 Interacting with the CJS – Pass or Punish

When the internal identities are not understood or perceived, harmful, stereotyped external perceptions can dominate, and individuals' needs are not effectively met. As a consequence of this mismatch, two very clear pathways for Irish speakers and deaf people arose in the data. Either they passed (Leary, 1999), underplaying or hiding their identity entirely in order to navigate their way through the CJS, or they overcommunicated and displayed their identity, and accepted the negative consequences which they anticipated. As a way of stigma management, they either passed or were punished. They could never be themselves and be respected/treated with dignity.

9.4.1 Passing

Many participants referred to passing and navigating their stigmatised external identity in their interviews. As noted in Chapter 2, passing is 'the management of undisclosed discrediting information about self' according to Goffman. It involves downplaying or 'undercommunicating' a stigma before a particular audience, with self-preservation at the core. Recall also how Leary explains that passing 'represents a form of self-protection that nevertheless usually disables, and sometimes destroys, the self it means to safeguard'. In the context of the data, participants understood the stigma attached to the external perceptions of their identity. And as a result, there was attempts made to pass, or undercommunicate their identity, in order to evade that treatment.

Passing features in deaf culture, perhaps most predominantly in the form of the deaf nod, as mentioned in Chapter 3. Deaf people will mimic common body language to feign understanding and communication so as not to expose their stigma (Vernon *et al.*, 2001). Lawyer2 referenced the deaf nod in their interview:

> Lawyer2: 'It was only because the interpreters explained to us that just because someone nods doesn't mean they understand. It's an appeasing gesture. But we didn't know that. We thought that if someone nods, they are showing understanding.'

In this instance, Lawyer2 and their colleagues were appeased by the client's passing. The nodding indicated to Lawyer2 that the client understood what was happening. It transpired that the client did not understand, and it was only when appropriate interpretation was provided that they were given access to the information. In avoiding 'appearing stupid', the client engaged in passing during their interaction with the CJS.

Similarly, Deaf4 and Deaf5 also engaged in passing. Deaf4 recalled sitting in the court, having no idea what was going on. The environment of a court was not conducive to lip-reading or their hearing aid (a loud, crowded place with many people and distractions, the speakers not facing Deaf4, the distance from Deaf4 to the speaker, etc). In managing their stigma through passing, Deaf4's action were detrimental to the self they were trying to protect, as Leary states. They were disabled by concealing their stigma. By protecting themselves from exposing that they were deaf, Deaf4 was disadvantaged and could not access the court.

Recalling Deaf5's case, throughout their interaction with Gardaí, they communicated with a Garda using spoken English. They passed as a hearing person. It was only when they revealed their identity as a deaf person that their otherness was exposed:

> Deaf5: 'And I said "No, I am deaf, I wear two hearing aids!"'

In Deaf5's account, the Garda was surprised by this, and their hostile attitude changed once Deaf5 revealed that they were deaf. This mirrors findings in the literature on passing. For those who effectively pass, only when their stigma has been exposed are they treated differently (Poindexter & Shippy, 2010). For Deaf5, the external aspect of their identity changed through the interaction. At first, they were a hearing person who had broken the law. Once Deaf5 exposed their stigma, the illusion was shattered and they no longer passed as hearing.

Passing was also a way to manage stigma used by Irish-speaking participants. Gael5 stated that where they did not have time to be brought to a Garda station or detained, they would pass as an English speaker:

> Gael5: 'If I am under pressure, or if there is someone in the car with me, I can't speak Irish because I wouldn't want the car to be taken, and they would be left. If I am by myself and if I didn't have anything else to do for the day... I'd think about it [using Irish]'

Gael5 noted that they 'can't' speak Irish where they do not have the time to be detained, showing that they perceived detention because of using Irish as an inevitability, and therefore passing to avoid this treatment was necessary. Gael6 admitted that they no longer engaged with An Garda Síochána in Irish, and therefore passed as a non-Irish speaker.

> Gael6: 'I said to myself, 'Feck it, I don't want the stress. I don't want to be stressed out.' So in recent times, I decided "just play it by ear"'

Gael6's life experience had made them alter the way they presented their identity to the world. While in younger years, they had attested to always communicating their identity as an Irish speaker, years of negative response had altered their stigma management. Now, they admitted to passing to avoid the negative response, and to engage in self-preservation against the external response to their identity. Again, as Leary notes, passing can have the effect of damaging the self that is intended to be protected. In protecting the 'True Gael' self, they need to contradict the very essence of the 'True Gael' self.

Gael7 shared this approach. They no longer engaged with Gardaí in Irish, due to their experiences in the past with the service. However, they specifically pointed out that they made efforts to engage with other official organisations (specifically the Motor Tax Office) in Irish, or to select Irish language services where they were otherwise available. The passing that they engaged in was particular to the Gardaí.

Gael8's experience also speaks to passing. They did not use Irish in their interactions with Gardaí and in their subsequent court interactions. Nevertheless, their name exposed their stigma and identity as an Irish speaker, and the judge displayed prejudice, in spite of Gael8's attempt to pass:

> Gael8: 'The judge said when my name was called out in Irish, he asked the lawyer I had – he was sneering when he said "*I suppose [their] name just happens to be in Irish now and [they] are looking to have [their] case heard in Irish?*"'

Their name alone exposed their otherness, even though they were engaging in passing behaviour, concealing and undercommunicating their identity (by not speaking Irish). Goffman references similar incidents in his work

> ...individuals excluded from some hotels on the basis of their ethnicity may have been ethnically identified through their names, so that here, too, an item of personal biography is exploited for categoric reasons. (Goffman, 1986: 79)

Information about a person's ethnicity and identity are garnered from their name, and they can then be excluded based on the perception of that ethnicity or identity. In Gael8's case, their name meant that they could not pass and so their identity as an Irish speaker was exposed.

Hylland-Erikson refers to instances whereby Sami people in Norway sought to conceal their identity as Sami, undercommunicating their stigmatised identity and overcommunicating their Norwegian-ness (1994: 36). This is an exercise in self-preservation: passing was used to protect individuals or groups from the negative perception of their identity. Goffman gives examples of homeless people in New York pretending to wait for an evening train so as not to have their true selves exposed and then be punished for their homelessness (1986: 60). Leary references Anatole Broyard, a Black American writer who passed as a white person until his death (Leary, 1999: 85). Similarities can be seen in the research. Deaf4, Deaf5, Gael5, Gael6 and Gael8 undercommunicated their identity, passing as hearing or English speakers as best they could to avoid a negative response to their identity. Their identity as Irish speakers and deaf people posed a risk when engaging with the CJS, as it would be perceived as negative and accordingly punished. In passing, they avoided the disadvantages which imminently flowed from their true selves.

In many instances participants did not seek to pass, rather overcommunicating their identity, and they were subsequently punished, as I now discuss.

9.4.2 Punish

If participants did not pass, or if they were unsuccessful in passing (see Gael8's experience, for example) then they were almost exclusively punished for their stigma. Again, Goffman's work is relevant here. In *Stigma*, he shows how otherness and stigmatised identities are penalised in society, through shame and ostracization (1986). The display of an othered identity in certain environments can result in punishment for the othered individual (Jefferson, 1993). When referring to 'punishment', I am referring to punishments such as fines, penalties, arrests, detentions, the use of force, convictions and prison sentences etc., but also to paternalisation. When participants were paternalised, rather than being treated as independent, autonomous individuals, the effect was indeed punishing, as the treatment was unfair and rooted in inequality.

As shown above, Deaf4 and Deaf3 were paternalised in their interactions with Gardaí, because their deaf identity was communicated. Deaf4 complained that in general, Gardaí think deaf people are stupid, and Deaf3 experienced a Garda ignoring them once they communicated their identity. Both Deaf4 and Deaf3 specifically referenced hearing people present who were treated differently, who were communicated with. Thus, the differential treatment they received because they were deaf was evident to both Deaf4 and Deaf3. It was easy to compare the punishment they received when their identity was made known to the experiences of hearing people they observed.

Gael participants were also punished, where that punishment varied from arrest and detention; fines; court proceedings. As noted in Chapter 12, Gael1 and Gael2 were arrested and detained when they refused to give a witness account in English or their name and address in English, respectively. Both Gael1 and Gael2 attributed their punishment (a night in a police station cell) with the Garda's reaction to their use of Irish. As cited in Chapter 12, Gael3 and Gael5 reported Gardaí admitting to elevating the punishment they received as a result of their use of Irish. Also in Chapter 12, Gael7 suspected that the Garda who attended the scene had elevated their punishment because they had used Irish, noting the numerous previous instances where they had been shown discretion. In all of these instances, participants presented their identity to Gardaí, and they reported that the observance of identity was punished.

As demonstrated in Chapter 2, there is a myriad of research showing how police punish stigma. Indigenous minorities (Chan, 2009), racial minorities (Reiner, 2010), sexual minorities (Reiner, 2010), those with mental illness (Brooker *et al.*, 2007), and the poor (Reiner, 2010), all experience being overpoliced (Kushnick, 1999). While the reasoning behind the punishment of stigma by police has been discussed in Chapter 2, ultimately, what occurs is a punishment for exposed stigma. An identity which is associated with deviance or otherness is punishable. This was evident in the data, as discussed in the previous chapter. What is clear so far is that the display of the self in the data resulted in punishment when that self is an othered identity.

9.5 Known-About-ness and Symbolic Access

In considering these research findings in light of access to justice, the pass or punish dichotomy is a multifaceted problem. There are obviously procedural access concerns at play, whereby there is a lack of facilities for dealing with minority language users, impacting on how these people experience the CJS. There is also a substantive access issue (Beqiraj *et al.*, 2017), whereby laws and policies do not exist, or are not strong enough and therefore lack substantive access to protect minority language users in the CJS. But there is also a lack of symbolic access, where symbolic access ensures that 'individuals from marginalised communities are fully included and empowered to participate as equal citizens' (Flynn, 2015: 16). The known-about-ness of Irish speakers and deaf people in society is limited. As discussed in Chapter 2, known-about-ness refers to how an individual or identity is observed by society. The individual's otherness will be understood in light of what the observer sees but also in terms of what they have previously known about the identity or stigma. This perception may be 'derived perhaps from gossip or a previous contact with the person when the stigma was visible' (Katz, 1981). When an individual's otherness becomes visible to an observer, what they understand about that otherness will be dependent not only on what they see but also on what they have been exposed to before, and what is known about that stigma. A society can have a known-about-ness for a particular group based on stereotypes which exist about that group. For example, Goffman refers to 'stigma symbols' which convey information about a stigmatised individual to observers, such as 'wrist markings which disclose that an individual has attempted suicide' or 'the arm pock marks of drug addicts' (Goffman, 1986: 61). When society sees these stigma symbols, people will be treated in light of what is known about that stigma. The person with the pockmarks will likely be treated as a stigmatised other, as an undesirable drug user to be avoided. The known-about-ness can often be harmful stereotypes that oversimplify or overrepresent just one aspect of the identity. And the effect is that when Irish speakers and deaf people present themselves as their True Gael and culturally deaf selves, they do not match the known-about-ness attributed to them and are accordingly punished.

For Irish speakers, the perception that Irish is the cúpla focal and limited in its function, ceremonial and often a waste of time or resources persists. Gael5 stated bluntly in their interview, 'They don't understand – like a lot of Irish people – that Irish speakers exist.' They acknowledged that societally, the known-about-ness of Irish speakers and Irish speaking does not perceive the 'True Gael' identity. Rather they are perceived in light of deviance, and assumed that when they do not play the 'Good Gael' (passing) they are the 'Bad Gael' who is a slíbhín and deviant (punishment). The known-about-ness of Irish is associated with tokenism and flourish, and the lived experiences of participants show that they are perceived as deviant when they do not match this known-about-ness.

For deaf people, the known-about-ness of a deaf identity is largely linked to a paternalised view of deaf people and the créatúr trope. As shown in Chapter 11, deaf people were often discussed using disability language during the debating of the ISL Act in the Dáil. As discussed in Chapter 3, this type of language does not necessarily differentiate between models of disability, which can cause deaf people to be seen in light of what they lack (Ladd, 2003), rather than in terms of who they are (Glickman & Hall, 2018a). Deaf4 in particular, noted the common perception that deaf people face where they are medicalised and paternalised.

The persistence of the general known-about-ness of Irish speakers and deaf people, above a nuanced understanding of the true identities points to a lack of symbolic access. When known-about-ness of Irish speakers and deaf people remains harmful, stereotypical external identities, then they are prevented from being treated as their true selves and being 'fully included and empowered to participate as equal citizens'. Symbolic access is absent. This was specifically noted by participants that their groups were not treated equally in society. As mentioned earlier Deaf3 did not feel they were 'on a par with hearing society'. Deaf4 alluded to a similar sentiment:

> Deaf4: The deaf community is a minority adapting to the majority. Deaf4 has felt like a second-class citizen.

Deaf4 was strong in their perception of the inequality in a society that deaf people experience.

> Gael1: 'When I was young, I didn't understand the negativity that there was about [Irish and Irish speakers] because I wasn't reading the English language newspapers...When I got older, I suppose I started to understand'

Gael1 is referring to negative stereotypes of Irish speakers which are common features in national media.

> Gael6: '*Well in terms of the state service, the state does not welcome us. As an Irish person, I am a foreigner in my own country in terms of language*'.

Gael6 is strong in their words, attesting that as an Irish speaker, they feel unwelcome in Irish society. It is important to once again recall the distinction used in the ECRML betweeen traditional and non-traditional language users, and in particular, Woehrling's justification that traditional language users do not experience 'problems of integration' (Woehrling, 2005). However, from Gael6's testimony it is clear that they did not feel any different from 'foreigners' or those who would use non-traditional languages. Their experiences were that of an outsider, where their language and their identity were perceived as exceptional to the normal. They felt a kinship with non-traditional language users in the treatment they received. Their problems could be said to be a lack of integration into society, where society does not accept their identity and symbolic access is denied.

These extracts show that participants acknowledged their lack of symbolic access. They show that their languages and their identities are not 'fully included and empowered' and that they are not treated as 'equal citizens'. This acknowledgement was not limited to discussions of the CJS. Deaf3, Deaf4, Gael1 and Gael6 were referring generally to the treatment of deaf people and Irish speakers in society. But many participants also had specific complaints about certain sectors demonstrating the inequality they experience in society. These experiences included problems with banks (Deaf1, Gael2); the social welfare office (Dr John-Bosco Conama); the revenue office (Gael6); the Motor Tax Office (Gael1, Gael7); and transportation services (Deaf1, Gael6). These instances demonstrated that Irish speakers and deaf people were an afterthought, or not thought about at all, and ultimately, that their identities were not valued enough to be considered. This added to the general sense from interviews that Irish speakers and deaf people were not fully empowered and equal citizens in society.

The findings of this research suggest that where there is no symbolic access, the benefits that substantive and procedural access can have in ensuring access to justice are limited. As can be seen from Chapter 7, actual substantive access measures are diluted and rendered unsubstantive where there is a failure to also ensure symbolic access. Legislative debates for both the OLA and the ISL Act showed the persistence of harmful, stereotypical known-about-ness of Irish speakers and deaf people, rendering the substantive access measures obsolete. This shows that in spite of efforts to include affected parties in laws and policies which affect them, they are undermined by the harmful societal perceptions that persist about said parties. Similarly, procedural access is also affected by symbolic access. Measures may be in place to remove barriers to access to justice for marginalised people. But those measures can only be effective when they are underpinned by symbolic access. If the Garda or the judge or the solicitor or the social worker enforcing the law perceives the Irish speaker or the deaf person only in terms of the harmful, stereotypical perceptions, and not in terms of their lived reality and true identity, then procedural access measures are also pointless.

If the societal known-about-ness of marginalised groups persists as a harmful, stereotypical external perceptions, the true identity of these groups is not understood. And when that true identity of these groups is not understood, this research's findings suggest that substantive and procedural access measures cannot match the appropriate needs of those groups. Without symbolic access, providing a more nuanced and accurate known-about-ness of marginalised people, true access to justice cannot be achieved.

9.6 Chapter Summary

The research in this chapter is novel. Not only have I continued to expand on the field of access to justice, by exploring symbolic access as it exists for minority language users, but I have also mapped access to justice literature onto identity literature, in order to offer a deeper understanding of how the CJS was experienced by those interviewed in light of their linguistic identity.

From the data presented in this chapter, a number of findings are clear. First, the internal identity of Irish speakers and deaf people does not match how they are externally perceived. A culturally deaf identity, visible in the literature, was held by the participants. Irish speakers demonstrated a 'True Gael' identity, where their language represented a core part of their identity and often superseded their need for self-preservation. The deep connection that participants showed to their language, community and culture was evident. However, this did not match how they were perceived in the CJS or the general known-about-ness of deaf people and Irish speakers societally. Only one participant (Gael4) recounted their true identity being externally observed. All other participants noted being misunderstood or misconstrued in light of the créatúr or the slíbhín tropes, as discussed in Chapter 8.

Second, as a consequence of the dominance of the harmful external identities, participants were left to manage their stigma by either passing or being punished. Knowing their identity would pose a problem, and represented a deviant, punishable other, interviewees needed to either undercommunicate their identities, or face the punishment head-on as methods of stigma management. Because their internal identity was not perceived, then they would not be treated in the CJS in light of the needs of their internal identity.

Third, this is linked to the lack of symbolic access and known-aboutness. The known-about-ness of both groups in society is largely limited to harmful, stereotypical perceptions of the créatúr and the slíbhín. This shows that there has not been adequate symbolic access underpinning access to justice measures for the groups. The persistence of these negative perceptions in the CJS and in society shows that Irish speakers and deaf people are not empowered, valued members of society. I have found that until the perception of these groups shifts from the external, harmful stereotypes to the internal, true identities, then access to justice cannot be truly achieved. The needs of Irish speakers and deaf people in the CJS and in society cannot be met unless we first perceive what actually it is to be an Irish speaker or a deaf person in the CJS and in society.

Note

(1) Cultural appropriation of by white people protective hairstyles for Black hair is relevant here. Where Black people (particularly women) are penalised in society for wearing natural hair or traditional hairstyles, those same styles are often lauded and deemed fashionable when worn by white, influential people. See Abdul-Jabbar 'Cornrows and Cultural Appropriation: The Truth About Racial Identity Theft' *Time Magazine* (26 August 2015), Smith 'Cultural Appropriation is Everywhere. But Is It Always Wrong?' *Time Magazine* (21 September 2016), Friedman 'Kim Kardashian West and the Kimono Controversy' *The New York Times* (27 June 2019).

10 Concluding Remarks

10.1 Introduction

In this final chapter, I draw together the findings of this research and return to the research questions posed in Chapter 1. The research has been an illuminating process, which sheds light on how minority language users can experience engaging with the CJS and using their language in Ireland. Using hermeneutic phenomenology to underpin the collection and analysis of empirical data, I have been able to engage with the research questions and explore the lived experiences of minority language users who use their language in the CJS. The research has shown how impactful language use can be and how central identity is to how an individual experiences the right to a fair trial, the CJS and access to justice.

I address the research questions in turn below, drawing to mind the data and findings which I have concluded.

10.2 How do Minority Language Users Experience the Right to a Fair Trial?

First, I address the question of how minority language users experience the right to a fair trial. I have found that language played a role in how deaf people and Irish speakers experienced the right to a fair trial. The use of their language had an impact of course on the minimum standards of the right to a fair trial. In particular, the right to trial without undue delay was impacted. It is clear that delay was a concern. That delay was rooted in both the availability of interpreters and in the availability of Gardaí or judges with appropriate Irish (in respect of Irish speakers). I have also found that where an individual is facing delay attributed to their linguistic needs, there may be a temptation to forgo those needs in order to avoid delay. The risk then is that although delay has been avoided, the individual is not given access as they are truly entitled to it. In forgoing linguistic needs to avoid delay, the fairness of trial is impacted.

I found that the right to be present at trial was also impacted. Physically, there were no instances of interviewees reporting being denied access to the court. However, there were issues around cognitive presence and the right to be *actively* present at trial. In being denied linguistic facilitations (interpreters or Irish-speaking CJS operative) individuals are unable to access the right to be present in practice. The benefits that come with being present – being able to understand the case against oneself, being able to participate, being able to hear the evidence against oneself – are unattainable. The findings of this research suggest that only when language is facilitated effectively, through appropriate interpretation or CJS operatives proficient in the language in question, can minority language users actually access the right to be present.

Connected to this is the right to communicate with counsel. Where counsel and the accused do not share a language, they cannot access their right to communicate without effective measures being put in place to bridge the language gap. What could be seen in the data is that interpreters were not always available, particularly outside of the formal court structures. For example, in police interviews and in consultations, interpreters were not always available. This of course, impacted the ability to effectively form a defence with counsel. Additionally, there were instances where interviewees reported no interpreter aid at all, therefore rendering communication with counsel disjointed or impossible. For lawyers, I found that there was also the concern that their communications with clients would be affected by a lack of interpreter ethics. Lawyer-client privilege does not necessarily extend to interpreters, and so lawyers showed concern that their presence would impact and undermine how they communicated with their clients and the quality of that communication.

Finally, interpretation was an underlying issue for many interviewees. Availability of interpreters was of course a concern. The right to an interpreter is undermined where there are insufficient interpreters to facilitate demand. There are multiple issues underpinning this lack of availability. Poor working conditions for interpreters were evident, where there is poor pay, long hours and a lack of appropriate and specialised training needed to interpret in legal context. In Ireland, interpretation is largely an unregulated field where there is no legislative oversight or regulatory monitoring. The poor working conditions then can have a direct impact on how minority language users will experience their right to an interpreter. Where the interpreters are poorly paid, overworked and undertrained with no oversight, these conditions can give rise to poor quality interpretations and ultimately to unfairness at trial. There is also an issue of entitlement, where interpreter access is gatekept by judges or Gardaí. There are no evident criteria for granting an interpreter and there is evidence to suggest that arbitrary decisions can be made based on an assumption that the accused is being deviant in their request for an interpreter, or on the belief that they *should* have a command of the court's language, irrespective of whether they do in fact.

In concluding this part, it must be noted that legal issues and minimum standards of the right to a fair trial formed only part of the lived experiences recounted by participants. In fact, I found that largely the minimum standards were not where participants had most issues or concerns. In recognising this finding, it was evident that experiencing the right to a fair trial is not limited to the minimum standards of the right to a fair trial. A broader look at the fair trial process was necessary to create a fuller picture of the lived experience of minority language users.

10.3 How do Minority Language Users Experience the CJS?

Secondly, I turn to addressing the question of how minority language users experience the CJS. I found through the research that language and linguistic identity impacted how minority language users experienced the CJS. For the most part, I found that Irish speakers and deaf people were not perceived in light of their internal identities when they interacted with the CJS. This had mostly negative effects, whereby simplified, harmful external identities were applied to Irish speakers and deaf people. I found that they were perceived in light of what I have called the créatúr or slíbhín tropes, which are underpinned by societal known-aboutness of the two groups. In addition, what I have called the 'Good Gael' is a sub-trope which was a performance used by Irish speakers, largely in an attempt to avoid what I have called 'Bad Gael' sub-trope, a harmful external identity applied to Irish speakers.

For deaf people, there was evidence to suggest that many had been treated in light of the créatúr trope. They were paternalised, treated as disabled in a medical model context, and their autonomy as individuals was undermined. No deaf person interviewed for this research identified as disabled, in any context of the term.[1] There was also evidence of deaf people being treated as the slíbhín, when they did not match the known-aboutness of deaf people. There was also evidence of deaf people being disbelieved about their identity as deaf people. I found that the internal culturally deaf identity which was held by participants was not perceived externally. Their internal identities were undermined by the créatúr and slíbhín tropes as external identities, and they were treated on the bases of those tropes when they interacted with the CJS.

Similarly, with the exception of one incident reported by Gael4, I found that Irish-speaking participants were not understood in light of their internal, 'True Gael' identities. Where they were perceived in light of their identities as Irish speakers, that external identity took the form of the slíbhín trope and the 'Bad Gael' sub-trope. In attempts to avoid the 'Bad Gael' external identity, and the associated punishments, Gael participants also alluded to performing the 'Good Gael' sub-trope, whereby they did not use Irish to be 'rude' or did not 'force' Irish on someone. This finding reflects the known-aboutness that Irish is a hobby language and not for actual communication (S. Brennan & O'Rourke, 2019; C.C. O'Reilly, 2014). This attempt to perform as the 'Good Gael' sub-trope was not always successful, and some participants were nevertheless perceived as the 'Bad Gael' sub-trope and accordingly treated.

In response to the conflict between the internal culturally deaf and 'True Gael' identities and the externally perceived identity as the slíbhín and créatúr tropes, I found that deaf people and Irish speakers managed their stigma by passing and concealing their true selves, or by overcommunicating their identity and be accordingly punished for that communication of identity. This placed deaf people and Irish speakers in a difficult position in the CJS: to either pass and conceal their true selves (Goffman, 1969), risking later exposure and the corresponding punishment, or suffer the consequences of concealing their identity, such as a lack of access to the language of the court; or to express that identity and be treated in light of the créatúr or the slíbhín tropes, whereby they are paternalised or treated as devious troublemakers, respectively.

This understanding of how minority language users experienced the CJS is underpinned by access to justice, which is concluded below.

10.4 How do Minority Language Users Experience Access to Justice?

Finally, I address the third research question, exploring how minority language users experienced access to justice. Access to justice has been the central focus of this thesis, through which the data is situated. It became clear from the data collected that a strict focus on the minimum standards of the right to a fair trial would only partially touch on the concerns that were expressed in interviews and the themes which arose therein.

In coming to this finding, access to justice scholarship provides an important lens through which to view the data. The experiences of participants were multifaceted and understanding them needs a multifaceted approach.

I found that procedural access issues arose for participants in respect of their minimum standards under the right to a fair trial. As noted above, their linguistic identity posed a barrier to procedural access in some instances. There was evidence of Irish speakers and deaf people being blocked from effectively engaging in the process against them, because of the CJS's reaction to their language or because of the lack of facilities in place. As addressed above, delays were common, participants' experienced difficulty in accessing their counsel, in accessing the benefits of the right to be present and in accessing an interpreter. These issues point to a lack of procedural access for marginalised minority language users. Again, these issues marked the narrowest part of the triangle for participants. These concerns, although impactful on the process of accessing the right to a fair trial in the CJS, represented the outcome of other access to justice concerns.

Substantive access issues were one such concern. In spite of initial attempts to include Irish speakers and deaf people in the creation of laws and policies that affect them, the ultimate result is one of compromise and tokenism. The legislative solutions do not point towards beneficial or equitable outcomes for the marginalised people they are designed for. In respect of training, where there is training for the engagement of CJS operatives with minority language users, that training can be wrought with harmful stereotypes and tropes, which reinforce the negative créatúr and slíbhín external identities, as shown above. It should be noted that in the creation of laws and policies for Irish speakers and deaf people, these negative, harmful tropes can also be seen by policymakers. This is possibly indicative of an overall lack of symbolic access.

Recall that symbolic access, according to Flynn, ensures that 'individuals from marginalised communities are fully included and empowered to participate as equal citizens...' (Flynn, 2015: 16). The lack of symbolic access in wider society was indicated by the presence of harmful stereotypes which dominate the known-aboutness of Irish speakers and deaf people. The findings of the research suggest that Irish speakers and deaf people experienced a lack of symbolic access in their interactions with society at large, not just in respect of the CJS. That lack of symbolic access manifested in the CJS as the slíbhín and the créatúr tropes. Were they valued, empowered and fully included citizens, they would have been perceived in light of their true selves. When the known-aboutness of a marginalised group persists as a negative trope such as the slíbhín or the créatúr, it indicates that there is a lack of understanding of the true needs and true identities of that group, and therefore a lack of symbolic access.

This lack of symbolic access, I believe, has underpinned a lack of substantive access, which has then underpinned a lack of procedural access. Where marginalised people are not valued and empowered, they are less likely to have a seat at the table when it comes to making laws and policy. It is less likely that their concerns will be heard by those who do make law and policy. Where their concerns have not been considered in the creation of law and policy, beneficial and equitable judicial outcomes are not provided for. Their concerns have not been built into the CJS. Their existence in the CJS is an exception. In being exceptional, they face barriers. They must either fight to remove those barriers (often experiencing punishment for such movement) or accept that they will not be treated equal (and conceal or pass their need for barriers to be removed.) Without a basis in symbolic access, substantive and procedural access are limited or absent outright.

10.5 Recommendations

It is difficult to neatly sum up this research into a list of clear policy or legislative recommendations. This book is a call for increased access to justice for minority language users. And if anything, access to justice research shows that real, meaningful access to justice must come from a wider, societal change, where marginalised identities are perceived as valuable, important members of society and are empowered to participate in that society. This research has seen multiple participants acknowledge the barrier to participating in society as their true selves, or the resistance in society to including their identity, either from a place of paternalism (créatúr) or disdain (slíbhín).

If we can have meaningful symbolic access, meaningful substantive access can follow, which can create meaningful procedural access. So how do we create meaningful symbolic access? Unfortunately, this is at the limits of my research, and although I can speculate, speculation is all I can offer. It may be that better education is the answer. If we include deaf history, ISL and deaf culture in Irish curricula it may be that hearing children become Deaf Aware, who then become hearing adults who are Deaf Aware. However, we can see that including Irish on the mandatory curriculum for all students in Ireland has not necessarily created a more inclusive environment for Irish speakers.

Rather, I think that there is a necessity for Irish society (which may begin at school) to *reexamine* its relationship to minority languages. This would mean interrogating the impact of postcolonialism on Irish society around Irish, and understanding on a deeper level, why the tropes of the slíbhín, the Good Gael and the Bad Gael are so pervasive over the True Gael identity. It would mean examining ableism and medical models of disability held in society which cloud and overwhelm more nuanced deaf identities. It would mean interrogating why disability is an undesirable trait in society, and why then we demonstrate pity when met with what we perceive to be a disabled identity. It would mean confronting the stark realities of disabled people, the barriers to accessing health, education, society and law that disabled people experience, before ever grappling with the nuances of deaf identity.

Certainly, we must have appropriately trained interpreters, with appropriate pay and good working conditions (McEvoy, 2025a). Certainly, we must have Gardaí, judges and lawyers who are able to conduct proceedings seamlessly in Irish and who are readily available. Certainly, we must have a wider implementation of laws which provide concrete, enforceable and clear rights for minority users (McEvoy, 2025b). But these solutions represent Band-Aids on bullet holes and are insufficient to tackle the root cause of the problem (De Meulder & Haualand, 2021). There must be deeper, more meaningful changes at the core of society. When change happens at the foundational layer of the Access to Justice pyramid, it can then seep upwards, first to substantive access and then procedural access, to offer real, meaningful changes and more and more specific places.

10.6 Summary

I began this book with a discussion of the cases of Maolra Seoighe and of John McGrotty; men, over 100 years apart, whose experiences of the

CJS were heavily impacted by their languages and their linguistic identities. In both cases, it is possible to observe a failure of access to justice. Both men experienced barriers to their effective participation in proceedings against them. Both men experienced a system, built on laws which did not perceive them, or consider them in the creation of beneficial and equitable outcomes. Both men were tried and convicted in societies which did not value them as empowered citizens. Both men experienced a lack of access to justice. In writing this book, I have not fixed the wrongs visited upon Maolra or John. I have not fixed the feelings of injustice, unfairness or discrimination which arose in interviews. What I have done, however, is highlight how language and identity are central to how minority language users experience the right to a fair trial, the CJS and access to justice in a way that is original. What I have shown is that in ensuring that minority language users are treated with equality, we must look beyond merely the narrow focus of the four walls of the court, or the police station interview room. I have provided an original contribution to research, by engaging with literature on identity, policing, human rights law and access to justice, and expanding on their scope to offer an understanding of the lived experiences of minority language users who engaged with the CJS. I have shown for the first time how individual Irish speakers and deaf ISL users in Ireland experienced using their language while engaging with their right to a fair trial in the CJS.

In concluding this work, in order to move forward and ensure that minority language users experience access to justice when they engage with the CJS we must look beyond the laws and policy which exist presently to help these marginalised groups. We must look at how these law and policies have been informed by societal known-aboutness of these marginalised groups, and how they in turn have built the walls of the court and the police station. We must first look to how these marginalised people – deaf people and Irish speakers – are perceived in the world and treated on the back of that perception. It is only when we can see, accept, value and appreciate the true identities of these groups that we can start to build a system fit for purpose, based on the principles of access to justice.

Note

(1) Be it a medical model, social model or a human rights model of disability.

References

A Guide to Good Professional Conduct for Solicitors, 3rd edn (2013) The Law Society of Ireland.

About Minorities and Human Rights (2024) OHCHR. https://www.ohchr.org/en/special-procedures/sr-minority-issues/about-minorities-and-human-rights

Access to Justice in Europe: An Overview of Challenges and Opportunities (2011) EU Agency for Fundamental Rights. https://www.refworld.org/reference/research/eufra/2011/en/78346

Adams, W.C. (2015) Conducting semi-structured interviews. In K.E. Newcomer, H.P. Hatry and J.S. Wholey (eds) *Handbook of Practical Program Evaluation* (1st edn, pp. 492–505). Wiley. https://doi.org/10.1002/9781119171386.ch19

Alcock, A. (2000) *A History of the Protection of Regional Cultural Minorities: From the Edict of Nantes to the Present Day*. Palgrave Macmillan. http://public.eblib.com/choice/publicfullrecord.aspx?p=344928

Alfredsson, G. (1991) 'Emerging or newly restored democracies – Strengthening of democratic institutions and development'. Discussion Paper of Workshop at the Strasbourg Conference on Parliamentary Democracy: Human Rights, Fundamental Freedoms and the Rights of Minorities, Essential Components of Democracy, Strasbourg: Council of Europe, 16–18 September 1991.

An Garda Síochána (2012) Coimisinéir Teanga.

An Garda Síochána (2019) *Competition for Selection of Garda Trainees.*

An Introduction to Irish Sign Language (ISL) in the Legal Setting (2021) Law Society of Ireland. https://www.lawsociety.ie/globalassets/documents/lspt/2020/s2059_brochure_isl-in-the-legal-profession-an-introduction.pdf

Aodha, G.N. (2017, February 6) Arlene Foster on Sinn Féin: "If you feed a crocodile it will keep coming back for more." *TheJournal.Ie*. https://www.thejournal.ie/arlene-foster-gerry-adams-3225834-Feb2017/

Appointment to Judicial Office (2024) *Association Of*. https://aji.ie/the-judiciary/appointment-to-judicial-office/

ATII (2009) *Code of Ethics for Community Interpreters*. Association of Translators and Interpreters Ireland.

Bacik, I. (2007) Breaking the language barrier-access to justice in the New Ireland. *10 Judicial Studies Institute Journal* 10, 15.

Bahdi, P.R. (2007) *Background Paper on Women's Access to Justice in the MENA Region* (p. 43)

Bairéad, C. (Director) (2018, April 4) *Murdair Mhám Trasna* [Broadcast]. TG4.

Baker, C. and Padden, C. (1978) *American Sign Language—A Look at its History, Structure And Community*. TJ Pub Inc.

Basser Marks, L.A. and Jones, M. (1997) The limitations on the use of law to promote rights: An assessment of the disability discrimination act 1992. In M. Hauritz, C. Sampford and S. Blencowe (eds) *Justice for People with Disabilities: Legal and Institutional Responses (Law, Ethics and Public Affairs)*. Federation Press.

Bates, E., Bond, J. and Wiseman, D. (2016) Troubling signs: Mapping access to justice in Canada's refugee system reform. *Ottawa Law Review* 47 (1), 72.

Baytar v Turkey, No. Application no. 45440/04 (European Court of Human Rights 2014)

Becker, H.S. (2018) *Outsiders: Studies in the Sociology of Deviance* (New edition, updated with two new chapters. Paperback edition) Free Press.

Benhadj v. Algeria, No. U.N. Doc. E/CN.4/2003/8/Add.1 (2001)

Beqiraj, J., McNamara, L. and Wicks, V. (2017) *Access to Justice For Persons With Disabilities: From International Principles to Practice*. International Bar Association.

Berezhnoy v. Russia, No. U.N. Doc. CCPR/C/118/D/2107/2011 (2011)

Bergova (2016) Trust in the state courts: Hispanic and African American communities. *International Relations and Diplomacy* 4 (12). https://doi.org/10.17265/2328-2134/2016.12.002

Berk-Seligson, S. (1998) The importance of linguistics in court interpreting. *Berkeley La Raza Law Journal* 2, 36.

Berk-Seligson, S. (2017) *The Bilingual Courtroom: Court Interpreters in the Judicial Process* (2nd edn). The University of Chicago Press.

Blot, R.K. (ed.) (2003) *Language and Social Identity*. Praeger.

Boddaert v. Belgium, No. App no 12919/87 (European Court of Human Rights 1992)

Boland (2016, May 30) Broadside: Can anybody truthfully say that Irish is a necessary language? *The Irish Times*. https://www.irishtimes.com/life-and-style/people/broadside-can-anybody-truthfully-say-that-irish-is-a-necessary-language-1.2663495

Boudreault, P. (2005) Deaf interpreters. In T. Janzen (ed.) *Topics in Signed Language Interpreting: Theory and practice* (Vol. 63) John Benjamins Publishing Company. https://doi.org/10.1075/btl.63

Bourdieu, P. (2010) *Outline of a Theory of Practice* (25. printing). Cambridge University Press.

Bradley, M.S. (2007) Girlfriends, wives, and strippers: Managing Stigma in exotic dancer romantic relationships. *Deviant Behavior* 28 (4), 379–406. https://doi.org/10.1080/01639620701233308

Brennan, M., Brown, R.K., MacKay, B. and University of Durham and Deaf Studies Research Unit (2004) *Equality Before the Law: Deaf People's Access to Justice*. D. McLean.

Brennan, S. and O'Rourke, B. (2019) Commercialising the *cúpla focal*: New speakers, language ownership, and the promotion of Irish as a business resource. *Language in Society* 48 (1), 125–145. https://doi.org/10.1017/S0047404518001148

Brooker, C., Sirdifield, C. and Gojkovic, D. (2007) *Mental Health Services and Prisoners: A Review* [Commissioned by the Prison Health Research Network]. University of Lincoln.

Brown, M.K. (1988) *Working the Street: Police Discretion and the Dilemmas of Reform*. Russell Sage Foundation.

Brunson, J.L. (2007) Your case will now be heard: Sign language interpreters as problematic accommodations in legal interactions. *Journal of Deaf Studies and Deaf Education* 13 (1), 77–91. https://doi.org/10.1093/deafed/enm032

Butler, J. (2004) *Undoing Gender*. Routledge.

Cahillane, D.L. (2016) *Judicial Diversity in Ireland* 6, 17.

Caldas, S.J. and Caron-Caldas, S. (1999) Language immersion and cultural identity: Conflicting influences and values. *Language, Culture and Curriculum* 12 (1), 42–58. https://doi.org/10.1080/07908319908666568

Canada, P.S. (2020, January 21) *Indigenous People in Federal Custody Surpasses 30% Correctional Investigator Issues Statement and Challenge* [News releases]. https://www.canada.ca/en/public-safety-canada/news/2020/01/indigenous-people-in-federal-custody-surpasses-30-correctional-investigator-issues-statement-and-challenge.html

Cao, D. (2007) *Translating Law*. Multilingual Matters.

Caollaí, É.Ó. (2013, December 5) Commissioner resigns over Government failures on Irish. *The Irish Times*. https://www.irishtimes.com/news/ireland/irish-news/commissioner-resigns-over-government-failures-on-irish-1.1616978

Capotorti, F. (1977) *Study on the Rights of Persons Belonging to Ethnic, Religious and Linguistic Minorities*. United Nations Economic and Social Council.

Cardi, V. (2007) Regional or minority language use before judicial authorities: Provisions and facts. *Journal on Ethnopolitics and Minority Issues in Europe* 6 (2), 1–24.

Chan, J.B.L. (1997) *Changing Police Culture: Policing in a Multicultural Society* (1st edn). Cambridge University Press. https://doi.org/10.1017/CBO9780511518195
Chan, J.B.L. (2009) *Changing Police Culture: Policing in a Multicultural Society.* Cambridge University Press.
Charlton, J.I. (2004) *Nothing About Us Without Us: Disability Oppression and Empowerment* (3. Dr) University of California Press.
Collaboration with An Garda Síochána and Trinity College Dublin to Pilot new service for Deaf community (2019, March 15) *Interesource Group.* https://interesource-group.com/2019/03/15/collaboration-with-an-garda-siochana-and-trinity-college-dublin-to-pilot-new-service-for-deaf-community/
Conama, J.-B. (2019) 'Ah, that's not necessary, you can read English instead': An analysis of state language policy concerning ISL and its effects. In M. De Meulder, J.J. Murray and R.L. McKee (eds) *The Legal Recognition of Sign Languages: Advocacy and Outcomes Around the World* (pp. 19–35). Multilingual Matters.
Conradh na Gaeilge (Director) (2017, March 16) *Myth #1: "Irish is a dead language"* [Video recording]. https://www.youtube.com/watch?v=XCEjILUJvFc
Conway, V. (n.d.) *17. Policed – Animal Rights – Tortoise Shack* [Broadcast]. Retrieved 26 November, 2024 from https://tortoiseshack.ie/17-policed-animal-rights/
Cooper, M. (Director) (2019, January 25) Students Exempt from Irish Are Studying Other Languages [Broadcast]. In *TodayFM.* https://www.todayfm.com/podcasts/the-last-word-with-matt-cooper/students-exempt-from-irish-are-studying-other -languages
Coulmas, F. (1998) Language rights — Interests of state, language groups and the individual. *Language Sciences* 20 (1), 63–72. https://doi.org/10.1016/S0388-0001(97)00012-0
Council of Europe, Guide on Article 6 of the European Convention on Human Rights: Right to a Fair Trial (Criminal Limb) (2019) Council of Europe.
Cradden, J. (2016, June 9) Deaf have human interpreter in court. *Village Magazine.*
créatúr—Translation to Irish Gaelic with audio pronunciation of translations for créatúr by New English-Irish Dictionary. (n.d.) Retrieved 25 November 2024, from https://www.focloir.ie/en/dictionary/ei/cr%C3%A9at%C3%BAr
Crenshaw, K. (1993) Mapping the margins: Intersectionality, identity politics, and violence against women of color. *Stanford Law Review* 43, 61.
Criminal Justice Fact Sheet | NAACP (2021, May 24) NAACP. https://naacp.org/resources/criminal-justice-fact-sheet
Crowley, T. (2005) *Wars of Words: The Politics of Language in Ireland, 1537–2004.* Oxford University Press.
Cusack, M., Jack, G. and Kavanagh, D. (2003) Dancing with discrimination: Managing stigma and identity. *Culture and Organization* 9 (4), 295–310. https://doi.org/10.1080/1475955042000195409
Cuscani v The United Kingdom, No. ECHR 625 (European Court of Human Rights 2002)
Darach Ó Séaghdha (Director) (2021, May 5) *Motherfoclóir ISL Episode* [Video recording]. https://www.youtube.com/watch?app=desktop&v=jsORJSesv48&feature=youtu.be
De Barra, C. (2017, February 4) The case for ending state support of Irish language is littered with dubious "facts." *TheJournal.Ie.* https://www.thejournal.ie/readme/fake-facts-irish-language-debate-3220676-Feb2017/
De Meulder, M. and Haualand, H. (2021) Sign language interpreting services: A quick fix for inclusion? *Translation and Interpreting Studies* 16 (1), 19–40. https://doi.org/10.1075/tis.18008.dem
Deaf people can deal with police using sign language (2019, November 20) *The Law Society Gazette.*
Degener, T. (2017a) A new human rights model of disability. In R. Cera, V. Della Fina and G. Palmisano (eds) *The United Nations Convention on the Rights of Persons with*

Disabilities: A Commentary (1st edn). Springer. https://doi.org/10.1007/978-3-319-43790-3

Degener, T. (2017b) The human rights model of disability. In P.D. Blanck and E. Flynn (eds) *Routledge Handbook of Disability Law and Human Rights.* Routledge.

Del Valle, S. (2003) *Language Rights and the Law in the United States: Finding Our Voices.* Multilingual Matters.

Delaney, E. (2019, August 12) Irish language should not be compulsory, especially for struggling school children. *Irish Independent.* https://www.independent.ie/irish-news/eamon-delaney-irish-language-should-not-be-compulsory-especially-for-struggling-school-children/38396171.html

Dibley, L., Dickerson, S., Duffy, M. and Vandermause, R. (2020) *Doing Hermeneutic Phenomenology Research: A Practical Guide* (1st edn). SAGE Publications.

Dodd, V. and Grierson, J. (2021, March 30) Sarah Everard vigil report strongly defends police's use of force. *The Guardian.* https://www.theguardian.com/uk-news/2021/mar/30/police-handling-of-sarah-everard-vigil-appropriate-says-watchdog

Dolan, T. P. (ed.) (1999) *A Dictionary of Hiberno-English: The Irish Use of English* (1. paperback edn). Gill & Macmillan.

Dzehtsiarou, K. (2015) *European Consensus and the Legitimacy of the European Court of Human Rights.* Cambridge University Press.

Ellis, R. (2015) *Understanding Second Language Acquisition* (2nd edn). Oxford University Press.

Enright, M., McCandless, J. and O'Donoghue, A. (2017) *Northern/Irish Feminist Judgments: Judges' Troubles and the Gendered Politics of Identity.* Hart Publishing.

Erard, M. (2017, November 9) Why sign-language gloves don't help deaf people. *The Atlantic.* https://www.theatlantic.com/technology/archive/2017/11/why-sign-language-gloves-dont-help-deaf-people/545441/

Eriksen, T. H. (2010) *Ethnicity and Nationalism: Anthropological Perspectives* (3rd edn). Pluto Press.

European Charter for Regional or Minority Languages Report of the Committee of Experts on Austria (2018) ECRML.

European Charter for Regional or Minority Languages Report of the Committee of Experts on Bulgaria (2016) ECRML.

European Charter for Regional or Minority Languages Report of the Committee of Experts on Croatia (2019) ECRML.

European Charter for Regional or Minority Languages Report of the Committee of Experts on Czech Republic (2015) ECRML.

European Charter for Regional or Minority Languages Report of the Committee of Experts on Finland (2001) ECRML.

European Charter for Regional or Minority Languages Report of the Committee of Experts on Germany (2006) ECRML.

European Charter for Regional or Minority Languages Report of the Committee of Experts on Romania (2012) ECRML.

European Charter for Regional or Minority Languages Report of the Committee of Experts on Slovenia (2014) ECRML.

European Charter for Regional or Minority Languages Report of the Committee of Experts on Spain. (2012) ECRML.

European Charter for Regional or Minority Languages Report of the Committee of Experts on Ukraine (2017) ECRML.

Ezendam, H. and Wheldon, F. (2014) Recognition of victims' rights through EU action: Latest development and challenges. In I. Vanfraechem, A. Pemberton and F. Ndahinda (eds) *Justice for Victims: Perspectives on Rights, Transition and Reconciliation.* Routledge. https://doi.org/10.4324/9780203094532

Fa'afete v. New Zealand, No. U.N. Doc CCPR/C/114/D/1909/2009 (2015)

Fact: Information on Irish Sign Language (2024) Irish Deaf Society. https://www.irish-deafsociety.ie/about/press-information/

FAQs (2024) An Garda Síochána. https://www.garda.ie/garda/en/faqs/?id=4851

Farrow, T.C.W. (2014) What is Access to Justice? *Osgoode Hall Law Journal* 51 (3), 957–988. https://doi.org/10.60082/2817-5069.2761

Fielding, N.G. (2013) Lay people in court: The experience of defendants, eyewitnesses and victims: Lay people in court. *The British Journal of Sociology* 64 (2), 287–307. https://doi.org/10.1111/1468-4446.12018

Find a Barrister (2025) The Bar of Ireland. https://www.lawlibrary.ie/find-a-barrister/

Find an interpreter (2025, January 9) *Register of Irish Sign Language Interpreters*. https://www.risli.ie/interpreters/find-an-interpreter/

Find an interpreter. (2025, March 7) *Register of Irish Sign Language Interpreters*. https://www.risli.ie/interpreters/find-an-interpreter/

Fishman, J.A. (1977) *Sociolinguistics: A Brief Introduction* (6. printing) Newbury House.

Fishman, J.A. (1985) Language, ethnicity and racism. In J.A. Fishman, M.H. Gertner, E.G. Lowy and W.G. Milán (eds) *The Rise and Fall of the Ethnic Revival: Perspectives on Language and Ethnicity*. De Gruyter. https://doi.org/10.1515/9783110863888

Fitzpatrick, P. (2014, June 2) *Tribes of Modern Ireland: None of Us are Just Irish | Irish Independent*. https://www.independent.ie/business/personal-finance/tribes-of-modern-ireland-none-of-us-are-just-irish/30312742.html

Flynn, E. (2015) *Disabled Justice? Access to Justice and the UN Convention on the Rights of Persons with Disabilities*. Ashgate.

Flynn, E. and Lawson, A. (2013) Disability and access to justice in the European Union: Implication of the United Nations Convention on the Rights of Persons with Disabilities. *European Yearbook of Disability Law* 4, 7–44.

Foclóir Gaeilge–Béarla (Ó Dónaill): Slíbhín (2021) https://www.teanglann.ie/en/fgb/sl%C3%ADbh%C3%ADn_

Foclóir Gaeilge–Béarla (Ó Dónaill): Créatúr (2024) https://www.teanglann.ie/en/fgb/cr%C3%A9at%C3%BAr

Foras na Gaeilge (Director) (2020, July 29) *Buntús Cainte Ceacht 60 | Foras na Gaeilge X RTÉ Archives | #LeChéile* [Video recording]. https://www.youtube.com/watch?v=gDlpH-QfLSE

Forde, M., Leonard, D. and Leonard, D. (2013) *Constitutional Law of Ireland* (3rd edn). Bloomsbury Professional.

Francioni, F. (2007) The rights of access to justice under customary international law. In F. Francioni (ed.) *Access to Justice as a Human Right*. Oxford University Press. https://doi.org/10.1093/acprof:oso/9780199233083.001.0001

Frydlender v France, No. 31 EHRR 1152 (European Court of Human Rights 2001)

Gaiba, F. (1998) *The Origins of Simultaneous Interpretation: The Nuremberg Trial*. University of Ottawa Press.

Gallagher, C. (2020, October 5) Galway woman makes history as first deaf person to deliberate on Irish jury. *The Irish Times*. https://www.irishtimes.com/news/crime-and-law/galway-woman-makes-history-as-first-deaf-person-to-deliberate-on-irish -jury-1.4370644

Gallagher, M. (1983) "The poor mouth": Flann O'Brien and the Gaeltacht. *Studies: An Irish Quarterly Review* 72 (287), 231.

García-Sánchez, I. and Nazimova, K. (2017) Language socialization and immigration in Europe. In P. A. Duff and S. May (eds) *Language Socialization* (pp. 1–16). Springer International Publishing. https://doi.org/10.1007/978-3-319-02327-4_30-2

Genn, H.G. (2010) *Judging Civil Justice*. Cambridge University Press.

Gertz, G. and Boudreault, P. (eds) (2016) *The Sage Deaf Studies Encyclopedia*. SAGE.

Gilligan, A. (Director) (2019, January 25) *The Irish Language* [Broadcast]. https://www.newstalk.com/podcasts/between-the-lines-with-andrea-gilligan/the-irish-language

Gillon, C., Figeroa, M. and Rios, A.A. (n.d.) *Borderlands/La Frontera* [Broadcast]. https://vocalfriespod.com/2018/09/19/transcript-8-borderlands-la-frontera/

Glickman, N.S. and Hall, W.C. (2018a) Introduction. In *Language Deprivation and Deaf Mental Health* (1st edn). Routledge. https://doi.org/10.4324/9781315166728

Glickman, N.S. and Hall, W.C. (2018b) *Language Deprivation and Deaf Mental Health* (1st edn). Routledge. https://doi.org/10.4324/9781315166728

Goffman, E. (1969) *The Presentation of Self in Everyday Life* (Nachdr.) Doubleday.

Goffman, E. (1986) *Stigma: Notes on the Management of Spoiled Identity* (26th pr) Simon & Schuster.

Grin, F., Jensdóttir, R. and Ó Riagáin, D. (2003) *Language Policy Evaluation and The European Charter for Regional or Minority Languages*. Palgrave Macmillan.

Guesdon v. France, No. U. N. Doc. CCPR/C/39/D/219/1986 (1990)

Hansen, J.G. and Liu, J. (1997) Social identity and language: Theoretical and methodological issues. *TESOL Quarterly* 31 (3), 567. https://doi.org/10.2307/3587839

Harkin, G. (2016, May 19) Deaf man banned from Donegal for harassing family. *Irish Independent.*

Hartley, J. (2000) Legal ease and 'Legalese.' *Psychology, Crime & Law* 6 (1), 1–20. https://doi.org/10.1080/10683160008410828

Harward v. Norway, No. U.N. Doc. CCPR/C/51/D/451/1991 (1994)

Haviland, J.B. (2003) Ideologies of language: Some reflections on language and U.S. law. *American Anthropologist* 105 (4), 764–774. https://doi.org/10.1525/aa.2003.105.4.764

Heavy-handed police response to Hong Kong protest unacceptable (2019, July 27) Amnesty International. https://www.amnesty.org/en/latest/press-release/2019/07/hong-kong-heavy-handed-policing-protest/

Heidegger, M., Macquarrie, J. and Robinson, E.S. (2008) *Being and Time.* HarperPerennial/Modern Thought.

Hermi v. Italy, No. App no 18114/02 (European Court of Human Rights 2006)

Heyerick, I. (2025) *The Sustainability of the Irish Sign Language Interpreting Profession: Research Report.* Trinity College Dublin. https://strategicinterpreting.blog/2025/01/09/the-sustainability-of-the-irish-sign-language-interpreting-profession-research-report-recommendations/

Hobsbawm, E. J. (1992) *Nations and Nationalism since 1780: Programme, Myth, Reality* (2nd edn). Cambridge University Press. https://doi.org/10.1017/CCOL0521439612

Hogg, M. (2006) Social Identity Theory. In P.J. Burke (ed.) *Contemporary Social Psychological Theories.* Stanford Social Sciences.

Holden, L. (2007, April 17) The rise of the gaelscoil—Is this the new playground of the elite? *The Irish Times.* https://www.irishtimes.com/news/education/the-rise-of-the-gaelscoil-is-this-the-new-playground-of-the-elite-1.1202171

Holland, K. (2017, October 20) Disproportionate number of travellers in prison population. *The Irish Times.* https://www.irishtimes.com/news/social-affairs/disproportionate-number-of-travellers-in-prison-population-1.3263524

Human Rights Committee, General Comment 13, Article 14 (Twenty-first session, 1984), Compilation of General Comments and General Recommendations Adopted by Human Rights Treaty Bodies (No. U.N. Doc. HRI/GEN/1/Rev.1) (1994)

Human Rights Committee, General Comment 32, Article 14, Right to equality before courts and tribunals and to a fair trial (No. U.N. Doc. CCPR/C/GC/32) (2007) UN Human Rights Committee.

Humphries, T. (2000, May 22) How to chat up a true Gael. *The Irish Times.* https://www.irishtimes.com/sport/how-to-chat-up-a-true-gael-1.273858

Humphries, T., Kushalnagar, P., Mathur, G., Napoli, D.J., Padden, C., Rathmann, C. and Smith, S.R. (2012) Language acquisition for deaf children: Reducing the harms of zero tolerance to the use of alternative approaches. *Harm Reduction Journal* 9 (1), 16. https://doi.org/10.1186/1477-7517-9-16

Hunter, R. (2015) More than just a different face? Judicial diversity and decision-making. *Current Legal Problems* 68 (1), 119–141. https://doi.org/10.1093/clp/cuv001
Irish (2024, November 18) UNESCO WAL. https://en.wal.unesco.org/languages/irish
Irish Deaf Society (2018, June 8) *Blanchardstown/Cabra Gardaí Learn ISL*. https://twitter.com/IrishDeafSoc/status/1005049893751226368
Irish Examiner (2020, May 1) Irish Examiner View: Do we need Covid-19 booklets in both English and Irish? *Irish Examiner*. https://www.irishexaminer.com/opinion/ourview/arid-30997200.html
Irish Language and the Gaeltacht Census of Population 2016 – Profile 10 Education, Skills and the Irish Language—Central Statistics Office (2021, June 4) Central Statistics Office; CSO. https://www.cso.ie/en/releasesandpublications/ep/p-cp10esil/p10esil/ilg/
Irish no longer a requirement to join An Garda. (2005, September 7) *Irish Times*.
Irish Sign Language (2021, June 4) Irish Deaf Society. https://www.irishdeafsociety.ie/irish-sign-language/
Irish Translators' and Interpreters' Association (2013) *ITIA Bulletin—April 2013*.
Jackson-Preece, J. (2014) *Beyond the (Non) Definition of Minority. ECMI Brief 30*.
James, W. (1995) *The Principles of Psychology: In Two Volumes. Vol. 1: ...* (Facsim. of ed. New York, Henry Holt, 1890). Dover.
Jefferson, T. (1993) *The Racism of Criminalization: Policing and the Reproduction of the Criminal Order*. Ethnic Minorities and the Criminal Justice System: 21st Corporal Roundtable Conference, 1992.
Judicial Appointment Commission—About (2025) Judicial Appointments. https://www.judicialappointments.ie/about-jac
Judicial Appointments Commission Act (2023) https://www.irishstatutebook.ie/eli/2023/act/33/enacted/en/html
Judicial Education (2024) *Association Of*. https://aji.ie/supports/judicial-education/
Kamasinski v Austria, No. App no 9783/82 (European Court of Human Rights 1989)
Katz, I. (1981) *Stigma: A Social Psychological Analysis*. L. Erlbaum Associates.
Kelleher, M. (2018, November 10) The shambles of Maamtrasna': The case of Myles Joyce, hanged and pardoned. *Irish Times*.
Kelly-Holmes, H. (2013) Sex, lies and thematising Irish: New media, old discourses? In H. Kelly-Holmes (ed.) *Thematising Multilingualism in the Media*. John Benjamins.
Kiernan, L. (2019, 04) Gardaí play their part in helping to make Portlaoise Ireland's first deaf friendly town'. *The Leinster Express*.
Knodel, R.K. (2018) Coping with vicarious trauma in mental health interpreting. *Journal of Interpretation* 26 (1), 25.
Koomen, J. (2014) Language Work at International Criminal Courts. *International Feminist Journal of Politics* 16 (4), 581–600. https://doi.org/10.1080/14616742.2014.947732
Kramsch, C.J. (2011) *Language and Culture* (12. impr) Oxford University Press.
Kushnick, L. (1999) 'Over Policed and under Protected': Stephen Lawrence, Institutional and Police Practices. *Sociological Research Online* 4 (1), 156–166. https://doi.org/10.5153/sro.241
Kusters, A., Meulder, M. D. and O'Brien, D. (2017) Critically mapping the field. In M. De Meulder, A. Kusters and D. O'Brien (eds) *Innovations in Deaf Studies: The Role of Deaf Scholars*. Oxford University Press.
Ladd, P. (2003) *Understanding Deaf Culture: In Search of Deafhood*. Multilingual Matters.
Lagerblom v. Sweden, No. App no 26891/95 (European Court of Human Rights 2003)
Lane, H.L. (1999) *The Mask of Benevolence: Disabling the Deaf Community* (new edn) DawnSignPress.
Larson, D.A. (2015) Access to justice. In J. Backhaus (ed.) *Encyclopedia of Law and Economics* (pp. 1–7). Springer. https://doi.org/10.1007/ 978-1-4614-7883-6_570-1

Laverty, S.M. (2003) Hermeneutic phenomenology and phenomenology: A comparison of historical and methodological considerations. *International Journal of Qualitative Methods* 2 (3), 21–35. https://doi.org/10.1177/160940690300200303

Law Society of Ireland (2019) *Law Society of Ireland Professional Practice: Legal Practice Irish Handbook Course I.*

Law Society of Ireland. (2021) https://www.lawsociety.ie/Find-a-Solicitor/Clar-na-Gaeilge/Ardchursa-Cleachtadh-Dli-as-Gaeilge/

Lawson, A. and Priestley, M. (2017) The Social Model of Disability. In P.D. Blanck and E. Flynn (eds) *Routledge Handbook of Disability Law and Human Rights.* Routledge.

LawUCC (Director) (2020, November 27) *Maintaining Access to Justice in the Pandemic* [Video recording]. https://www.youtube.com/watch?v=3bbyAvc-5PQ

Leach Scully, J. (2012) Deaf identities in disability studies. In N. Watson, A. Roulstone and C. Thomas (eds) *Routledge Handbook of Disability Studies.* Routledge.

Leary, K. (1999) Passing, posing, and "keeping it real." *Constellations* 6 (1), 85–96. https://doi.org/10.1111/1467-8675.00122

Leeson, L., Flynn, S., Lynch, T. and Sheikh, H. (2020) You have the right to remain signing: A snapshot of the Irish justice system and deaf signers. *TEANGA, the Journal of the Irish Association for Applied Linguistics* Special Issue (11), 142–173.

Leeson, L. and Saeed, J.I. (2012) *Irish Sign Language: A Cognitive Linguistic Account.* Edinburgh University Press.

Leeson, L. and Venturi, L. (2017) *A Review of Literature and International Practice on National and Voluntary Registers for Sign Language Interpreters* (p. 104) A report commissioned by Sign Language Interpreting Services.

Legal Practitioners (Irish Language) Act (2008)

Leigh, I., Andrews, J. and Harris, R. (2018) *Deaf Culture: Exploring Deaf Communities in the United States.* Plural Publishing.

Leonard, C. (2023) *Deaf People in Ireland: Education, Poverty and the Law, 1851-1922* [PhD]. Trinity College Dublin.

Loftus, B. (2010) Police occupational culture: Classic themes, altered times. *Policing and Society,* 20 (1), 1–20. https://doi.org/10.1080/10439460903281547

Lopez, C. (2010) *Disorderly (mis)Conduct: The Problem with 'Contempt of Cop' Arrests.* American Constitution Society for Law and Policy Issue Brief.

Lord, J., Guernsey, K., Balfe, J., Karr, V. and deFranco, A. (2012) *Human Rights. Yes!* (N. Flowers, ed.; 2nd edn). University of Minnesota Human Rights Center.

Lowney, R. (2023) *Clár na Gaeilge (An Dlí-Chumann)/Irish Language Register (Law Society)*

Mac Giolla Chríost, D. (2012) *Jailtacht: The Irish Language, Symbolic Power and Political Violence in Northern Ireland, 1972–2008.* University of Wales Press.

Madaraka Festival (Director) (2019, April 25) *Ngugi Wa Thiongo – Why Africans hate their own languages | Diaspora Connect: Ep. 23* [Video recording]. https://www.youtube.com/watch?v=tnF6XdOh5HY

Manhart, M. (2019) "Backpack Refugee Rights Lawyering" in Greece – Access to Justice through Legal Empowerment. *International Human Rights Internship Program Working Paper Series* 38, 7 (1), 38.

Martin, N. (2012) Disability identity – disability pride. *Perspectives: Policy and Practice in Higher Education* 16 (1), 14–18. https://doi.org/10.1080/13603108.2011.611832

Maume, P. (1998) Nationalism and partition: The political thought of Arthur Clery. *Irish Historical Studies* 31 (122), 222–240. https://doi.org/10.1017/S0021121400013924

May, S. (2012) *Language and Minority Rights: Ethnicity, Nationalism and the Politics of Language* (2nd edn). Routledge.

McCaffrey, A. (1999) Don't Get lost in translation teaching law students to work with language interpreters. *Clinical Law Review,* 347.

McCarthy, T. (2020, June 2) Police criticized over heavy-handed response to peaceful protests across US. *The Guardian*. https://www.theguardian.com/us-news/2020/jun/02/police-criticized-heavy-handed-response-peaceful-protests-across-us

McElhatton, S. (2020) *Kevin Barry: What Really Happened. RTÉ*. https://www.rte.ie/news/2020/1101/1174753-kevin-barry/

McEvoy, G. (2025a) *Barriers to studying and working as an ISL interpreter: Developing an evidence base in order to launch a campaign to increase the number of ISL interpreters in Ireland*. Irish Deaf Society. https://irishdeafsoc.wpenginepowered.com/wp-content/uploads/2025/10/IDS-Full-Report-Working-as-ISL-Interpreter-Research.pdf

McEvoy, G. (2025b) 'Pretty words on a page': Disappointment in sign language laws in Ireland, Finland and the UK. *TEANGA, the Journal of the Irish Association for Applied Linguistics* 32. https://doi.org/10.35903/teanga.v32i.9964

McIntosh, J. and Mendoza-Denton, N. (eds) (2020) *Language in the Trump Era: Scandals and Emergencies* (1st edn). Cambridge University Press. https://doi.org/10.1017/9781108887410

McNamara, D. (2018) *The Criminal Investigation of Suspects with Disabilities: The Impact of the UN Convention on the Rights of Persons with Disabilities*. Dublin City University.

Michael and Brian Hill v. Spain, No. U.N. Doc. CCPR/C/59/D/526/1993 (1997)

Millen, N. and Walker, C. (2001) Overcoming the stigma of chronic illness: Strategies for normalisation of a 'spoiled identity.' *Health Sociology Review* 10 (2), 89–97. https://doi.org/10.5172/hesr.2001.10.2.89

Miller, K.R. and Vernon, M. (2002) Assessing linguistic diversity in deaf criminal suspects. *Sign Language Studies* 2 (4), 380–390. https://doi.org/10.1353/sls.2002.0021

Minogue, C. (2021, March 5) *Irish Sign Language Expert Shares Some Examples of ISL*. TodayFM. https://www.todayfm.com/podcasts/dermot-dave/irish-sign-language-expert-shares-some-examples-of-isl

Namakula, C.S. (2012) Language rights in the minimum guarantees of fair criminal trial. *International Journal of Speech Language and the Law* 19 (1), 73–93. https://doi.org/10.1558/ijsll.v19i1.73

Napier, J. (2002) The D/deaf-H/hearing Debate. *Sign Language Studies* 2 (2), 141–149. https://doi.org/10.1353/sls.2002.0006

Napier, J. and Spencer, D. (2008) Guilty or not guilty? An investigation of deaf jurors' access to court proceedings via sign language interpreting. In S.B. Hale and D. Russell (eds) *Interpreting in legal settings*. Gallaudet University Press.

Nardi, P.M. (2018) *Doing Survey Research: A Guide to Quantitative Methods* (4th edn). Routledge.

Newton, E. (1979) *Mother Camp: Female Impersonators In America* (Phoenix edn) University of Chicago Press.

Ngugi wa Thiong'o (2005) *Decolonising the Mind: The Politics of Language in African Literature* (Reprint) Currey [u.a.].

Nogueira López, A. (2012) Article 8.1 Education (i) In A. Nogueira López (ed.) *Shaping language rights: Commentary on the European Charter for Regional or Minority Languages in light of the Committee of Experts' evaluation: Commentary on the European Charter for Regional or Minority Languages in light of the Committee of Experts' evaluation*. Council of Europe Publ.

Nugent, D. (1994) Judicial Bias. *Cleveland State Law Review* 42 (4), 1.

Ó Beoláin v Fahy, IR 279 (2001)

Ó Cadhla v. Minister for Justice, 503 IEHC ___ (High Court of Ireland 2019).

Ó Caollaí, É. (2013, December 4) Commissioner resigns over Government failures on Irish. *Irish Times*.

Ó Caollaí, É. (2021, April 26) Garda Síochána reported to Oireachtas over Gaeltacht service. *The Irish Times*.

Ó Cuirreáin, S. (2017) *Éagóir: Maolra Seoighe agus dúnmharuithe Mhám Trasna*. Cois Life.

Ó Cuív, É. (2015, February 22) About. *Éamon Ó Cuív TD*. http://www.eamonocuiv.ie/aboutme/

Ó Deá, A. (2016, September 12) We just want to speak our own language, in our own country. *TheJournal.Ie*.

OAO Neftyanaya Kompaniya Yukos v. Russia, No. 853 (European Court of Human Rights 2014)

O'Brien, T. (2018, August 21) Government wants to lower Māori prison stats but hasn't set specific target | Newshub. *News Hub*. https://www.newshub.co.nz/home/politics/2018/08/government-wants-to-lower-m-ori-prison-stats-but-hasn-t-set-specific-target.html

Öcalan v. Turkey, No. App no 46221/99 (European Court of Human Rights 2005)

O'Higgins, L. (2007) (In)felix Paupertas: Scholarship of the eighteenth-century Irish Poor. *Arethusa* 40 (3), 421–450. https://doi.org/10.1353/are.2007.0025

Oliver, M. (2017) The social model in action: If I had a Hammer. In P.D. Blanck and E. Flynn (eds) *Routledge Handbook of Disability Law and Human Rights*. Routledge.

O'Reilly, C. (1996) The language – litmus test for equality? Competing discourses of identity, parity of esteem and the peace process. *Irish Journal of Sociology* 6 (1), 154–178.

O'Reilly, C.C. (2014) *Irish Language in Northern Ireland: The Politics of Culture and Identity*. Palgrave Macmillan.

O'Rourke, B. (2011) Whose language is it? Struggles for language ownership in an Irish language classroom. *Journal of Language, Identity & Education* 10 (5), 327–345. https://doi.org/10.1080/15348458.2011.614545

Ortoleva, S. (2011) Inaccessible Justice: Human Rights, Persons with Disabilities and the Legal System. *ILSA Journal of International and Contemporary Law* 17 (2), 41.

Over-Representation (2018, January 9) ALRC. https://www.alrc.gov.au/publication/pathways-to-justice-inquiry-into-the-incarceration-rate-of-aboriginal-and-torres-strait-islander-peoples-alrc-report-133/3-incidence/over-representation/

Packer, J. (1993) On the definition of minorities. In J. Packer and K. Myntti (eds) *The Protection of Ethnic and Linguistic Minorities in Europe*. Institute for Human Rights, Åbo Akademi University.

Padden, C. (2002) The deaf community and the culture of deaf people. In S. Gregory and G.M. Hartley (eds) *Constructing Deafness*. Continuum in association with the Open University.

Parker, C., Scott, S., Geddes, A., Atkinson, P., Delamont, S., Cernat, A., Sakshaug, J.W. and Williams, R.A. (2020) *Snowball sampling*. https://methods.sagepub.com/foundations/snowball-sampling

Pawlosky, M. (1996) "When Justice is lost in the "Translation": Gonzalez v. United States and "Interpretation" of the Court Interpreters Act of 1978. *DePaul Law Review*.

Phelan, M. (2011) Legal interpreters in the news in Ireland. *International Journal for Translation and Interpreting* 3 (1), 76–105.

Phelan, M. (with Irish Legal History Society) (2019) *Irish Speakers, Interpreters, and the Courts, 1754 –1921*. Four Courts Press, in association with the Irish Legal History Society.

Piatt, B. (1993) *Only English?: Law and Language Policy in the United States*. University of New Mexico Pr.

Piller, I. (2016) *Linguistic Diversity and Social Justice: An Introduction to Applied Sociolinguistics* (1st edn). Oxford University Press.

Pirotta, M. (ed.) (2017) *The Graz Recommendations on Access to Justice and National Minorities & Explanatory Note*. OSCE High Commissioner on National Minorities.

Poindexter, C.C. and Shippy, R.A. (2010) HIV diagnosis disclosure: Stigma management and stigma resistance. *Journal of Gerontological Social Work* 53 (4), 366–381. https://doi.org/10.1080/01634371003715841

Police to look into who gave order to pepper spray Helsinki protesters (2020, October 4) YLE News. https://yle.fi/a/3-11578440

Purkey, A.L. (2014) A Dignified approach: Legal empowerment and justice for human rights violations in protracted refugee situations. *Journal of Refugee Studies* 27 (2), 260–281. https://doi.org/10.1093/jrs/fet031

R v MR, No. ONSC 408 (Supreme Court of Canada 2020).

Re Manitoba Language Rights, 1 SCR 721 ___ (Supreme Court of Canada 1985).

Recognition of Irish Sign Language for the Deaf Community Bill 2016: Report and Final Stages – Seanad Éireann (25th Seanad) – Tuesday, 17 Oct 2017 – Houses of the Oireachtas (2017) https://www.oireachtas.ie/en/debates/debate/seanad/2017-10-17/4

Recognition of Irish Sign Language for the Deaf Community Bill 2016: Second Stage: Hearing on 13 (2016a)

Recognition of Irish Sign Language for the Deaf Community Bill 2016: Second Stage: Hearing on 13 (2016b)

Reiner, R. (2010) *The Politics of the Police* (4th edn). Oxford University Press.

Riley, P. (2007) *Language, Culture and Identity: An Ethnolinguistic Perspective.* Continuum.

Rogers, R.A. (2006) From cultural exchange to transculturation: A review and reconceptualization of cultural appropriation. *Communication Theory* 16 (4), 474–503. https://doi.org/10.1111/j.1468-2885.2006.00277.x

Romaine, S. (2006) Planning for the survival of linguistic diversity. *Language Policy* 5 (4), 443–475. https://doi.org/10.1007/s10993-006-9034-3

Rose, H. and Conama, J. B. (2018) Linguistic imperialism: Still a valid construct in relation to language policy for Irish Sign Language. *Language Policy* 17 (3), 385–404. https://doi.org/10.1007/s10993-017-9446-2

Rousseau, A. (2019, December 11) People who speak Irish need to be given jobs! *Newstalk.* https://www.newstalk.com/podcasts/highlights-from-the-hard-shoulder/people-speak-irish-need-given-jobs

Russell, D. (2000) Interpreting in Legal Contexts: Consecutive and Simultaneous Interpretation [PhD, University of Calgary]. https://www.collectionscanada.gc.ca/obj/s4/f2/dsk2/ftp02/NQ54808.pdf

Salinas, L. S. and Martinez, J. (2010) Right to confrontation compromised: Monolingual jurists subjectively assessing the English-language abilities of Spanish-dominant accused. *American University Journal of Gender* 18 (3), 21.

Sąman v. Turkey, No. App no 35292/05 (European Court of Human Rights 2011)

Schneider, E. and Crombie, M. (with British Dyslexia Association) (2003) *Dyslexia and Foreign Language Learning.* Fulton.

Seanad Debate: Hearing on Vol 169 No 21 (2002)

Shepard, R.T. (2007) Access to justice for People who do not speak English. *Indiana Law Review* 40, 643.

Shugart, H.A. (1997) Counterhegemonic acts: Appropriation as a feminist rhetorical strategy. *Quarterly Journal of Speech* 83 (2), 210–229. https://doi.org/10.1080/00335639709384181

Shukuru Juma v. Australia, No. U.N. Doc. CCPR/C/78/D/984/2001 (2003)

Shulman, M. (1993) No hablo ingles: Court interpretation as a major obstacle to fairness for non-English speaking defendants. *Vanderbilt Law Review* 46 (1), 175–196.

SI 658/2020 Irish Sign Language Act, 2017 (Commencement) Order (2020)

Sign language course a first for Law School (2020, August 5) *The Law Society Gazette.*

Skelton, T. and Valentine, G. (2003) "It feels like being Deaf is normal": An exploration into the complexities of defining D/deafness and young D/deaf people's identities. *The Canadian Geographer/Le Géographe Canadien* 47 (4), 451–466. https://doi.org/10.1111/j.0008-3658.2003.00035.x

Skinner, R. (2024) 'When he comes into police custody, he has certain rights': The burden for achieving access in a video-mediated interpreted custody interview. *International Journal of Police Science & Management* 26 (3), 381–394. https://doi.org/10.1177/14613557241245585

slíbhín—Translation to Irish Gaelic with audio pronunciation of translations for slíbhín by New English-Irish Dictionary (2021) Focloir.Ie. https://www.focloir.ie/en/dictionary/ei/sl%C3%ADbh%C3%ADn

Stafford, M. (2017, May 6) *Only a true Gael could name these 10 players based on their Wikipedia entry*. SportsJOE.Ie. https://www.sportsjoe.ie/gaa/true-gael-name-10-players-based-wikipedia-entry-122523

Submission from the Irish Translators' and Interpreters' Association to the Working Group on the Jurisdiction of the Courts (2002)

The Recognition of Irish Sign Language for the Deaf Community Bill (2016)

Trenz, H.-J. (2007) Reconciling diversity and unity: Language minorities and European integration. *Ethnicities* 7 (2), 157–185. https://doi.org/10.1177/1468796807076839

Tyan v. Kazakhstan, No. U.N. Doc CCPR/C/119/D/2125/2011 (2017) U.N. Doc CCPR/C/119/D/2125/2011 (2017)

US Ex Rel Negron v. New York, No. 434 F.2d 386 (2nd Circuit 1970)

US v Mayans, No. 17 F3d 11745 (9th Circuit USA 1999)

Vernon, M., Raifman, L.J. and Greenberg, S. F. (1996) The miranda warnings and the deaf suspect. *Behavioural Sciences and the Law* 14, 121–135.

Vernon, M., Raifman, L.J., Greenberg, S. F. and Monteiro, B. (2001) Forensic pretrial police interviews of deaf suspects avoiding legal pitfalls. *International Journal of Law and Psychiatry* 24 (1), 43–59. https://doi.org/10.1016/S0160-2527(99)00031-X

Vizgirda v. Slovenia, No. App no 59868/08 (European Court of Human Rights 2018)

Walker, S. and Archbold, C.A. (2020) *The New World of Police Accountability* (3rd edn). SAGE.

Walsh, J., O'Rourke, B. and Rowland, H. (2015) *Research Report on New Speakers of Irish*. Foras na Gaeilge.

Walshe, J. (2003, July 2) Irish lessons "are a waste of time"' The Irish Independent. *Irish Independent*.

Waterhouse, K. (2014) *Ireland's District Court: Language, Immigration and Consequences for Justice*. Manchester University Press.

Wattman, J. (2018) Interpreting for deaf people with dysfluent language in forensic setting. In W.C. Hall and N.S. Glickman (eds) *Language Deprivation and Deaf Mental Health* (1st edn) Routledge. https://doi.org/10.4324/9781315166728

Woehrling, J.-M. (2005) *The European Charter for Regional or Minority Languages: A Critical Commentary*. Councial of Europe Pub.

Woodward, J. (1975) *How you gonna get to heaven if you can't talk with Jesus: The educational establishment vs. The Deaf community*. Annual Meeting of the Society for Applied Anthropology, Amsterdam.

Woodward, J. and Horejes, T. (2016) deaf/Deaf: Origins and Usage. In *The SAGE Deaf Studies Encyclopedia*. SAGE Publications.

Zeynalov v. Estonia, No. CCPR/C/115/D/2040/2011 (European Court of Human Rights 2015)

Index

access to justice, 7, 44–45, 162, 164
barrier, 1–2, 6, 48, 55–56, 58, 60, 66, 92–95, 97–98, 101, 162, 164
procedural access, 9, 15, 44, 46–50, 53–62, 64–71, 75, 77, 81, 84, 93–94, 96–98, 100–102, 124, 155, 157, 162–164
substantive access, 9, 15, 46, 48–51, 53, 75, 102–106, 109–110, 114–116, 121–122, 124, 155, 164
symbolic access, 9, 15, 44, 46, 51–53, 105, 109, 122, 124–125, 127–129, 132–133, 135, 137–139, 141–143, 145, 155–158, 163–164
An Garda Síochána, 1, 7, 12–14, 39, 49, 106–108, 110–111, 114–115, 123, 129, 139–140, 152
Garda, 1, 7, 12–14, 39, 49, 71, 74, 78–80, 90, 94, 106–108, 110–117, 123, 127–129, 131–132, 134, 137–140, 148–152, 154, 157
Gardaí, 53, 72, 74–76, 78–80, 91, 94, 102, 107–108, 110–111, 113–116, 122, 127, 129, 131, 135, 137–140, 149, 151–152, 154, 159–160, 164
Guard, 116

court, 1, 6, 7, 25, 44–48, 51, 54–65, 69–71, 73–74, 76–77, 80–82, 88, 90–93, 95–100, 103, 106, 117–118, 120, 130–131, 138, 151–152, 154, 159–160, 162, 165
barrister, 1, 117, 122
CJS, 2, 6, 8–9, 10, 14, 16–17, 19–21, 23–27, 36, 41, 43–44, 47–55, 63, 71, 79, 81–82, 84, 89, 100, 102–103, 109–110, 122, 124–125, 127, 129, 134–135, 137, 141–143, 145–146, 149–151, 153, 155, 157–163, 165
judge, 23, 25, 35, 66, 80, 91–92, 99, 110, 117–118, 120–123, 153, 157
solicitor, 90, 98, 117–118, 120, 122, 157
crime, 1, 6– 7, 22, 28, 128, 137–138, 140
criminal, 1–2, 6–12, 14–16, 19, 28, 41, 44, 49, 53, 57, 61–62, 65, 82–83, 88–90, 92, 96–97, 108–109, 123, 147

deaf, 1, 3, 7–14, 16–17, 20, 26–36, 41–42, 64, 66, 71, 73, 75–76, 78, 89–91, 94–95, 98, 102–105, 114–116, 121–122, 124–129, 131–133, 141–146, 150–159, 161–165
CODAs, 29
deaf children, 29, 34–35
deaf community, 1, 13, 29–31, 33–34, 42, 90, 104–105, 114–115, 121–122, 128–129, 143–145, 156
deaf culture, 11, 28–29, 31, 35–36, 105, 121, 144, 146, 151, 164
deaf people, 3, 7, 10–14, 16–17, 20, 26–31, 33, 35–36, 41, 64, 66, 73, 78, 90–91, 102–103, 105, 114–116, 121, 125–129, 132–133, 141–143, 145–146, 150, 153–159, 161–163, 165
deaf schools, 34
disability, 20, 28–33, 36, 44–45, 48–50, 61, 105–106, 114–115, 126, 128–129, 145–146, 155–156, 164–165
disabilities, 30
disabled, 15, 20, 29–31, 36, 50, 53, 105, 114–116, 126, 145, 151, 161, 164

ECHR, 6, 9, 23, 54–56, 59, 61, 63–64, 84–85, 92, 96, 101

ECtHR, 51, 56, 59–62, 64, 66–68, 70–71, 81–82, 85, 87–88, 93, 96, 101

ICCPR, 6, 9, 15, 23, 44, 54–56, 58, 63–64, 84–85, 92, 96, 101
HRC, 44, 51, 56–59, 62, 64, 66–68, 71, 81–82, 85–87, 93–94, 96–97, 101
identity, 4–6, 8, 10–11, 13–21, 23–32, 34–44, 53–54, 57, 63–64, 100, 105, 107, 115, 122, 124–126, 128–130, 132–133, 135–159, 161–162, 164–165
external identity, 21, 25, 42, 128, 161
internal identity, 25, 41–42, 115, 142–143, 146–147, 149, 158
known-aboutness, 52
othered, 4, 8, 15, 17–25, 42, 44, 71, 129, 130–131, 153–154
passing, 17, 19–21, 63–64, 104, 120, 143, 150–153, 155, 158, 162
stigma, 16–21, 23, 25, 28, 33, 36, 53, 126, 129, 135–136, 142, 150–155, 158, 162
interpreter55, 56, 64, 72–73, 77, 80, 89
interpreting, 50, 60, 65, 67, 70–71, 78–79, 91, 95
Irish language, 2, 14, 37–39, 80, 91–92, 106–110, 113, 117, 120, 133, 138–139, 147, 152
Gaeilge, 38, 106, 118, 125, 129
Gaeltacht, 2, 36–38, 106
in Irish, 12–13, 23, 34, 36, 39–40, 42, 63, 99, 103, 106–110, 117–118, 120–123, 132–133, 135–140, 148, 150, 152–153, 156, 164
Irish speaker, 2, 13, 36–37, 40–41, 63, 120, 133, 136, 139, 143, 146, 152–153, 156–158
Irish-speaker, 10, 137
speaking Irish, 133
spoke Irish, 11, 94, 106, 138
Irish Sign Language, 1, 3, 7–8, 63–64, 78, 89, 102–105, 121
ISL, 1–3, 7–9, 11–14, 28–29, 34–35, 42, 63–65, 72, 76, 78, 83, 89–90, 94, 102–106, 110, 114, 121–122, 131, 156–157, 164–165

linguistic, 3, 5, 10, 20–21, 23, 25, 29, 34, 38, 57–59, 61–64, 73, 79, 85, 88–89, 101, 121, 129, 158–162, 165

minority, 3–5, 16, 19, 27, 130, 159, 161–162
indigenous, 3–4
marginalisation, 94–95
marginalised, 8–9, 16, 19, 24, 26, 44, 48–53, 100, 102, 109–110, 121–122, 124, 141, 155, 157, 163–165
minorities, 4–5, 15, 21, 26, 32, 50, 154

oralism, 34
oralist, 35

participant, 13–14, 29, 80, 98, 115, 140–141, 144, 149, 158
AGS1, 110–111, 113, 120, 139–140
AGS2, 72, 89–91, 114–116, 128–129
Deaf1, 131–132, 145, 157
Deaf2, 143–144
Deaf3, 66, 72, 78–79, 91, 115, 127–128, 144–145, 154, 156–157
Deaf4, 98, 114–115, 127, 144–145, 151, 153–154, 156–157
Deaf5, 128, 132, 144, 151–153
Dlíodóir1, 71, 120
Dlíodóir2, 71, 118, 120–121
Gael1, 107–109, 113–114, 137–140, 147–150, 154, 156–157
Gael2, 107–109, 114, 137–139, 147, 154, 157
Gael3, 107–109, 113–114, 137–139, 147, 154
Gael4, 80–81, 134–135, 137, 139–140, 147, 149, 158, 161
Gael5, 99, 107–108, 113–114, 118, 121, 137–140, 147–150, 152–155
Gael6, 113, 137, 147, 152–153, 156–157
Gael7, 72, 91–92, 113–114, 134–135, 137–139, 147, 152, 154, 157
Gael8, 134–135, 137, 152–153
JBC, 144
Lawyer1, 71, 74–75, 91, 94–95
Lawyer2, 71, 73–76, 91, 95, 98, 132, 151
LL, 72, 76, 89, 104–105, 116
SÓC, 107–108, 147

police, 1, 7–8, 15–16, 19–26, 43, 46–47, 49, 54, 65–72, 76, 79, 87, 89, 100, 115–116, 127–129, 131–132, 137, 142, 154, 160, 165
cop culture, 21–23, 25, 114, 116, 125
cops, 116
police culture, 21–22, 116
punishment, 1, 5, 137–138, 142–143, 147–148, 150, 154, 158, 162–163
punished, 132, 137–139, 149–150, 153–155, 158, 162

right to a fair trial, 6, 84, 92, 159
Article 14, 9, 23, 44, 51, 54–58, 67, 84–85, 88, 92–94, 96
Article 6, 6, 9, 23, 31, 54–55, 68–69, 84–85, 88, 92, 96
communication with counsel, 92
presence at trial, 85, 96, 98
right to an interpreter, 6, 42, 51, 55–64, 67–72, 75, 81–82, 84, 97, 100–101, 160
undue delay, 6, 55, 76, 84–85, 87–88, 92, 100–101, 159

trope, 18, 41–42, 125–137, 140–141, 143, 147, 150, 155, 161–163
Bad Gael, 42, 125, 131, 133–137, 139–142, 147, 150, 155, 161–162, 164
créatúr, 41–43, 125–129, 141–143, 155, 158, 161–164
Gael, 13, 37, 39, 41, 63, 120, 122, 134, 136, 140, 146–147, 149, 154, 161
Good Gael, 42, 125, 131, 133–135, 140–142, 147, 155, 161, 164
slíbhín, 41–42, 125, 129–134, 136, 141–142, 155, 158, 161–164
True Gael, 42, 141–142, 146–147, 149–150, 152, 155, 158, 161–162, 164

For Product Safety Concerns and Information please contact our EU Authorised Representative:

Easy Access System Europe

Mustamäe tee 50

10621 Tallinn

Estonia

gpsr.requests@easproject.com

www.ingramcontent.com/pod-product-compliance
Ingram Content Group UK Ltd.
Pitfield, Milton Keynes, MK11 3LW, UK
UKHW021008120926
8556IPUK00028B/216

9781800419094